The *Cottager's* Handbook

The Cottager's Handbook

...a guide for all seasons

BOB PHILLIPS

Canadian Cataloguing in Publication Data

Phillips, R. A. J. (Robert Arthur John). 1922-
   The cottager's handbook

ISBN: 0-13-181306-4

1. Vacation homes — Handbooks, manuals, etc.
I. Title.

TH4835.P48 1987   643'.2   C86-094617-7

Prentice-Hall Inc., Englewood Cliffs, *New Jersey*
Prentice-Hall International Inc., *London*
Prentice-Hall of Australia, Pty., Ltd., *Sydney*
Prentice-Hall of India Pvt., Ltd., *New Delhi*
Prentice-Hall of Japan Inc., *Tokyo*
Prentice-Hall of Southeast Asia (Pte.) Ltd., *Singapore*
Editora Prentice-Hall do Brasil Ltda., *Rio de Janeiro*
Prentice-Hall Hispanoamericana, S.A., *Mexico*

ISBN: 0-13-181306-4

Production Editor: Sharyn Rosart
Manufacturing: Don Blair
Design: Bruce Bond
Illustration: Sarah Jane English
Cover Photograph: Michael Peake, Hide-Away Island
Composition: Fleet Typographers Ltd.

Printed and bound in Canada by Gagné Printing Ltd.

1 2 3 4 5 GP 91 90 89 88 87

Table of Contents

Foreword   viii

A

Absences   2
Algae   3
Anchors   4
Animals   5
Architecture   11

B

Barbecues   13
Beaches   15
Biological Toilets   16
Blueberries   18
Boathouses   19
Boating Safety   21
Bonfires   23
Books   24
Boundaries   25
Buoys   27
Burglars   29

C

Canoes   31
Chain Saws   34
Checklists   35
Chisels   37
Closing Up   37
Cold   39
Comfort   41
Communications   42
Compost   44

D

Docks   45
Dogs   47

Domestic Chores   49
Drains   51

E

Electric Wiring   53
Excuses   55

F

Fans   57
Fences   58
Fireplaces   60
Fire Precautions   64
Firewood   68
First Aid   69
Fish   71
Flags   76
Food Storage   79

G

Games: On the Way   81
Games: At the Cottage   83
Garbage   86
Gardening   88
Generators   93
Guests   95

H

Hammocks   96
Harmful Plants   100
Heat   102

I

Insects   108

K

Kites   118

L

Ladders	120
Leaves	122
Lifejackets	124
Lighting	126
Lightning	128
Local People	131
Locks	132
Log Buildings	134
Log Splitting	138

M

Manuals	140
Maps	143
Mushrooms	145

N

Names	147
Newspapers	148
Northern Lights	150

O

Oil Lamps	152
Opening Up	153
Outhouses	155

P

Paints and Preservatives	157
Parking	159
Photos	160
Planning	161
Plumbing	163
Politics	169
Pollution	171
Power Boats	173
Pumps	176

R

Rafts	182
Rainy Days	184
Renting	185
Resuscitation	188
Roads	191
Rocks	194
Rot	195
Rowboats	197

S

Safety	199
Sailing	202
Saunas	206
Security	209
Septic Systems	212
Signs	215
Snow	216
Snowmobiles	218
Storms	219

T

Tools	221
Trees	226

W

Water	229
Weather	231
Weeds	233
Wells	236
Winter	238
Wood Cutting	242
Wood Storage	245
Woodstoves	248
Woodworking Projects	252

To Mary Anne, and to Margaret, Brigid and Jennifer,
whose cottage days enriched the lives of us all.

Foreword

This book is dedicated to the idea that cottaging is the world's great breakthrough in the search for mental health, and perhaps also to the idea that Canadians can be the mentally healthiest people of all.

One of the great clichés about Canada, repeated by natives and envious foreigners alike, is the glory of our geography — the great open spaces, the lakes, the rivers, the snow-capped peaks, the call of the loon, the sound of young voices abandoned to the joys of nature. And yet most of us, most of the time, live in cities that could as well be anywhere.

Cottaging is the great escape to our natural heritage. Even if the stereo and VCR are standing conspicuously in one corner and the purring ice-cube maker in another, we enjoy the illusion of being close to nature and to our roots in the soil. And there is truth in our fantasy. We are staring at trees and waters instead of asphalt and brick. We walk in woods, perhaps where no one has trod before. We create a world of our own in a dinghy slapping the gentle waves of our lake. We learn how night-time comes and goes in all its tranquillity, a phenomenon unrelated to the passage of time on rushing clocks.

And we do more. We cope. We are on our own. We have new problems to solve for ourselves and for the pleasure of our families. We have scope to be creative, whether in making that recalcitrant pump yield its flow of precious water, or building things of our own, or improving upon nature by sweeping open the curtain of trees to reveal that most perfect scene of summer peace. We not only plunge into a new environment, but both consciously and unconsciously, we try to shape it to our dreams.

This is as true as we care to make it in cottages of every degree. It happens whether we live in a cottage whose every board we have nailed with pride, or we are renting someone else's investment. We discard routines and climb quickly out of city ruts. Maybe, too, we start shedding inhibitions and do things we enjoy without wondering how they will be judged on our urban block.

Then why on earth do we need a guide book?

For some of the same reasons that such a book is valued by travellers in a strange land. It is meant to enhance enjoyment of the cottage life by making available the experience of others to solve problems which might otherwise subtract from our hours of cottage enjoyment. It shows the detours around the risks inherent in this new life, to avoid pleasure-destroying catastrophes. It suggests ideas to plumb the fullest potential of our great release from city existence. For many questions, it may simply provide the answers you always wondered about.

A first glance through these pages may cause the timorous to wonder if they should stay at home. Fire precautions? Water safety? Blackfly wars? But they would be wrong. A similar guide to city dwelling would surely persuade many readers never to leave the countryside. For cottagers who employ good sense and accept some guidance, the likelihood of disasters is slim; we just want to make the odds even better in your favor. That is why we may seem to dwell more on life's little complications than on the joys of the season, which you will surely discover in your own personal way.

It is far easier to write a guide for travellers in a far-off land than for cottagers. Travellers use the same few methods of transportation to reach the same few objectives. Cottagers and their cottages vary enormously, from temporary camps to country mansions, from third-generation cottagers to those on new voyages of discovery. In this guide we lean toward the new-comer, who may be thirstiest for help. At the same time we hope that veteran hands will find rewards in sharing the experiences and ideas of others. The capacity for enjoyment of cottage life is infinite, and there is no limit on the paths to its discovery.

Thus we hope that readers will use their guide according to their diverse interests. Especially those starting anew may wish to glide through the pages to find a picture of the unsuspected details of life in the country. Those who are well-etablished may want to look up the subjects of special interest or concern to them, perhaps in the search for new horizons. And within months we trust that the pages will be well-thumbed by every kind of reader who wants a fast reference when meeting a new situation or planning a new activity or project.

On subjects like cottaging, is there any final word? Some may disagree with the approaches taken in this book, out of philosophical differences or out of other experiences. It is, after all, difference of opinion that makes horse races. This book is intended to resemble a personal conversation with a friend and neighbor rather than the ultimate encyclopedia, and the writer would be especially happy if that conversation moves beyond the pages of this book. On all matters of personal safety, however, we have left minimum room for difference of opinion by seeking a consensus of all authorities within reach. If it does nothing else, we hope that this project has lessened the hazards in an unfamiliar world for you and your family, and given you the sense of security to enjoy its glorious benefits.

Bob Phillips

Cantley, Québec
January, 1987

Julian Smith

A

*A*BSENCES

Regret is usually the predominant emotion when leaving the cottage. Fear that the place may come to harm is often a close second. There are many sources of potential damage to the cottage, both natural (see **Storms, Animals**) and unnatural (see **Burglars**). What can be done to protect the cottage when you are absent?

There are two schools of thought. One is to secure the place as if it were the Bank of Canada. The other, which appeals to the less energetic among us, is to assume that nothing is impregnable, and leave the place virtually open. If you choose the first, turn quickly to **Security**. In either case, you will need to do some creative writing.

Do not fail to leave near the front door a notice which gives a phone number for the honest passer-by to call in case of trouble. If a roof is on the verge of collapse, or a window is broken, it is necessary for you to receive that information in order to repair the damage. Those of you who are cautious may not wish to give your own names or phone numbers on the note. As well, the city number will probably necessitate a long-distance charge which may discourage the passer-by. So try to give the phone number of a local person who will pass the message on to you.

Then, inside the cottage, on a prominent table, leave notepaper and a pencil with a notice to the effect: "If you have been in the cottage, please write your name and the date." That may sound pointless in catching the criminal element, and it probably is. (Although stranger things have happened. Our cottage was once broken into by youthful intruders who seized a camera, took pictures of one another and left the undeveloped film behind.) But it could add greatly to your peace of mind when your first springtime entry gives you a vague sense of someone having been here. Instead of suspecting that something has been stolen for months to come, you will see a note, "Forgot my hammer. Merry Christmas, Sam" and know that it was your faithful local helper. Or "Sank in lake with snowmobile. Lit your stove. Thanx. Undecipherable" may give you charitable thoughts depending on your view of snowmobiles. Or perhaps your nephew Ronnie and his girlfriend did break in; it will please you to know that he can write his name.

Anyway, you can't lose by leaving that pad and pencil, and you may collect some unexpected literary gems.

ALGAE

To cottagers, algae is not just a character in a P.G. Wodehouse novel. It is an insidious green aquatic plant that makes boats slimy, swimming unpleasant and fishing dubious. Algae, like most aquatic plants, does not thrive in fast-moving water, or in lakes or rivers with clean sand or rocky bottoms. Though it has its place in the natural scheme, most cottagers wish algae would do its thing elsewhere.

To control the growth of aquatic plants, do *not* use chemicals, or the local authorities may come around to arrest you. If the stagnant pond is completely on your own property, you may be legally entitled to do so, but the unforeseen consequences of the chemicals make their use a bad idea. Manual labor is the best way to attack most aquatic plants, though you can't do much to eliminate algae permanently without changing the conditions for its development.

At the first sign of aquatic plants growing where you do not wish them to, use a stiff rake on the bottom to yank them out (if the water is shallow). Some people recommend scything, but if you have ever tried to swing a scythe smartly under water you will see why we don't. Besides, raking is more likely to get the roots up. Where the water is deeper, position a person at each end of a heavy chain and drag the bottom with it, thus creating employment for the junior member of the family who will be assigned to clean up your chain. If you do not own a reasonably long welded steel chain with at least ¼-inch links, you can make do with a lighter one by attaching weights (such as scrap iron) every few feet.

With some planning, you can avoid that task. Buy a 10-foot-wide roll of 6 mm polyethylene — the kind of plastic sheeting used for vapor barriers in house construction. As early in spring as your lower parts can stand the cold, spread it over the bottom of your swimming area and anchor it with stones tied or wired to the edges, with more stones in the middle. As long as it stays in place, nothing will grow there. If you like, you can safely take it up by early August and store it for next year.

A more ingenious-sounding strategy is to spread the same sheet on the ice anytime in winter. It is less likely to work close to the shore, where ice will grind and heave against an obstacle. Elsewhere — at least in theory — it will sink into place at spring break-up. In practice, it will not spread out nearly as evenly as with the first method, and some hand-adjustment will probably be called for after it drops into place.

Beware the lure of bullrushes. They look so attractive that you may be tempted to pull up some from the roadside to transplant to your shores. They will probably either disappear forever, or suddenly spread in such profusion that you will rue the day you welcomed them.

*A*NCHORS

You may need anchors for stationary objects such as buoys, slightly mobile craft like rafts (see **Buoys, Rafts**) or for your boat. For the first two, you may well opt for angular rocks or cement blocks. If you are using a rock, secure a stout wire, like galvanized braided clothesline wire, to the rock, tighten it with pliers and secure it with a wire fastener, then attach your line to it. This avoids the big problem of ropes slipping off rocks.

For boats you may think a rock or block too cumbersome, but before investing in an expensive anchor from your friendly hardware merchant, consider the bottom where it will be used. The big hazard is sunken logs, which tend to become woven into other sunken logs and need a bulldozer to dislodge. If you are on a river that has been used for logging, or near the heavily wooded shore of a lake, you may have trouble. In this case the flukes — those two or more hooks on the bottom of the anchor — could fasten you irretrievably to the bottom; you may have to sacrifice the anchor to get home for supper. Maybe the old rock or block is not such a bad idea after all.

Whenever you carry an expensive anchor, remember to leave in your boat some light cord and a float, such as a small closed plastic bottle. Then if you do have to cut free, tie the cord to the anchor line to mark the spot. If you come back with friends in their boats, together you may salvage it.

ANIMALS

There is a tendency among cottagers, at the beginning, to love all animals. Without detracting from this noble sentiment, we think it wise to suggest that cottage country is not necessarily a Peaceable Kingdom in which all creatures, human and otherwise, co-exist in idyllic harmony.

No matter how long you have been cottaging, it might be wise to engage the locals in conversation about the fauna. You may well get some useful information after sifting through the tales about fish of shark-like proportions, bears that move houses, and the snake that bit young Billy's foot. Especially if you have children, it is well to be forewarned of the possibilities of encounters of the animal kind.

Aquatic Types

Bloodsuckers (leeches) Though not life-threatening, bloodsuckers are unpleasant at best and terrifying at worst. They are less likely to be found in the moving waters of a river than in a quiet lake. Use gentle propaganda to allay the fears of young children and to persuade them not to panic if they encounter a bloodsucker. Keep a damp-proof container of salt by the beach. When the need arises, sprinkle the bloodsucker liberally with salt, and it will curl up and fall off harmlessly. If you have no salt, or are in a real hurry, just pull it off.

Crayfish In the fresh waters of most cottage country, there are unlikely to be many hazardous biting creatures. Children can, with luck, be persuaded what fun it is to have a toe tweaked by a crayfish. If you have too many large crayfish for comfort near your dock, you can catch them with a simple trap made of ½-inch hardware cloth rolled in a cylinder about 20 inches long and 8 inches in diameter. Out of the same screening, make a cone for each end with a hole 4 inches in diameter at the small end. To avoid having to remove the cone each time you get a catch, on the top of the cylinder you can make a little doorway, which only you can open. For bait in the center you can put dead fish or even the remnants of a tin of fishy catfood, open at both ends.

Clams We have no record of cottagers being attacked by giant man-eating clams. In fact, the only risk seems to be cutting a tender foot on a sharp shell no longer inhabited by a clam.

Turtles Snapping turtles, which many people consider a delicacy, are often found by the shore or in the water, where they live to a great age. Their bite can be dangerous. Most people consider the best way to handle them is to run, or even walk, away from them. Warn children not to approach them. If you must catch a turtle, grab the shell just behind the head.

Small Land Animals

Bats Bats, which are really flying mice, have a far worse reputation than they deserve. They may touch a human being inadvertently in their gyrations, but the stories of bats that try to fly into women's long hair are unauthenticated myths. Bats are beneficial to cottage life because they eat enormous numbers of insects. It is therefore best to ignore them, but few cottagers do.

To get rid of the bat now flying around the bedroom, the best instrument is the kind of net used in fishing. Failing this, a tennis or badminton racquet has pushed many an unwanted bat towards the open door or window; but the racket may injure the harmless creature, and it is far less effective than a net in getting it out quickly. The morning after such an episode, search for evidence of a nest built inside your cottage attic or even in a hidden corner of your bedroom. It may have a family of young in it; you will have to persuade them firmly of the desirability of moving off your premises.

Beavers They are picturesque and their well-organized communities are fascinating to observe, but they can be a nuisance if they fell your prized trees or flood your land. Ordinarily, beavers are as shy as most animals, but when you are out of sight or asleep they can be very bold in invading your land, even close to the cottage. If you have a problem, do not try to deal with it yourself. Ask the local game warden about setting a trap and moving the offenders to a new home.

Groundhogs They are unlikely to cause you harm unless you have a garden, where they can be devastating. If you have a dog, groundhogs will probably stay away, for they are not an aggressive animal — except with someone else's vegetables. One way to eliminate them is to use a humane trap, available from good gardening stores. A better solution to the groundhog problem is to make your garden unwelcoming enough that they avoid it altogether. Ammonia bags hung from knee-high wire fencing will put off even a persistent groundhog very effectively, but they must be renewed often.

Porcupines The only justification for the existence of porcupines in the animal scheme of things is their ability to provide the main ingredient of porcupine stew, much favored by lost and starving trappers. Porcupines eat your plastic water lines, the hoses in your car, your cottage. (They love salt, even the traces left by sweaty hands; therefore, wear gloves when handling plastic pipes or wood.) They kill defenceless trees by nibbling bark; once their chewing has encircled a tree, it cannot be saved. They cause excruciating pain to inquisitive family pets. We hesitate to say it, but there is virtually no way to deal with resident porcupines aside from "termination with extreme prejudice." If you have a severe porcupine problem, we suggest that you call your local Humane Society for advice.

Rabbits Rabbits may well be lovable, but overnight they can destroy months or even years of gardening effort. In some ways they are worse than groundhogs; the season of their voracious appetite is longer, and they certainly move faster. Rabbits hopping across the spring snow may nibble the bark of young trees and thus kill them, sometimes above the protective wire mesh you so carefully installed when there was no snow.

A dog may solve the problem, but most rabbits know they are much faster than the family pet and therefore may safely ignore it. Shooting at rabbits may upset young members of the family. Use of a humane trap, and subsequent removal of the rabbit to the woods is one solution. Giving up gardening is another.

Raccoons The raccoon is one of the most intelligent and intrepid animals that may trespass on your property. It is also dexterous; having what passes for a thumb, it can translate devilish plans into effective action. It is also an extraordinarily attractive animal, which becomes almost a pet for many cottagers. Raccoons are even reputed to wash their hands after meals. If one becomes tame enough to sit on the back porch pleading for food, do not let young children near it, for it could inadvertently cause injury with its powerful paws. If you do

not want raccoons around, our only advice is to take great care in depriving them of your food. In particular, your garbage must be kept in foolproof metal containers, or in a virtually indestructible wooden cupboard.

Skunks The only thing people have against skunks is their smell. If they make a home under the cottage, or under the floorboards of a garage, shed, porch or outhouse, their smell is noticeable even though they have not been spraying. Camphor or mothballs spread in such places may persuade skunks to live at your neighbor's place instead — but then you must cope with the smell of mothballs. It is not a foolproof deterrent, and the crystals must be renewed each season.

If your dog, cat or any other furry pet is sprayed by a skunk, the only practical remedy is a tomato juice bath. Be lavish with the juice, and leave it in the fur to dry. Repeated applications may be necessary.

Snakes Most snakes in cottage country are harmless, and try to be friendly, but you should find out from the local people if there is any serious chance of meeting a poisonous snake. If so, please do two things. Take the trouble *now* to find the address of the nearest medical treatment centre with anti-venom serum, and quietly plan just what you would do in such an emergency. Second, buy a book or pictures identifying snakes and launch a small family education project. The object is only partly to warn of danger; knowledge will dispel the silly notion that all snakes are dangerous and thus encourage a healthier attitude to nature. Against that tiny chance of impending disaster, those few minutes of planning now could save a life.

Squirrels There are dozens of identifiable types of squirrels, and even more if you add chipmunks to your list. Their cycles of population are more obvious to cottagers than those of other animals. They may be a minor nuisance around gardens, where they have a tendency to dig up and consume bulbs. Planting mothballs with the bulbs may discourage squirrels, but don't sprinkle mothballs anywhere where there are young children who may eat them like peppermint candies. If you are at your cottage in winter, you will find squirrels to be major and expensive consumers of bird seed at feeders. If you are not there, they may break into your house and use your upholstery, blankets or clothing to make nests. If they become a nuisance, you can catch them easily in a humane trap baited with apple or peanut butter, and move them elsewhere. Never, of course, set a trap unless you will be there promptly to deal with the caught animal.

Rabies

Even animals that are normally no threat to humans — such as foxes — may be dangerous if they have rabies. Watch for signs of abnormal animal behavior, including a tendency to easy friendliness to humans, and keep an eye open for small animals which have died for no immediately apparent reason. If there is any suspicion of rabies, do not approach the animal, and report the occurrence promptly to the game warden or public health clinic. If there is any chance that you have been bitten by a rabid animal, speed to the nearest medical center. Ensure that the rabies vaccinations for your family pets are up-to-date before even approaching cottage country, and if your pet is bitten, consult a veterinary promptly.

Large Animals

Bears Unless your cottage is in the distant wilds where voracious and undiscriminating creatures abound, about the only life-threatening quadruped you may see is a bear, which may venture into so-called civilization in search of food, generally in late summer. If you keep well out of their way, travelling eastwards calmly and unprovocatively while they head west, the chances of unprovoked attack are remote. If, most improbably, a bear comes in your door (without opening it), when you are in the cottage, just distance yourself. Without getting near the animal, open every possible door and window to ease its exit. Do not try to frighten it by banging on the microwave oven. (It may eat the whole thing.) Don't use food as a bait to lure it outside: it will only remember that this is a good place for a free meal. If a bear comes, just wait till it goes. Then do what you should have done before the crisis: check that you have no food or garbage in unsecured containers. That precaution will not eliminate visits from bears; they may still wander by in search of berries. Removing temptation will lessen the chances that they will stay, return, or settle down for the winter. If a bear is showing signs of being a constant nuisance, ask the help of the nearest game officer.

Deer Deer, or even moose, may venture surprisingly close to towns in search of food in late summer. If you see one, count it as an interesting experience, even more so if you got a photo. Deer cause no harm and require no precautions. Don't let your dog persecute deer by chasing them to the point of exhaustion.

ARCHITECTURE

Cottages are the last refuge of closet architects. Perhaps you bought a cottage already firmly built, but do not despair. Even if it is not a handyman's dream, you can manufacture opportunities for new wings, decks and outbuildings for many purposes. Here is your chance to create your own Taj Mahal, St. Paul's Cathedral or even — depending on the neighbors — Great Wall of China.

It is a pastime to be highly recommended whether you intend to build it all with your own creative hands, or contract it out to Sam from the village. The dream carries you through the dreary winter as designs flow across the backs of envelopes. An important step in the process is the trip to the local library to look up books of cottage designs. They are less likely to inspire you than to trigger a desire to burst the bonds of conventionality on your own small turf. If your present buildings meet all conceivable needs, you might be moved to create a "folly" in the spirit of rich eighteenth century European landowners — a tower to be equipped with a telescope to view the skies and neighboring beaches; an orangery for intimate entertainments; a mad fountain which responds to music.

This is your chance. You would never have the nerve in the city — nor would you get past the building inspectors there. Cottage country is the place for the unleashing of creative instincts. If you have no artistic talents whatsoever, you can still build something. (If you don't believe it, look at what some developers do.)

B

BARBECUES

It is not by accident or even through aggressive marketing that the barbecue has become the central rite of cottage life. It brings food preparation to the great outdoors, liberating the preparer from standing over a hot stove so that he or she may stand over a hot barbecue surrounded by mosquitos. It makes food preparation the central entertainment of the social occasion, rather than a discreetly hidden adjunct.

The development of the cottage barbecue within a generation or two has progressed quickly from a campfire to a light metal container on legs to a hibachi to propane-fired high-tech. Along the way, those lovingly constructed brick or stone barbecues, which were once the altars for worshipful cottagers, are now overgrown with ivy. The fuel has evolved from local twigs to charcoal to products of the chemical industry.

The evolution of the barbecue has not been without its detractors. There are those who swear that the steak or freshly caught fish tastes distinctly better when it has been cooked over burning pine and hardwood, or at least over charcoal, than after being gassed. The evidence is controversial. The best is what the chef considers best.

Those using the campfire are unlikely ever to run out of fuel, unless they have forgotten to store some in a dry place. The stones on which the fire is built can give a long, intense and flameless heat conducive to temperature control by the skilled practitioner. And when the meal is over, it is the social center of the evening's crowd. How many people roast marshmallows on a gas barbecue? There is, of course, no need to be overly primitive. Wire racks from your old refrigerator or electric stove (or from a junk shop for a dollar or two) make cooking far easier and probably better. You can rig up a picturesque tripod of wooden poles or steel rods on which to hang a pot to boil the water for coffee, but a little preheating with a concealed electric kettle will save your waiting guests from dehydration. Campfire users must always remember to take careful measures to extinguish their fires before leaving.

The ordinary sheet metal barbecue or the hibachi, both using charcoal or charcoal briquettes, are faster to organize and can be lit in places (like the deck) where you really would not favor a campfire. Considering the innate ugliness of a rusting charcoal barbecue which no one gets around to putting away after use, the hibachi is the better bet of the two — if it is well-made. Insist on cast iron rather than sheet steel to give a more even, longer heat. Price is not necessarily a guide, for the imported cast iron models without gadgetry are among the cheapest. The hibachi has a smaller capacity than the portable barbecue, but this disadvantage is easily overcome by using two or more together. These devices give less risk of fire than campfires, but you cannot safely douse them with water without risk to the metal, especially cast iron. They should be covered with a piece of sheet metal at the end of the evening, or you can spray the coals very lightly with water without wetting the metal.

Any culinary disasters from the use of these types of barbecues usually arise because the operator does not take enough time for heating. Typically, the hungry guests assemble over drinks, the operator lights the charcoal with a flourish — or with an electric charcoal lighter. (The electric lighter is much better than an inflammable liquid if you value your eyebrows.) Rude enquiries such as "When do we eat?" and "What are you doing there anyway?" soon are heard from the starving guests. The chef, under intense social pressure, puts the meat on the grill where it is lost to sight in flame-filled clouds of greasy smoke. Soon people are eagerly clawing at the charred shapes on their paper plates. The eagerness does not last long. When the meal is all over, the charcoal is burning in a perfect glow for gourmet delights.

Instead, of course, the chef should light the charcoal at least half an hour before the guests are in sight, and have enough of it burning that none need be added for the rest of the meal. For many meats, and especially for fowl or lamb, we hold that the secret of success is how slowly the food is cooked, and how few are the explosions of flame from dripping fat. The favored place for the racks should be far up from the source of heat.

The gas barbecue, whether table-top or of piano dimensions, invokes other special skills, the most notable of which is knowing when the propane cylinder is about to breathe its last. If you do not own a gadget to show the amount of gas left, the presence of a spare, unused cylinder is a must for every meal.

There is no doubt that the gas barbecue gives the operator more control over the cooking than does any other outdoor method. There is no waiting period for heat-up, and no fire hazard when the meal is over. The only apparent disadvantages are the price and nuisance of storing the brute. Well, there is one other drawback. If your meal is a total failure, how do you find an alibi?

BEACHES

If your beach is a gleaming expanse of pristine sand, there is nothing much you need do, except boast about it. If, however, your swimming area is marred by rocks, sunken logs, weeds, or water too deep for small children, you may wish to take action.

Before you begin any alterations to your waterfront, check that local regulations do not make your fondest dreams illegal. In some jurisdictions, dumping sand in a waterway is forbidden through concern for pollution. It would be best to check with local authorities, for if you think dumping sand is hard work, wait until you have to scoop it out on the way to court. Thus, the first step is to surmount any legal hurdles.

Next, remove any sunken logs or branches. If the logs are really stuck, whether in a vertical or horizontal position, put a chain around one end and try to pull them ashore with a come-along dolly attached to a tree. If you are unlucky enough to have a small forest of upright deadheads, first try attaching two ropes to the upper end of each, and have two volunteers with firm footing try to loosen them by regular motion from two directions. (You can supervise.) You may still have to use the come-along dolly.

To move larger rocks, invite a lot of friends and neighbors (the terms are not necessarily mutually exclusive) for a rock bee with promises of generous hospitality. You will also need rakes, shovels and wheelbarrows. After the most obvious obstacles are out, have the crew form a line and move forward, kicking every bit of sand in the chosen area as they advance. When someone yells in pain, stop and extract the rock. When that is done, give them a drink and stiff iron rakes to comb the bottom.

If you can, examine the sand before you contract for it. It is worth a few extra dollars to get good sand, of a quality for mixing cement. Sand with humus material will stir up more easily and encourage the aquatic plants you do not want. When your sand is delivered — probably to a spot far away from the water — make a rock-free path to the shore for wheeling it out. Some old planks may be handy, but they will be useless when you enter the water. You can wheel out until the barrow is completely submerged, but the workers should generally be allowed to keep their noses above the surface. If the way is not bumpy, it is best to start dumping at the deep end, for the turbulence is more annoying when you start at the shore. If the wheelbarrow keeps hitting irremovable rocks, make your own underwater path with sand; it does not take much work to smooth out the piles with rakes. By the next day the water should be clean and sparkling again.

Especially if trees grow near the water's edge, it is important to rake the bottom, preferably both in autumn and in early spring. If any sharp rock still creates a hazard to tender feet, mark it with a small float. If you don't remove it before freeze-up, chances are it will be lost by spring.

That's how they built the beach at Ipanema — we guess.

BIOLOGICAL TOILETS

Environment-conscious cottagers will rejoice at the growing strictness of government inspectors in enforcing the regulations designed to prevent pollution of our waters. For cottagers whose soil is deep and conducive to the creation of septic fields, compliance with these rules poses no problem. But what of those countless others who, like St. Peter, have founded their house upon a rock? The trouble is that as standards of disposal become more strict, the means available to rock-bound cottagers to meet them seem to diminish.

There are two ways to reduce solid waste by bacterial action. It may decompose without oxygen, as in a septic tank. Since the temperature is not high enough to incommode all those microscopic bugs, it can create quite a stink. Aerobic bacteria, on the other hand, love oxygen, develop a real sweat while eating up the stuff and end up smelling like sweet violets — or almost. So much for science.

The old outhouse was the best known example of those deep-breathing microbes, and much has been written about its social benefits. Yet unless you live far from the reach of sniffing officialdom, forget it. The old leaching pit is equally frowned upon, even for your bathwater. Septic tanks are fine where they can be built, be financed and pass inspection. A holding tank is also permissible, but there are things most people would rather hold than the contents of a holding tank. Also, who is going to empty it for you and where?

So we have problems, and they are all the worse because sewage has become one of our biggest growth industries; we leave it to others to discern why we produce so much more than we used to. Another problem is that we consume so much water just to sloosh it away: some forty percent of the 30 gallons of water each of us uses daily. That, however, is something for the septic tank owners to worry about. What about those of us who have no place to install one?

So-called chemical toilets used to be so common and relatively cheap that you could pick them up at the corner convenience store. You simply added some pretty blue or green crystals to the mix and periodically, when no one was looking, carried out a couple of buckets of harmless guck for burial. But, alas, no longer. Most of them have given way to much more sophisticated "packaged aerobic systems" with motors, fans, temperature controls, bells and whistles. The main difference between these models and the old chemical toilet is a couple of thousand dollars. They are also hard to find, except in larger cities. Since, when operated properly, they do the job without too much smell or too many buckets to carry away, they are apparently revered by their owners, and they may be the only alternative.

In the view of some seasoned observers, government rules have become so unrealistically strict that they are self-defeating, hence the great grey water controversy. Grey water is the stuff which comes from your sink or shower. Common sense persuades most people that it is not as hazardous to health as other effluents. In short, if you can drain away this less risky liquid into a good leaching pit, the problem of serious waste disposal is enormously eased. It may be solved even by a holding tank or at least by a relatively small packaged aerobic system. We have known government inspectors who secretly have agreed with this technique, but regulations in most provinces prevent them from giving official approval to draining away sink water in a leaching pit.

Perhaps public pressure could provide simple and economic means to dispose of waste at cottages. What we need is a national movement. (See also **Outhouses, Septic Systems**.)

*B*LUEBERRIES

Unlike other small fruits such as strawberries and raspberries, which have been taught to grow luxuriantly in market gardens, blueberries are usually the possession of wild places, which means cottage country. To impress the city neighbors it may not be necessary to serve vintage champagne: far cheaper is a pie "from our very own blueberries."

You should search them out in early summer when they are green and useless. You can watch as they begin to turn to that magic purple-blue, and resolve to start picking them tomorrow. In that case, it is predictable that the birds will consume them that very evening.

In the great blueberry race between man and bird, the latter always seems to win. That is partly because birds cheat. They do not wait until the berries are ripened to your standard. Your only hope is that plants are so lavishly spread along the rocks that the birds do not have time to eat them all before you arrive. If you are really keen, never mind the witticisms of your neighbors. Go out and spread cheesecloth or light netting over your favorite patch in its final stage. It's more effective than scarecrows and better than bare bushes.

BOATHOUSES

There seems almost as great a variety of designs for boat-houses as for cottages, but there are some special warnings before you begin

The first step must be to make absolutely certain that you can legally put the boathouse at the spot you have in mind. Not only must your deed leave no doubt about your ownership of the land there, but you must also check that no by-law restricts construction on the edge of a waterway. If the situation is at all clouded, a wise precaution is to apply for a building permit at an early stage of planning.

The boathouse may be a magnificent retreat that includes living quarters, or a simple cupboard that protects light craft from weather and vandals. If there is any problem about authority to build, a cupboard up the shore may be the solution. It has the advantage of being cheap and probably will not need a building permit, but it serves only canoes, rowboats, small dinghies and other craft which can be lifted overland with reasonable ease.

There are two kinds of conventional boathouse: those which are built on the water, and those which are not. The first is far more difficult and expensive to build and maintain, but almost a necessity if you want protection for a large and heavy motor boat. Trouble comes from two directions: rot and ice. The danger of rot will be much reduced if you use pressure-treated lumber both for all underwater parts, and for construction near enough to the water's surface that it will often be damp from splashing. Continuously wet or continuously dry conditions are not nearly the risk of intermittently wet and dry.

Ice is the other problem that few boathouse builders seem to have solved. Rarely is it practicable for the amateur to sink concrete piers into the lake or river bottom deep enough that no freezing will ever occur beneath them. Therefore, the building will shift like any cottage on shallow foundations, and it may be even worse when one end is on land and the other on the water. Another winter enemy is the river or lake ice, which may press against the foundation with enormous force and shift it.

The solution is simple if the boathouse has only one floor and is therefore light enough to be adjusted by the owner. (If there are living quarters above, that is another storey.) You can even let the whole building float like a huge raft, but since it is too heavy to be hauled ashore, you will still need to protect it from the river ice. If the building is put on foundations, just assume that it may need annual adjustment. Anchor one end well on the shore. For the other end, make stout cribs at least 3 feet square and fill them with the largest rocks that can be shifted by hand; the crib will extend from the river bottom to whatever height you have decided for the lowest board of the boathouse. Each spring, check that the cribs are still secure and use a spirit level on the boathouse. Chances are that a small shifting with a jack, or perhaps just a large crowbar, will put it right, and you can fix it for the year by adding a few rocks to the cribs. Eventually you may have to rebuild the cribs, but meanwhile it is important never to neglect the structure for a season, or it may go far enough out of true to start wrenching out nails and warping boards.

If you are building the boathouse after you have occupied the cottage property for a few years, you will have the advantage of continuous observation of ice habits. If the chosen site is at a river bend where ice tends to pile especially heavily, it is probably a poor place to build. In most circumstances, the only protection against the power of the river or lake ice is rock in the form of breakwaters or cribs built away from the foundation work. It need not be farther away than a foot or two, provided the pushing ice, which will inevitably damage your protective barrier, does not push it into the foundation. Remember to repair that rock barrier each summer, preferably when the water is at its lowest, in August.

We leave designs of boathouses, with or without living quarters, to your own imagination. We ask only that you think of the future. If you are ever likely to have a large motor boat, why not plan for it when you build your first boathouse? Unlike cottages, boathouses do not lend themselves to new wings as families grow: they have to be torn down and rebuilt. If you may ever wish to add a room for guest accommodation on top, it will cost little more to build the lower part heavily enough now to accommodate it. If you are thinking of a simple structure on dry land for a boat, make it big enough to be a changing room and to house the unimaginable collection of junk you will accumulate in the years to come.

At the other end of the spectrum, if you do not want even a boat cupboard, consider a rack for the canoe or rowboat as an alternative to leaving it on the beach. You can make it in an hour with saplings or 2 × 2s, preferably attached to a stout tree. Lifting the boat onto it will probably bring less wear than the customary dragging up the beach, and there should be no rot problems if the craft is stored even a few inches above the ground. A good chain around the seats will give almost as much security as a boathouse.

BOATING SAFETY

Boating safety and fire are the two subjects which wise cottagers take very seriously.

For boating safety, don't wait till spring. From your local Red Cross or Transport Canada pick up the excellent literature they have prepared for free distribution. Those members of the family who claim to have reached the age of discretion should be required to read it, *and then to discuss it in a family conference.* At that conference, safety measures can be explained to the younger progeny, and *all* will be asked to contribute to a set of family rules. If the family together wants to set penalties for infractions, the rules are more likely to be respected and remembered than if parents alone try to lay down the law.

Those rules should cover such items as:
- who is allowed to use what boat;
- who is allowed to go out alone;
- a strict procedure for notification before any use of the boat;
- hours for boating (for example, be home an hour before sunset);
- safety equipment to be carried in boats (life preserver, life jackets, paddles or oars, whistle or horn, possibly flares, fire extinguisher);
- responsibility for periodic monitoring of safety equipment and of the condition of the boat;
- conduct in the boat;
- what to do if the boat capsizes, catches fire, loses a rudder or mast, hits a reef, encounters an electric storm, or other emergency situation;
- what to do if you find someone else in trouble;
- eligibility and rules for water-skiing;
- loss of privileges for breaking the rules.

The late winter family session on boating safety should be followed up by a refresher course — perhaps over the cottage dinner table — when the season opens. Especially if there are young family members, it is an appropriate time to broaden the discussion to all water safety: for example, setting limits on times, places and boundaries for swimming, designating supervision, setting summer targets for youngsters learning to swim, fixing a time for practice in life-saving and resuscitation. (See **Resuscitation**.)

BONFIRES

Are you sure you want one? There are two possible objections: fire and the law.

You must find out whether there are local restrictions on open fires. It is common to find that a permit, costing very little, is required, although in dry seasons it may not be easy to obtain. You might get away with breaking the law, but you will be taking a chance that at the climactic moment of your party the law will arrive with much water and an ugly summons. And if an unauthorized fire gets out of hand, you are in trouble.

These details attended to, you will prepare the site. Building a bonfire beside the lake is a sensible way to reduce the risks, but that is not precaution enough. If you have running water, leave the hose ready for action close by: if you live more primitively, make sure there are many buckets handy. Be certain there are no overhanging branches nearby, for it is easy to underestimate the power or range of the flames. Unless the spot you have chosen is surrounded by nothing but rock, or pure sand with no vegetation, make a ring of rocks around the site to form the perimeter beyond which no sparks will be allowed to go.

Need we say that starting the fire with gasoline is out? Take the trouble to find dry kindling. Although we discourage the use of any liquid fuel, stove oil is a good deal safer, and kerosene somewhat safer, than gasoline, provided you handle it very carefully. Do not throw a large dollop on the flames and wonder where your eyebrows went. Pour very little on some pieces of wood, just inside your stone ring, let it soak in, and then throw the pieces into the middle one at a time.

After the fire is burning well, you need not worry about how dry the wood is. Even green branches will catch from the intense heat. Forget about toasting marshmallows until the fire has died down to coals. Otherwise you risk scorched hands and culinary failure.

If you don't want a lot of charred wood to clean up, you will have to wait around for a long time until the bonfire burns out, then take a stiff iron rake, its handle often dipped in the lake, to roll out the coals. Whatever you do, don't leave those coals unattended to expire by themselves. That is how forest fires start. Soak the whole thing until the grey ghastly soup is cool to the touch, then soak around your perimeter ring some more. And when you wake up next morning, run right down to the site. If the ground is even warm to the touch, soak the area again. You may not believe it, but the remains of a bonfire can start a conflagration even two days after it seems safe.

Now, are you sure you want that bonfire?

Books

We do not presume to trespass on your summer reading, whether it is that pile of detective novels or those dubious magazines tucked on the back shelf of the storage room. We do suggest spending some of your relaxing moments exploiting the joys of cottage country. Such a self-education project can also solve the problem of Christmas giving for years to come.

The many books on nature can add a new dimension to the country experience for both adults and young people. Rocks are as good a place as any to start. A paperback on geology for the amateur and a rock collection (often available from your local museum) may be a stimulant to starting your own rock collection.

To learn about flora, buy separate books that will help you recognize trees, wildflowers and so-called farm weeds. If you plan to start your own first garden, of course, books on gardening abound. For fauna, look for books on birds, freshwater fish and small animals.

Don't overlook astronomy, even if you have no intention of buying a telescope. In the country you will see far more stars than city dwellers. Monthly sky charts, available from many sources, including the National Museum of Science and Technology, will give point and purpose to your skyward staring.

In the country you are more conscious of weather. An amateur's book on meteorology could equip you to become a local forecaster — you may do better than the professionals.

Your proximity to nature may encourage more curiosity about frontier times. Reading an old classic like *Roughing It in the Bush*, by Susanna Moodie, will be even more pleasing in the country. This is also a good time to interest your family in more contemporary books of historical fiction written for a younger audience. Your family is more likely to enjoy the possibly tedious drive to the cottage if they become interested in the older architecture they pass. There are simple books on architectural history which tell the story of styles still common in the towns and the countryside, as well as specialized works on barns and railway stations.

Then, of course, there are the more practical references. A book on first aid is a must, and a paperback medical dictionary can be comforting (or the reverse) if medical aid is far away. On that same shelf you could collect leaflets on poisonous weeds (like poison ivy and poison oak) or poisonous snakes. (See **Animals**.)

Your books on operating the cottage will depend on your ambition to build or maintain the structures yourself, or to rely on others. Since "readily available local help" is usually a contradiction in terms, it seems desirable for even the least manually dexterous cottager to have some printed guidance. Try a general book on household maintenance which ventures into items like water pumps and explains something of residential electrical systems to the totally uninformed. A quite separate volume should deal with construction for those with dreams. If you have not had much experience with structural carpentry, don't rely on plans alone, but first give yourself a fast course from books.

If reasonable self-sufficiency is your goal, you might want to buy a book on maintaining small motors to help you with boats, chain saws, lawnmowers and similar equipment.

Of course, before you even start on your cottage career, you may think it wise first to study the latest bestseller on how to become a millionaire — fast.

BOUNDARIES

When you acquire your foothold in cottage country, building a fence may seem a low priority, but knowing your exact boundaries is important. Without delay you should resolve any doubts about your deed or what it means on the ground.

There are many horror tales of people who had long assumed — wrongly — that they knew where their land went, and then were forced to abandon plans for that new guest house, or even to tear down part of the cottage itself. Never assume that your neighbors will always be kindly and understanding. Next year their property may be in less sympathetic hands. Even public utilities have been known to have fallible records which lead them to assert — perhaps incorrectly — the right to cut down half your forest.

If there are no survey markers on any corner of your property, you would do well to convince your neighbor(s) to share the costs of employing a surveyor to establish them. If there is even one metal pin, you should be able to figure out where the lines go, if you are willing to accept a small error. You do not need surveyors' instruments to plot your boundaries. All you require is a long tapeline, a simple celluloid protractor, two sticks of 1 × 1 inch wood about 2 feet long secured by a single screw at one end, a reasonably good compass, and a buddy equipped with 6-foot marker sticks. That buddy should be your next door neighbor, or neighbors, to avoid future argument. Identify the pin from the deed. For example, it could be at the corner near the hydro pole on the shore, or at the end of the entrance road.

Use the compass to find as exactly as possible where true north is; if you don't know the variation between true north and compass north in this region, find out from the planning branch at the town hall, and adjust the compass reading accordingly. Read the angle of your property line from the survey plan or deed, and find the angle on the protractor. Then pivot the two sticks to the same angle and don't let them slip. With the screw towards you, line one stick towards true north, and the other to the required angle. Have your buddy stand far away and sight along the stick to guide him or her for the placing of a temporary marker. Then measure on the line the distance noted on the deed or survey plan.

If your lot is huge, you will have to repeat the process with your buddy until you get to the end of that property line. Put a semi-permanent wooden marker there. That should be a boundary angle marked on your survey plan. Try again to find a pin in that vicinity. If you can't see it, repeat the process with angle, tape and buddy. If you are lucky, there will be only four sides, but even so your final reading will put your fourth peg a disconcerting distance from the first one instead of on top of it. Repeat the whole process, but this time go in the opposite direction. You can then average your error by putting your permanent markers midway between your two attempts at each corner. If you do it all summer, and get a hundred readings to average, you should be mighty close.

Or maybe you should phone that surveyor.

However you do it, put at each corner of your property a low metal stake with its top painted red — so it won't be lost or tripped over. Then write a note saying what you have done in whose company, initial and date it, copy it, attach one copy to your deed and give one to your neighbor(s).

Buoys

There are four common uses for buoys:
- to serve as an anchorage for boats;
- to mark the limits of safe swimming;
- to identify something on the bottom — a jagged rock, for example, or Uncle Walt's golf ball;
- to attach the foot valve of your water system.

As an anchorage for boats, the buoy has some great advantages over dragging the vessel onshore. Storms do less damage to boats that are moored out on the water than to boats that are by the shore where they may be dashed on rocks or even sand. You can moor a boat to a buoy by yourself from shore, or launch a boat without heavy lifting.

A simple design requires flotation material, such as a scrap of styrofoam left over from building the raft (see **Rafts**). Enclose the material in a box no more than a foot square. It should be made of scrap cedar, preferably 2×8 sides, with 1×3 slats on top, and a piece of 2×3 or 2×4 across the bottom to keep in the styrofoam and to hold the anchor wire or chain. Be sure that the 2-inch lumber is well secured with spiral nails, at least $3\frac{1}{2}$ inches long.

The anchor can be an angular rock or cement block. Its size depends on the kind of boat you plan to attach to it, and the kind of bottom, for you do not want it to drag in a strong wind.

For a small boat, it should weigh at least 50 pounds. The cable can be wire or chain. If the water in your lake or river drops a lot during the summer, you might choose a chain and a U-fastener with bolt; the chain loops around the board on the bottom of the buoy and is attached back to itself with the fastener; or, it is attached with the fastener to a hitching ring screwed into the bottom of the buoy. It is not very difficult later in the season to pull the chain a bit tighter to compensate for the lower water levels.

Attach two hitching rings to the sides of the buoy, and fix galvanized rope pulleys to each of them. When the buoy is anchored in place, provide yourself with enough 1/4-inch polypropylene rope to reach just over double the distance of the buoy from shore. Thread the rope through a pulley and leave both ends, one with a snap fastener, lightly tied to some object onshore. Your boat must have a painter as long as the distance from the buoy to shore.

To tether your boat, just snap onto it one end of your buoy rope and pull the other end until the boat slides out to the buoy, meanwhile keeping one end of the painter onshore. When the boat is out there, secure the other end onshore. To get your boat again, just undo the shore line, and pull on the painter until the craft is at your feet.

To mark the limits of your safe swimming area, or an object on the bottom, you don't need to be nearly as elaborate. Plastic 4-liter jugs are the usual solution, with a rope from handle down to anchor. To mark the limits of the swimming area, stretch between the buoys a light rope with obvious floats (wood or smaller plastic bottles) every 3 or 4 feet. An anchor and buoy every 25 feet or so is a good idea. Even if the distance is relatively short, it is sensible to use at least three such devices in a straight line, so that you can easily detect any drifting on your boundary.

For securing your water line, you need the first kind of buoy. It can be attached to the anchor line so that the plastic pipe is out of the way of boats, but well above the bottom. A far better procedure than letting the foot valve rest on the bottom, it will prevent trouble with sand mucking up the valve and discoloring your water.

BURGLARS

One of life's unhappier episodes begins in the middle of the night when you hear a sound evidently caused by an intruder. We would like you to live to dine out on the story.

But don't worry unduly. The chances are strong in cottage country that the burglar did not intend to break into an occupied dwelling, and he or she will quickly disappear on realizing the mistake. If you do suspect a burglary to be in progress at your cottage, here is what to do: first, quietly slip out of bed and latch your bedroom door. You really do not want to meet this class of visitor.

Second, when you are reasonably satisfied that it is not the cat, your drunken bother-in-law or a poltergeist, reach for the intercom, phone or panic button by your bed (See **Communications, Security**) and quietly share your concerns with your neighbor or the police.

Third, after checking that other windows are closed and locked, open one just wide enough to scream your head off. Since this performance is largely for the benefit of the burglar, don't just yell "Help." Call a person's name (fictitious or real) to give the impression that (a) you know someone is nearby, and (b) that you regularly call this heavily armed, 250-pound friend to destroy burglars. This strategy will probably send the intruder running.

In the highly unlikely and unfortunate circumstance that the burglar wishes to confront you and succeeds in doing so, avoid heroics. Try to give the impression that you will not cause trouble. Your object is not to apprehend the intruder, but to persuade him or her to leave as quickly as possible. While you are together, concentrate on memorizing every detail of the burglar's appearance and voice to help the police in their investigation.

When the incident is over, report it immediately to the police.

C

CANOES

Of all the water craft available to the cottager, the canoe has had the most appeal. It evokes idyllic hours of slipping through unfamiliar waters to explore, like our forefathers, beyond that final bend. It suggests effortless gliding on the lake when the heat of the day has seeped into a cool moonlit night. It is the lightest of all craft to carry, whether portaging or putting it on the family car en route to some secret fishing spot. It is an efficient form of motive power. It is relatively cheap, though the costs of different models vary enormously. It is kind to the environment, a visual adornment rather than a noisy blight. Its only notable drawback is that it is less safe than other boats for the very young and for the unpracticed amateur. But canoeing is an easily learned skill well worth acquiring.

Someone inexperienced in canoes should not go out and buy one. It is important first to try different shapes, sizes and materials. It is not enough to practice on your neighbor's canoe, though any experience will help you make a better decision as to the characteristics important to you. If there is an opportunity, rent a succession of different canoes and put them to the tests you have in mind as a future owner. Do you want appearance, grace, stability, speed, manoeuverability, lightness, toughness, suitability for shallow or deep water or for white water, adaptability for sailing (or even for a motor) large cargo and passenger capacity?

The variety embraces birchbark, cedar, canvas, aluminum, fibreglass and other plastics. You can eliminate the first unless you are a special collector, and cedar canoes are out of the price range of most cottage buyers. The aluminum, which is the least beautiful and the noisiest of all, is by far the most popular because it is sturdy and easily maintained. Canvas, meaning canvas stretched over wood, is light and quiet, but it does not stand up to sharp rocks and needs continuous work. The plastics are gaining greater favor because of their toughness, lightness, relative ease of repair and low maintenance.

Size depends on your projected use. Canoes of about 17 or 18 feet are most popular for family use. They should not weigh more than about 80 pounds, for even if you are not planning to portage, you will probably be carrying it to the shore, or heaving it onto the roof of the car. And the heavier it is, the more work paddling will be.

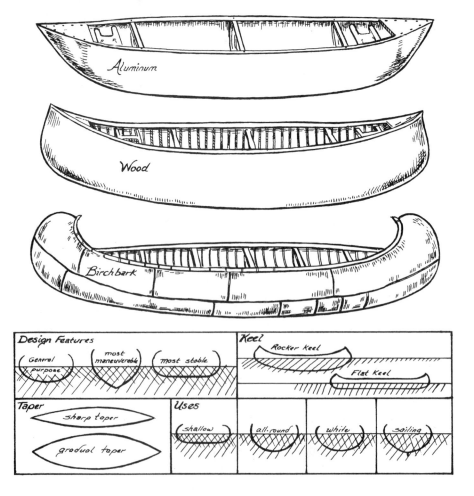

Then there is the shape. The most stable canoe has a flat bottom from side to side, but it is the least manoeuverable. A keel that goes deeper in the middle than at either end eases turning, but creates steering problems in strong crosswinds. Most families compromise and choose a canoe with a slightly rounded bottom and fairly flat keel. When the sides curve in, you may get a bit wetter in rough water, but the craft is stronger and paddling is easier. Don't be too carried away by graceful high peaks at the ends; they look nice, but they catch crosswinds.

There is also the kayak, which is a marvellous craft but an unlikely choice for your first boat. In the hands of the expert, the kayak is enormously fast, manoeuverable and exciting. A kayak can also be an open invitation to drowning unless great care is exercised by the learner or high skill by the veteran. Today they are usually made of reinforced plastics with one or two cockpits which are chosen or designed for the user; in fact, one talks about "wearing" a kayak.

Canoe paddles come in wood, aluminum or plastic. A good paddle should flex slightly and be about 6 inches wide. Ideally, the bow paddler should have a paddle that reaches from ground to chin, and the stern paddler, who does the steering sternly, has one that is a bit longer but with a wider and shorter blade.

When carried by car, the canoe must always be inverted on roof racks. A wise precaution is to run ropes or web straps around the canoe and under the car roof (with the doors open) in case the rack itself should ever work loose. Then attach ropes from the bow and from the stern down to the underpinnings of the car as a defence against the enormous pressure of the wind which may otherwise wrench it sideways. Stop the car to check the load often en route.

And before you launch your canoe, remember safety: have flotation cushions and/or life preservers in the boat. Any passenger who is not a strong swimmer must wear the life preserver at all times in the canoe, and all must wear them if there is a chance of being in difficult water. To help the uninitiated to enter the canoe from a dock, instruct them to put their weight equally on their hands grasping the gunwales while stepping squarely in the middle of the bottom. Finally, do not allow anyone to even think about changing places when you are away from shore.

CHAIN SAWS

The chain saw is the most lethal instrument in cottage country. Obviously, a sharp chain designed to speed through rock elm will do an even more efficient job on fingers, legs and necks. In relation to its size and weight, it is one of the most powerful instruments ever put in the hands of amateurs, and one of the most dangerous.

It is, however, enormously useful. Before buying one, please do two things. The first is to buy or borrow a good book about chain saws. Some excellent manuals are published by manufacturers. Don't worry if the publisher's brand is not yours; ninety percent of the information will apply. Then read it with strict attention. Be sure to take it with you to the cottage, and scan it again just before your first try at sawing. The second chore is to study the latest available non-commercial testing reports in a publication such as *Canadian Consumer*, published by the Consumers Association of Canada, *Protect Yourself*, published in both official languages in Québec by l'Office de la protection du consommateur, or the American *Consumer Reports*.

The marketing of chain saws is highly competitive, particularly in the range designed for the do-it-yourself owner. Within this range, differences in performance of brands and price are generally not great. There is, however, a significant price gap between this type of chain saw and models designed for the professional woodsman. There is little point in crossing that gap for ordinary cottage use. Within the do-it-yourself group, there is a price range depending on size and extras. If you intend your saw only for pruning, a small, light one will do. If you are going to cut down many dead trees or collect all your firewood, a 16-inch blade is normal. If any of the extras are clearly related to safety, try to stretch your budget to get them. Useful devices to look for include the tip on the end of the blade to prevent kickback, the protective plastic guard on top in front of the hand — both for safety— and an automatic oiler with a manual override. The automatic feature is helpful for a beginner who may forget to keep the blade lubricated; the override is a good idea, because the automatic device may gum up, or you may be in really tough wood and want to be lavish with the oil.

Commit yourself to the essential maintenance equipment, some of which will come with the saw: wrench and screwdriver, grease gun (if needed for the model you buy), at least one spare chain, and chain-sharpening equipment. Chain sharpening can be quite difficult. Many amateurs wisely prefer to get a professional to sharpen the chain, and equip themselves with enough spare chains to serve between visits to the sharpening expert. The alternative is to become an expert yourself, and save both time and money. The true expert is likely to use nothing but a $3 file and an incantation, but you will not be one of these for a while. You may want to invest in a device (for about $35) which ensures you get the right angle. If you sharpen the chain yourself, you are more likely to keep it constantly touched up, which is a good thing.

We have left to the last the most important supplement. Don't let us ever catch you out in the woods without a hard hat, safety glasses and steel-toed boots. Ear protectors are also a thoroughly good idea if, at the end of the day, you want to be able to distinguish Mozart from the top forty. Heavy leather gloves are a good idea if you can wear them comfortably.

Finally, once you are committed to this lethal but wonderfully useful instrument, never go out in the woods without a buddy. It saves time when they come to look for the mortal remains.

CHECKLISTS

Next to the deed and maybe the diagram of the sewer, the most important cottage document is the checklist. Although your memory is undoubtedly phenomenal, you could just have a costly off-moment. But that is only part of the reason. If you lend your cottage to someone else, or if your growing family is reaching the age of discretion, equipping them with checklists will save you a lot of trouble, and ensure that maintenance procedures are consistent.

The two most important checklists cover the things to do on first arrival in spring, and at the close-up in the fall. In between, periodic checklists can save time and effort.

Writing up the first draft is an agreeable pastime when one is still in the city, impatiently awaiting the spring thaw. Visualize every detail on arrival at the cottage in a reasonably logical order. ("1. Clean up the car seat where the dog was sick.") A sample list:

Before entering, walk around the building to see if anything was disturbed by man, woman or beast.

Unlock the door.

Check every room for any untoward disturbance before the family really disturbs them.

Switch on the power.

Remove the plywood from the windows and store it beside the woodshed.

Remove the winter cap from the chimney.

Take the matches, soap and other items beloved by mice from the oven.

Connect the water. (Detailed instructions are posted over the tank, of course.)

Turn on the refrigerator.

And so on. And so on. The list is personal to each cottager, and it will not be complete until you have test-driven it on your arrival.

There could be lists for weekends later in the season, which give details for putting the boat and dock into operation, dragging out the lawn games and hammock, checking for fallen trees and branches for disposal, road mending, firewood supply, roof repair, screen installation, and much, much more.

At the end of the season, more than a simple lock-up is required. This is the time to list tools that need to be sharpened, repaired or replaced, and a time to wipe a thin film of oil over anything that will rust. This is the time to remind yourself of other purchases "we'll never go another season without." Then comes the sad ritual of putting away and winding down. Remember to make your list so detailed that someone totally unfamiliar with the premises can follow it. (See **Closing Up.**)

Finally, if you are really well organized, you will see that a copy of each list remains in the cottage, and a copy goes with you to the city to be lovingly elaborated on in the dead days of winter when cottages are only for dreams.

CHISELS

Wood chisels are part of every handyman's kit. Their number, variety and quality depend on your skill and ambition. If you have neither, at least furnish yourself with a one-inch chisel of medium quality. It will come in handy for all sorts of things, such as getting the old putty out of a broken window and opening the bedroom window, or even for opening the pork and beans when the power has deserted the electric can opener.

Many cottagers overlook cold chisels, the kind that are needed for cement and even rock. The great Precambrian Shield, on which so many cottages are built, is impervious to screwdrivers and nail files. So are the cement blocks which may be in your foundation. We suggest having two chisels: one narrower than an inch, one wider.

Then there is the 4-foot monster called the 16-pound chisel. (They come in other weights.) The uninitiated may refer to it as a bar or crowbar. It is invaluable for levering away heavy rocks which nature has perversely placed on roads or cottage sites. It is also good for levelling the lighter parts of the cottage itself (the veranda, for example) when you find that frost has made the doors or windows behave badly. Sometimes it may be useful at grass-cutting time when there is no other way to get the eldest son out of the hammock.

CLOSING UP

This sad ritual varies according to the cottager. After all, it is not everyone who must take home the Van Dycks from the dining room.

That brings up an important question: how much do you leave behind? There are those who like to leave the cottage totally ready for use as soon as the door is open. There are other cottagers, generally those who have entertained vandals every winter, who take away virtually everything movable. This is a decision you have to weigh according to your evaluation of local risks. If you choose something in between, bear in mind that most thieves and vandals tend to the lower end of the age spectrum. Their first interest seems to be sharp knives, with which they practice on your furniture. Next most vulnerable are items which they think they can sell, notably audio-visual equipment. Stereos and television sets rank higher than grandmother's antique china. Don't encourage them to mayhem by leaving around destructive tools like axes, crowbars and hammers: hide them well. Fire extinguishers are a tough question. Young vandals seem to get a charge from discharging fire extinguishers and leaving your premises under a thick layer of greasy white dust which is almost impossible to clean up. But since they also may light a fire — carelessly — should there be fire extinguishers to be used by those with a little conscience? These are moral dilemmas which only cottagers know.

In general, there seems little point in trying to make a cottage super-safe. It is impossible anyway; it takes a lot of trouble and the damage from frustrated vandals may then be all the greater. You may think it worth the effort to cover windows with plywood, which also protects them from birds or flying branches, and may even prolong the life of wood frames. If you decide on plywood, ask at your local lumber company for damaged sheets which sell at a fraction of normal cost and may be quite adequate for the purpose.

Your biggest job after covering of windows is likely to be draining the water system, and that means draining, not just closing down. The foot valve must come out of the lake, to be cleaned and dried. The tank and pump have to be emptied. Take special care to see that the lowest drain cock is opened and the pump run for a minute after all seems empty. The plastic pipe should be emptied as far as is reasonably possible. If it froze in a low place last year, and you had to fix the split with a joiner, loosen off that connection (to allow the water to drain out) so that it will not happen again. If you have hot water, the power should be switched off at the tank as well as at the circuit breaker, then drain the water carefully. Repairing copper pipe is such a bore that it is worth the effort to clear water from it by blowing through it very hard. If it has a low place prone to freezing, put a drain cock there.

If you are particularly anxious that your stove or any other electrical equipment not be used in your absence, remove and hide the fuses. Taking away the circuit breaker is a bit extreme, but the amateur can do it.

Putting a simple wooden cap on the chimney will discourage birds or squirrels from coming in by that route and will also stop snow and rain.

If there is a record snowfall next winter, you may be glad that you had put in temporary roof supports. (See **Snow.**)

Closing up is the time to take inventories of tools and supplies in order to avoid frustrations on the first spring trip. It is also the time for all those winter precautions like winterizing the boat motor, the lawnmower and any other internal combustion engines which seemed so labor-saving in July. It is also time for smearing oil on anything likely to rust.

Now you will come to the smaller things which require attention. Have you emptied the electric kettle and everything else holding freezable liquid? If you have a flush toilet, are you sure all water is drained, or should you put some anti-freeze in the bowl just in case? Is everything that mice might eat — short of the chesterfield — tucked into the oven or metal containers? Are all flammable materials, such as gas for the chain saw, stored outside, far from harm's way? Did you leave that paper and pencil on the table so that legitimate users can record their presence? Is your "in case of accident please notify _____" note on the front door?

It's time to close the door on the season. Half an hour down the road, you will be thinking of next summer. The new season has begun.

COLD

Cottagers may have the illusion that their country retreat means only long hot days, the splashing of swimmers and the scent of warm pine brezes. Yet it is not always like that. Even during the balmy days of summer, cold weather can unexpectedly descend upon cottage country occasionally during the day and more often at night.

For those with a generous budget, winterizing the cottage is the ultimate solution, though we delete from our visiting lists those who introduce air conditioners. For the rest of us poor folk, it is a matter of compromise between a frigid interior and a frigid banker.

Of course, insulation will yield dividends on hot days as well as cold nights. If you can't insulate everywhere, the roof or ceiling is the highest priority, followed by the walls. Insulation under the floor will be appreciated in winter, but you may not notice the improvement during cool summer nights. If you happen to be panelling a room, the investment in 6 mm polyethylene sheeting to form a vapor barrier will help you evade the draft.

To do a good job (which takes little money and not very much time), discover where those cold breezes are entering. Make the cottage as dark as possible on a bright day, and watch where the sunlight dances in. Alternatively, you can light the cottage brightly at night, and go outside to see the extent of your problem. Then caulk each of those cracks and holes with a caulking gun or with caulking cement and a spreader.

If you are serious about winter use, but your pocketbook does not run to double-glazed windows, put plastic sheeting on the outside of all the windows and all the doors but one. Stapling is fastest, but tacking with thin wood strips is better proof against windstorms and more economical, for you can then re-use the plastic. It is not sufficient to close the flue in the fireplace: whenever it is not in use, close it off with a tight-fitting board or blanket.

Don't forget the benefits of passive solar heat in any structure. If you are using the cottage only in summer and if heat is your main problem, give tender loving care to the nearby shade trees which point sunward. If you are thinking also of winter, discourage coniferous trees in that direction, for they will obstruct heat. A high cedar hedge is a great windbreak, provided it is far enough away not to give shade in winter.

To lessen that damp feeling on cool nights, check that the ground under the cottage is dry. If roof run-off is finding its way underneath the structure, the dampness is bad for you and — much more important — it will speed deterioration of the wood of your cottage. Somehow you must divert the flow and get rid of all stagnant water. If you are on rock covered with a thin layer of soil, it is best to scrape the rock clean under the building. (Don't you wish you had done it before construction?) This procedure will also discourage animal life.

And, if you haven't already, think about heating. A fireplace is hopeless except for romantic thoughts. Don't waste money on an ordinary stove: buy an energy-efficient stove that will keep your family warm for hours while you are outside getting warm by splitting wood. A cookstove may be tempting, but remember how it will heat the house in July when you are trying to cool it; for such days you will need a standard range or microwave as backup. Unless you are already an expert on stoves, remember to consult those non-commercial consumer reports before entering the retail jungle.

Electric heating also makes sense, especially if it is a matter only of removing the damp chill of August evenings. After checking that your electric service will handle electric heating, you might want to think of one or two baseboard units (perhaps of 1500 watts each) in the main room and a 500 watt unit in the bathroom, particularly if it is equipped with a tub or shower. In the bedrooms, electric blankets are a reasonable and cheaper substitute when the power is working. The advantages of electric heat are that you will not get too hot, as from a stove, there is no hassle with firewood, and it is the safest type of heat if properly installed. Also, it may well be less expensive to purchase than a good energy-efficient stove. Please don't rely on portable electric heaters, which can be fire hazards. If you feel tempted to use one regularly, call in the electrician to install safer baseboard heating.

COMFORT

Whether your cottage is a distant dream, or already a family institution, please stop a moment and think about your philosophy of cottaging.

Is the cottage designed to be a complete escape from your lifestyle in the city, or is it a relaxing change of scene?

By the first we mean a romantic back-to-the-land philosophy in which you teach yourselves and your children the joys and travails of primitive living. You do not regard hauling buckets of water from the lake as an inconvenient way to prepare for dinner. You know that a trip in the rain to the outhouse is just one of those things that must be done. These aspects of cottage living are part of the ritual of placing the cares of the city as far away as humanly possible. For philosophical as much as economic reasons, you may turn your back on electricity, knowing that it brings in its wake the mayhem of television and noisy motors. You see rewards in your ability to cope, the self-reliance and interdependence that your family learns, and the total change as you move from city to country.

At the other extreme are those who want a change of scene from the city, but also a rest. They do not fancy heating water over an open fire, or finding that it's bedtime before the dishes are even washed. They favor certain labor-saving devices and are not averse to enjoying some of the entertainments that modern technology can provide. They believe in the law that the joy of a cottage is measured in the ratio of hard work to time in the hammock. At the end of the holiday they are rested.

Perhaps you should consider to which end of the spectrum you are nearer. It is quite possible that your views will change with the years, usually in the direction of less work and more leisure. That was typical of our hard-pressed ancestors who started out with little choice in the matter.

We raise this question as more than a philosophical point. However strong your views, you will probably admit that there are some points to be made by each side. Are you sure that you are not unconsciously changing your cottage lifestyle, perhaps in ways that will later make you wonder why your enthusiasm for the country has dwindled? Is that new gadgetry really important enough to erode the sense of family self-reliance you once enjoyed? Do you really balance this new convenience against the dangers of making the cottage a city clone? And horrors, are you sure that this new project is not a response to what you have seen the neighbors doing?

There is a tremendous value in cottage living for everyone — sometimes it is worth wondering if you are getting from it everything that you really want.

COMMUNICATIONS

Whether your idea of a cottage emphasizes primitivism or creature comforts, communications are worth a passing thought. If telephone service is available, do you decline it with scorn, proclaiming that you come here to escape the phone? Maybe it is worth a second thought.

We can cite sad cases of cottagers without a telephone who have spent precious summer days by the phone booth down at the village awaiting that important call. It may not be the year's business deal at all, but a message about illness in the family. Isn't there some advantage in receiving a phone call from Sam Jones before he arrives unexpectedly, so that you can tell him and his five children that you have just contracted leprosy with no visitors allowed, instead of hearing the crunch of gravel under the wheels of his overladen station wagon? When the children reach that age when the company of their friends becomes more vital than the isolated tranquillity of the cottage, are you not more likely to keep them in the family bosom if they can communicate with the outside world? Would you not like the feeling that you could phone instantly to the fire department, police or doctor?

If you have a phone, you might want to consider two accessories to reduce the hassle of running for the phone just as you are flexing for a superb jack-knife from the diving tower. One is the remote unit, which you can take to the beach or even fishing (if you are near shore). The other is the answering machine, which lets you ignore all phone calls until you decide to run the tape once a day. Of course, your city friends who pay long-distance charges to talk to your machine may not be pleased.

If the telephone is not an option, you may wish to create a simple local communications system. It can be as easy as two wires strung along the ground with some cheap equipment at either end to let you communicate with your nearest neighbors. There are two justifications for it. One is security. A remote place in the country can sometimes seem scary at night to city people; if one happens to be alone when that creaking begins to sound more and more like footsteps, it is comforting to know that you can press a buzzer to summon company. Or if the children are old enough to be left alone when you are out visiting, you and they may feel better if they can get help should they be worried.

The other justification is privacy. If you have a line to your neighbors, and perhaps a call box out at the end of the road, you can make it known that you do not welcome guests who have not first phoned to see if their visit will be convenient. A cottage is the place to do your own thing, and it's just possible that it is a thing you would prefer not to continue in front of an unexpected audience.

The simplest version of such systems is similar to the old party line on which each subscriber responds to his own series of long and short buzzes that ring on every phone. They can cost as little as $10 each plus cheap wire. Sophisticated versions, which run to around $100 per unit plus expensive wire, give the same privacy as dial phones on single-party lines. Neither requires great skill to install.

The kind of FM communications unit which you simply plug into the electric circuit is another option, but you would be wise to borrow one to try before investing. They will not work if a hydro transformer is between units, and are therefore useless between two buildings, each of which has a transformer between the main line and the house. Also, in some places, they pick up so much static as to be almost worthless. Don't count on walkie-talkies unless you have tried them first on the site. The cheap ones are low on range and reliability and serve best as toys. The better ones may have a place in boat-to-shore communications when the boaters are within sight.

COMPOST

It really is true that you can convert grass clippings, garden cuttings and much kitchen waste into beautiful muck, even though surveys prove that out of every 7.32 people starting a compost pile, only one reaps the rewards. Even if you do not succeed, it is a nice lesson in how hard nature has to work.

You can't just throw all that garbage into a pile. You must make layers, each about 8 inches thick. The experts say that the first layer ought to include old vegetables; the fish you caught, but the family wouldn't even cook; and green weeds. Next you spread manure (not every home admits to having a ready supply), wood chips, pine needles, hay, straw and shredded newspaper. Then comes a layer of grass cuttings and leaves. On top of that is soil, lime and bonemeal, and, if you want to cheat a little, one of those packages you can buy from the seed store to make composts. Then you start it all again.

After two weeks, you turn over the whole pile from top to bottom, thoroughly mixing the layers as you go. Then every week you do it again. Finally, when it is half-decomposed, you shovel away the snow drifts and use it on the garden.

And it is excellent exercise.

D

DOCKS

If this is your first approach to docks, you must decide why
you want one. Is it just to swim from? That may be a good
idea if the lake bottom is lined with sharp stones, muck or other
undesirable walking ground. But if the bottom is easy to walk
on, and shelves so gently that you would not be able to dive from
the end of the dock anyway, perhaps a raft is a better answer. It
can serve as a small dock while fastened to the shore, or it may
be moved out for safe diving or even fishing. Its portability is
also a great advantage when you want to store it safely at the
end of the season. (See **Rafts**.)

But you may still want a dock for the boat.

The decision on dock design depends on whether you want
a temporary or a permanent installation. If you have no large
rocks around, the decision is probably made for you: it can't be
permanent. The permanent dock, which is far cheaper, and
creates less problem of storage in autumn, will still need maintenance every spring. If you have lots of large rocks and willing
arms, you can, in effect, make one or two rock piles up to the
high water level and place a wooden frame on it, but it is not a
good idea. The rocks will spread out, especially with ice, and be
in the way of bathers' feet. It is better to make rough cribs,
slightly narrower than the proposed dock, and high enough to
reach from the bottom to just above high water. If you want to
reduce future maintenance, invest in pressure-treated lumber of
a nominal thickness of 2 inches. Use light cross bracing, for the
crib may well tilt next winter, and you want to be able to right it
with ropes from shore without destroying it. Put enough rocks
in each crib to enable you to adjust it firmly on the bottom and
in a straight line from shore, then fill them up. Cedar is the best
material for the frame and decking.

An alternative to the permanent dock is a rock-anchored dock,
which is put out every year. This may be a better choice if you
have reason to believe that ice action would be strong enough

to damage those cribs each winter. In this version, you use standard trestles made of 2 x 4s. The length of the legs on the trestles
will have to be adjusted to your water depth; if your beach
shelves steeply into deep water, the outer trestle will obviously
need much longer legs than the shoreward trestle does. In
choosing the height of the dock, bear in mind the annual drop
in water level from May to August. You will probably want to
make the sub-structure just high enough to have a dry surface
at the beginning of the swimming season.

Joining the trestle's four legs near the bottom are horizontal
2 x 4s, needed both for bracing and to support a shelf made of
scrap lumber. The idea is to sink those trestles to the bottom,
level them, and place large rocks on the shelves until they are
stable. You need a miminum of two trestles not more than 8 feet
apart. If you want a longer dock, add as many trestles as you
wish, but make the decking in units no more than 8 feet long.
At the end of the summer you will remove the deck units and
the trestles, and re-position them the following spring.

Each deck unit can be made of 2 x 8 cedar with 1 x 4 or 1 x 3
cedar slats nailed across, leaving ¾-inch gaps between. There
should be bracing in the shape of an X underneath, preferably
neatly dadoed into the 2 x 8s. Use only galvanized nails throughout. If the distance between the trestles is less than 8 feet, you
can use 2 x 6 for the side rails. Cedar will cost much more than
spruce, but it will last much longer and be far lighter to handle
each spring and fall. You can, of course, use saplings instead of
sawn lumber to save money, but they will probably be heavier
to lift and the dock will be harder to walk, sit or lie on.

One disadvantage of this dock may be that by late August it
will be far above the water. If that bothers you, you can go back
to the anchored raft, design a floating dock, or make a dock from
aluminum framing. The floating dock is an adaptation of the
raft, but it does not need as much flotation material if one end
is always to be anchored on the shore; you can put the flotation
material only at the floating end. As the summer passes you will
gradually move out the floating dock so that the shoreward end
is always just at the receding water's edge. If such a floating dock
is too short for you, you can extend it in units of 8 feet, but of
course the units out in the river really are rafts, completely
floating. Although they will be attached to one another by galvanized wire or chain, which permits a little play, you will probably need more support than that to keep a long dock at right

angles to shore in heavy winds or sharp current. The farthest
end of the floating dock may need ropes or wires at a 45 degree
angle to the shore. These attachments, which can be a nuisance
to swimmers, should be marked with small buoys made of
plastic bottles or bits of flotation material.

Aluminum supports for docks are the most expensive solution, but the neatest. You can find them at builders' supply or
marine stores. The aluminum framework is put in place in the
water each spring and removed each autumn. With a little effort,
the decking can be adjusted to the dropping water level without
removing the whole framework.

DOGS

Dogs may be man's best friend, but they can also be the
neighbor's worst enemy. They are the source of much tension
amongst cottagers.

Dogs themselves are the keenest cottagers of all. All winter
they dream of freedom to roam the woods, upset garbage pails,
frighten timid people, tangle with porcupines and howl beautiful
canine songs at midnight. If you have neighbors, especially dog-
less ones, your dog has to be curbed.

Since restricting freedom is harder than bestowing it, you may
as well start tough. No matter how pathetically your dog com-
plains, you should be firm about controls until it is demon-
strated that they are not needed. This could mean placing a long
clothesline wire near the ground level on a large plot, which is
to become his domain. A reasonably long lead is snapped onto
the wire, allowing the dog to take lots of exercise, choose
shade or sun, and always have fresh water within reach.

You then explain to the dog in convincing tones that he is
allowed to run free when under supervision. Without a lead, he
can join the family swimming or scamper into the woods as long
as he returns when his owner bellows. If, however, he trots off,
or if he sneaks out the screen door by himself, it will go hard
with him. If he gets the message, he can then be let out whenever a member of the family is outside with him and willing to be
responsible for keeping him within acceptable reach. This seems
a pretty reasonable degree of freedom and it will certainly help
neighborly relations.

If this is your regime, mention it to neighbors before trouble starts. Say that you would consider it a favor if they would tell you if your dog is ever seen disturbing the peace within their boundaries. (They could call you on the intercom, if you have one!) Explain that, since the dog is free only under supervision, normally a loud scream would bring one of you running.

Be understanding of neighbors who complain about your pets messing up their lawns and gardens: the deposits may not only look and smell bad, but destroy prized vegetation. Let your neighbor know that you are prepared to stoop and scoop promptly.

A less direct approach is to call a meeting of neighbors, both owners and non-owners, to consider how peace and good relations can be maintained. If that is your plan, be sure that everyone invited knows the subject to be discussed and that you have a good representation from both sides. It may need tact and persuasive diplomacy to overcome latent hostility or defensiveness. There should be no surprises, nor should dog-owners feel that they are being persecuted.

What happens if you have no dog, but your neighbors do? We've made that easy for you. Just give them copies of this book with this page prominently marked in red.

On reflection, your dog might be glad he spent the summer with this limited freedom. He didn't find porcupine quills up his nose, choke on stolen chicken bones or get hit by a car out on the highway.

There are also health hazards which you can predict and arm yourself against. Be sure your dog has had annual shots to protect against rabies before you leave for the country. This is essential both for your pet and for your family. Also consult your veterinarian about protection against heartworm, a potentially fatal, mosquito-carried disease, which has been moving northward from the southern United States. Your dog probably should be tested and then regularly receive protective pills throughout the mosquito season.

Still, the unforeseen may happen. If your dog argues with a skunk, tomato juice is about the only effective remedy for the smell. Wash the dog thoroughly with the juice, and let it dry on the fur before combing and brushing it out. If the dispute is pet *vs* porcupine, have strong tweezers or needle-nose pliers to remove a few quills, but if there are many, go to the animal hospital fast. Do not let any quills remain in the animal for longer than overnight, as they may soon become infected.

Finally, to reduce the chance of unnecessary stress, equip yourself with a manual on the care of dogs so that you will be better able to handle less serious canine problems yourself, and judge when an emergency trip to the nearest veterinary is necessary.

DOMESTIC CHORES

How many domestic chores should you have at the cottage? Should you do the family washing on the rocks by the lake, or get a washing machine? Do you buy a dishwasher in order to have more time to listen to the call of the loon?

Of course, the answer depends on your philosophy of cottage living, your lifestyle, your pocketbook and, to some extent, on the availability of alternatives. Take washing, for example. If you go into the local town weekly, would it not be easier to use the coinwash there than to give space to a washing machine which may break down and require still more labor to have repaired? On the other hand, if the local coinwash is inadequate and you are coping with diapers, an unsophisticated so-called apartment washer may be the answer: reasonably priced, simple, needing little space. Washing on the rocks is not popular, except with those who have a severe budgetary problem or a sense of masochism about country living. And environmentalists may object to the soap in the lake.

The most important labor-saving device to reduce domestic chores is a tap. Maybe it is acceptable to run to the lake for pails of water when you are young, or even when the children are still there to do it for you, but it eventually becomes a tedious chore subtracting from cottage enjoyment. If you have a water pressure system, all kitchen chores will seem enormously easier. Your second ambition may be hot running water as well, because three or four hundred dollars more will give you not only convenience at the sink but the cleanliness of a shower. Third on the list of water systems could be the septic tank, which will permit a flush toilet, thus ending one of the most disagreeable of maintenance chores and adding to the pleasures of cottage life. (See **Septic Tanks**.)

But this may not be your priority list. Very close to the top may be electricity, without which few labor-saving devices are possible. If you have that, it may be a toss-up whether a tap or an electric refrigerator comes next. In the unlikely event that local farmers are still cutting ice each winter, your supply of ice may be relatively easy and cheap, but an ice box is messy, it does not protect food as well as an electric refrigerator and it does not make ice cubes. If you have to drive to town or far down the highway for ice, you will appreciate electric refrigeration even more.

If we are thinking of how to reduce chores, firewood and stove maintenance is a target. If the fairly reasonable cost is not a barrier, electric heat, at least in the living room, will mean less shivering as well as less tracking for firewood, less clean-up, and less stove cleaning.

For other domestic chores, we urge you find out about the local labor supply before assuming that gadgetry is the answer. If you are lucky enough to have some reliable local young person come regularly for everything from house clean-up to grass-cutting and firewood collection, you may be financially ahead of the game, have far more services, and be doing a favor to the local economy. Every labor-saving device that you install is a potential problem, especially in the country where you are more likely to get sand in the water or have surges in electric power. We acquired some labor-saving devices only as a last resort because we could find no human being to help us. We hope that you will be luckier.

For those whose cottage is close enough to their city home to make weekly visits routine, the attitude to some domestic chores may be different. You can simply bundle up the washing for the city machine, and use whatever other mechancal gadgetry you can while you are there. That may be logical, but we ask you to consider whether it is wise. Your stay at the cottage is an escape from city routines, a recharging of the batteries, a rekindling of the flames, or whatever metaphor you choose. Don't let the new life become eroded by making your cottage just an extension of your city porch. The fewer trips you have to make to urban reality, the more decisively you can separate the two worlds in which you are lucky enough to live, and the greater will be your enjoyment of both. It may even be worth putting your city home out-of-bounds for the duration of your holiday.

DRAINS

Even if you never wish to learn the finer aspects of plumbing, you may gain a nodding acquaintance with drains. The two most common problems with drains are things that go down them, and things that don't.

If you've lost your ring down the sink, and want to get it back before your mate finds out, don't let any more water run down. Find a pipe wrench, or any other large wrench. Lie down uncomfortably amid all that clutter under the sink (you could move it). If you are lucky, at the bottom of the U-shaped plastic trap there will be a large nut, which you can unscrew with the wrench. Otherwise, loosen off the two retaining nuts which usually hold the whole trap in place. Remove the trap carefully (it has water and guck in it) and dump it in a pail. Either the ring is in it, or you had better think up a good story. The only other possibility is to probe the septic tank itself. Is your marriage worth it?

If, on the other hand, the problem is that liquid in the kitchen sink or in the toilet will not drain out, the first step is to get out the rubber plunger. Remove the drain plug, if any, and stuff the overflow vent at the back of the sink, if any, by jamming a rag into it. Run in a couple of inches of water unless it is full to overflowing (in which case, bail out some). Then plunge repeatedly. If it is not clear in a dozen strokes, sterner measures are needed.

One is to remove the trap on the sink. (See above.) Another is to try a snake — it's a sort of auger and cable that plumbers use. If you don't have one of those, you can try chemicals sold under various trade names.

Using chemicals on a toilet is generally not a good idea. They will probably become too diluted to be effective, and the presence of strong caustic substances will not make it easier for whoever may have to take the beast apart later. Before calling in the plumber, you may wish to know whether the fault is around the toilet, or somewhere farther down the system. If all other drains in the cottage work well, the problem is presumably localized to the toilet — for whatever comfort that may be.

If the problem of clogged drains in sinks arises often, you may have a combination of two problems: letting too much grease and other refuse go down the sink, combined with too gentle a slope on a long drainpipe. You can help the first by family discipline. You probably cannot readily have the drainage system changed, but you could ask your plumber to install an inspection port which will make cleaning easier. You should also consider preventive maintenance: a strong drain cleaner dumped down the drain once a month, before the grease builds up. These chemicals are not especially good for septic tanks, but the amount you would use each month should not cause harm.

E

*E*LECTRIC WIRING

If it is your policy to call in a good licensed electrician to do any work more complicated than changing a light bulb, most of this section is not for you. (We assume that your wiring conforms to all building and safety codes.)

Those who like to do it themselves are likely to be tempted by the prospect of a morning's work with the wire strippers and boxes as a faster and cheaper alternative to calling up the local electrician. There should be curbs on your enthusiasm.

First, as always, there is the law, which varies from province to province and from state to state. Some areas sensibly allow the householder to do minor wiring as long as a permit is first secured, so that there can be inspection. Others, less inclined to the welfare of the consumer than of the union, threaten to send you to prison if you so much as change a switchplate. In the latter circumstances, householders do their thing anyway, and there is no record or inspection. Such activity is hardly conducive to safety. We leave it to you to examine the applicable law and your conscience.

If you take over a cottage with wiring over 25 years old, we recommend you call in an electrician for an estimate on necessary updating. In particular, you should not continue to use two-hole, ungrounded outlets, and you should worry a little if some of your wiring is aluminum. In either case, you may be facing an expensive rewiring job, but the stakes in terms of personal injury and property loss are high. An honest electrician will also tell you if squirrels or mice have been dining on your circuitry, or if the insulation is so oxydized as to be unsafe. There is no real need to replace fuse boxes with circuit breakers, but there is an advantage in safety and convenience in doing so; if you are having other work done, you may as well get an estimate.

Even if you are ambitious for work and economy, think twice about wiring your whole cottage unless you have had training. If your electrician is sympathetic, you may be able to arrange that he puts in the service panel, you install all the boxes with associated carpentry and wiring, and he comes back to connect it. This method will greatly reduce your cost with little risk of diminished safety — if you are careful, that is. It is wise to precede such a project with a winter evening course in residential wiring at the local technical school. You will also want to read up on such regulations as where boxes are to be placed relative to the floor, kitchen sink and so on. You must still be extremely careful if you are to be safe. Your friendly electrician may spot obvious blunders, but he may not see if you have cut the leads too short in the junction box, carelessly installed connectors, or driven a nail through the wiring buried in a wall.

These remarks apply also to that new wing you may be building. There you certainly may cut the holes for boxes, and string the wiring as the carpentry goes along, whether or not you use an electrician to make the connections. Doing all the electrical work later will cost more and be messier.

If you are still in the planning stage of cottaging, get involved in the decision about the size of service you will have. The usual 100 amp service may seem fine now, but if you later decide to add a wing or new building, or opt for electric heating or other heavy power consumers, you will face far heavier costs for upgrading the panel than if you accept the small margin for a bigger service now.

What about ground fault interrupters? On new electrical installations you must have them for outlets in bathrooms or outside, but no one will force you to change existing equipment. At least get an estimate for conversion for the sake of safety. You will probably decide in favor of it, especially if you have children, who are even more likely than adults to get shocks and suffer seriously from them.

EXCUSES

Our dreams of cottaging always seem to center on the idyllic sounds of happy young voices, the call of the loon, the brilliance of the setting sun. All very true, but experienced cottagers know that Things Go Wrong. That things do go wrong is more than an inconvenience: it tends to destroy credibility. "Gee mom, there's a funny thing in the outhouse...." "I told you that you couldn't install that pump yourself...." "You really think your cottage was a good buy, eh?" You can't prevent misfortunes, but you can be prepared by using the long winter months to develop instant excuses for every unfortunate occasion. We start you on your list.

1. The road in is absolutely impassable. "It's never been like this before. I graded it myself. I understand it was a reaction to that volcano in Outer Mongolia."

2. You forgot the key. "Oh no, I didn't forget it. I left a spare in the crotch of that willow tree, but a chipmunk must have taken it."

3. No water in the tap. "I expected that. It is perfectly installed, but there has been a recall of the ratchet-scratchet gear on the output impeller, and the suppliers ran out of the part."

4. You didn't tell me the Formbys were arriving this morning for a week. "I thought you might have seen their letter, but I guess Canada Post lost it."

5. The dock has floated away. "Yes, I was afraid of that. It was perfectly installed, but in this lake there is a type of fish that devours the moorings of docks. Nothing we can do about it."

6. The roof is leaking. "Not really. You don't understand that it is necessary to have airspaces in it to prevent dry rot."

7. You've got to do something about the mosquitoes. "Oh no. It is very important to preserve the ecological balance upon which all creatures depend."

8. When are you going to put up the hammock? "Perhaps next summer, but now it would unbalance the growth of the trees." OR "The latest scientific information is that hammocks are conducive to problems of the lower back, and I did not want you to risk trouble."

9. The outboard motor won't start. "Quite right. I think it would be healthier to use the oars."

10. The kindling is all wet. "Yes. I didn't want to risk a fire through spontaneous combustion."

11. Didn't you build that front wall crooked? "No, I modelled it on the Parthenon which has no straight lines."

12. The flies are coming in through all those holes in the screens. "I don't think so. They come in through the door, but the holes in the screens are to let them out."

F

F_{ANS}

Fans are used to extract odors and to keep cool. Since the addition of unwanted smells makes a hot summer day in the cottage seem stifling, let's start there. If you have a decent window which opens in the bathroom, an exhaust fan in that room is not a priority. It may be more important around the stove. You can opt for a stove hood containing a fan that exhausts air — but does not recirculate it — or you might consider instead an exhaust fan installed in the wall. You can get a much more powerful fan and it will probably cost no more than the hood. It will extract food odors, tobacco smoke and hot air from the whole building when the doors and windows are closed. If you wish to spend a little more money, consider buying a fan which works on a very low, relatively noiseless speed as well as at full blast. Then you can leave it on all night.

The other place to exhaust air is under the roof. If you have a space between ceiling and roof, you already have, or should have, ventilators to prevent wood rot. On a warm day, that is still a very hot place. You could help cool it with a motorless fan that extracts air by the turning of a circular louvre above the roof, or — far more effective — with a conventional electric attic exhaust fan of a size that the dealer will specify according to your attic's dimensions. Here you can paint the lily by putting it on a thermostat so that it works automatically when the temperature reaches a predetermined level. It will help to cool the cottage, though psychologically it is less effective because you will not feel the moving current of air.

If your cottage ceiling is high enough, you can consider a ceiling fan. (Before you order it, check your ceiling height and its vertical length. It must be not only above head level, but well above it.) From movies such as Casablanca we know that a ceiling fan is just the thing for tropical weather, and it has the pleasant effect of moving drafts across your skin. It probably won't do much more: indeed, it will tend to push the warmer upper air down at you. In fact, the ceiling fan's greatest use may be to circulate the heat from the stove or fireplace in cooler weather. Despite the popularity of the practice, it is not a good idea to buy a ceiling fan with a light attached; the heat from the light can overheat the fan motor.

Small portable fans are great psychologically, and we don't knock anything that makes you feel cool, especially when you may be trying to have a siesta. Unless you can contrive to put them where they pull in cool air from the floor or below it, they won't lower the temperature much. When choosing fans, make a selection appropriate to the age of your family. If you have small children, or if some are likely to visit you, be extra careful to choose models with safety blades — those that are made with soft plastic that are not dangerous to fingers or with steel well-enclosed in a safety grille.

If you are ambitious, you could experiment with putting in the floor some grilles that allow you to draw in the cool air lying underneath the cottage. You would feel that air only if your fan is near the grille. If it works, it has the secondary benefit of clearing out stale air, which may be conducive to rot, underneath the building. You will, of course, need covers to put over the grilles in cooler weather.

*F*ENCES

Before thinking of fences you will, of course, be certain about where they will go. (See **Boundaries**). Then decide their purpose.

If they are to stop the unwanted passage of fauna, such as domestic animals from a neighboring farm, chances are that you will opt for standard farm wire fencing. It is not picturesque, it costs more than using local wood, but it can usually be erected relatively quickly. The notable exception is when you are cursed with a surplus of rock and a shortage of soil in which to dig post holes. Particularly in such difficult conditions you may find yourself wanting to deviate from the property line to take advantage of living trees as fence posts or to avoid enormous boulders. For this reason alone, it is essential that you persuade your farming neighbors to join you in fence-making. You will thus avoid future quarrels about where the fence line leaves the property line. Besides, you will probably find their long experience in fence-making a great help to the enterprise. If you are protecting your property from their straying animals, you have a good case to ask them to share the cost of materials and to help with the future maintenance. However, if they are uninterested in a fence, there is no way to make them pay.

If you are on your own and working in reasonably rock-free soil without many tree roots along the way, you have a choice of cedar or steel posts. The latter cost more, but can be pounded in quickly with a sledge hammer. They do not rot, but since they will rust, we suggest prolonging their life somewhat by a coat of metal paint before they are used, even if they seem to have a red undercoat already. Almost no one treats cedar posts, but since their vulernable part is just below ground level, we see no harm in giving them a generous slathering of preservative (see **Paints and Preservatives**) around the bottom before setting them in place. For digging holes in good conditions, borrow or rent a post hole digger, either the old-fashioned hand-driven kind, or one equipped with a gas motor. If conditions are bad — for example, buried boulders or big tree roots — the solution is incredibly hard work with crow bar, axe and shovel, or some kind of barrier that does not depend on fence posts. The pioneers had effective fences which were entirely built on the surface: ask your librarian to help you find a design.

There may be other reasons for a fence than to keep out farm animals. Maybe you want to indicate to very young members of your family the bounds beyond which they must not go. Maybe you have an understandable sense of pride in these private acres, and want to mark them suitably. Maybe you believe that good fences make good neighbors, and that it is just as well to have a barrier before any misunderstanding arises.

For any of these purposes you will probably want some kind of wooden fence with certain artistic virtues. Please see **Woodworking Projects** for a few simple designs. But before you build, talk to your neighbor, and if possible make it a joint project.

Another possibility is a living fence or hedge. It may be slow to complete — it could take ten years — but it is attractive, it can be cheap and it needs little maintenance. In this case, there is some advantage in doing it on your own. Your neighbors, or the new people who buy that property next year, are entitled to cut back what grows on their side and they may make it look ridiculous, if not downright unhealthy. That could be heart-breaking after you have patiently and lovingly watched it grow. Therefore, plant it far enough back of the property line to give you full control. On the other hand, take care not to let it grow so high that your neighbors can complain about the shade ruin-ing their favorite garden; their legal case may be murky but there is no point letting any kind of fence lead to bad relations.

The subject of fences brings up the question of rights-of-way, either your access road across a farmer's property, or a right-of-way across your own property, for someone to walk, to drive or to maintain power lines. Is your deed crystal clear, and are the legal limits being observed? Laws vary from place to place, but you may have difficulty proving that someone else does *not* have a right-of-way on your land if a path or lane has been used for many years without question. You may wish to consider the advice of a lawyer before closing it off, installing a gate, or offer-ing a short-term right-of-way. Be careful about investing in any structure on an unusued right-of-way, near power lines, for example. The utility company does not have to use the right-of-way to keep its rights, and one unexpected day it could demand that the right-of-way be cleared. If the company is in the habit of destroying or pruning trees below its lines, it may be a good idea to mark the edge of its right-of-way (often 50 feet on each side of the center line) with spray paint on trees or with pickets; that may dissuade the company from damaging your trees.

One of your trickier problems could be shared rights-of-way, such as an access road used by many cottagers whose views on the degree of maintenance that it requires vary sharply. Some may be content with a stony lane which is barely accessible in July; others may opt for a good, well drained road which will not inflict mortal injury on your car in any weather. If you want the higher standard, you may have to pay a disproportionate share of the costs. Even though you may resent your neighbors for freely benefitting from your carefully crafted freeway, it may be worth the money to do it. (See **Roads.**)

*F*IREPLACES

Evenings by a roaring fire are certainly a major theme of cottage fantasies. That's just fine, as long as the roaring fire is in the fireplace. Consider the fireplace for what it is — a pleasant thing to watch, a focus for the cottage, a device to dispel the damp chill — but not an efficient means of heating the building in the cool or cold off-season. If you want to be comfortable as late as Thanksgiving, you should also have a stove or electric heating.

If you have no fireplace and itch to build one from all those free stones lying around, you can do it if you are patient and handy. The first step is to buy or borrow a book on the subject. Whether you or the local handyman takes on the job, you can both reduce the risk of problems and ensure better interior heating if you invest in a steel liner, sold under various trade names. It is really a small furnace with a plenum which heats cold air drawn in from ducts, and expels it by convection through the room. In addition, you can install a fan which provides forced air — and noise. If you are feeling lavish, get the fan anyway: you do not have to leave it on always. With this equipment, all you have to do is build around the device, which is still no mean feat for the amateur.

You can reduce the construction problem by buying a prefabricated insulated chimney, which may look jarring attached to your cottage, but is safe and easy to clean. If you build the chimney in the traditional way, be sure to use vitrified clay liner to avoid endless problems in cleaning and repairing mortar between your stones. Your book will tell you the size according to your fireplace opening: don't guess, or the fireplace may convert your cottage into the largest smokehouse around.

If you have a fireplace already, you need consider only maintenance. Most important is the annual cleaning. The time-honored method is to carry up to the roof a sack of stones attached to a stout rope that is longer than the chimney. Disaster will follow quickly if that rope is not very securely attached to the sack. You then lower the sack down the chimney, twisting it and working it up and down as you go to dislodge soot and hardened creosote. This system works well enough — it served for centuries — but it is not as efficient or convenient as modern wire brushes with fibreglass wands made specifically for chimney cleaning. Also, over-enthusiastic use of the sack of stones risks damage to the liner. Be sure to quote the exact inner dimensions of your liner when you buy the brushes; you also need to know the chimney's length when you get the connecting wands. If you and your neighbors share the same size chimney, it might be a good idea to share the cleaning equipment.

On completion of this rooftop operation, you can descend to find your family in consternation over the soot on the floor because you forgot to close off the front of the fireplace. (Didn't we tell you that?) Now you have to reach up, and with garden trowel or small dust pan, collect all the loose junk which has fallen on the ledge above and behind the place where the fire is set. You will be glad of a vacuum cleaner with a flexible tube to get the last remnants and clean up the mess in general. To say that this is a very dirty job, indeed, is not to exaggerate. If you try to clean yourself off in the lake, the anti-pollution authorities may apprehend you.

Even with the flue closed, the fireplace is like an open window. That may be fine in summer, but when days are cool it is a cause of drafts. For more comfort, cut a piece of thin plywood or particle board just larger than the fireplace opening, and make your own invention to hold it tightly in place. (High-tech folks install magnets; people with lower standards lean a log against it.)

There are cottagers who are very particular about what is burned in fireplaces because of the creosote that may build up in the chimney (See **Stoves**.) If your chimney is in good shape and is cleaned regularly, you need not worry about burning softwood, carpentry scraps, newsprint or other such materials that worry the purists. Nevertheless, the fireplace is not a great vehicle for burning garbage, except for the most combustible elements of it. (Dead mice are better buried.)

Some birds like chimneys and fireplaces as much as you do. A bird that makes its way down the chimney in your absence can do unbelievable harm to your decor while in frustrated captivity. To keep out birds or squirrels, make a simple chimney cover with a piece of 2 x 4 nailed to plywood cut just larger than the protruding liner. When you put it on in autumn, be sure to leave a large sign in the fireplace as a reminder to remove it before starting a fire.

But what if the fireplace, new or old, does not work? There could be many reasons for this problem, the worst of which is poor construction. In the city you might first check if your dwelling is too airtight for the necessary draft, but that is much less likely to be a cottage problem. Does the flue open properly? (When it is closed, hang a small block of wood from it as a reminder.) Is the chimney clean? Can you see light by poking your now filthy head far up into the chimney on a sunny day? The device of lighting a newspaper and holding it up the flue until you scream is most likely to help if you have a long chimney and damp cool air which responds to the flaming paper more easily than to a normal fire. Apart from that, it is a matter of becoming skilled in lighting the fire for that particular fireplace: lots of paper, dry, thin wood well away from the front, not too much old ash, but a covering of about an inch of it on the bottom.

If you like playing with newspaper, here are two hints for lighting fires. One is to fold a few pages diagonally, roll them, and twist them into a doughnut. Lit with ordinary crumpled paper, these doughnuts may even substitute for kindling if you are short of small pieces of wood. Second, after you have ignited the paper, spread two single-thickness newspapers on your fire screen so that the opening is completely blocked, except for an inch left at the bottom. That will create a powerful draft, but *never* leave it unattended: in a few minutes it will be so successful that it will catch fire. Bellows, which are really a must, are less dramatic and harder work, but safer.

Finally, when the evening is grown old, take care with the remaining hot coals. You are probably all right if you have a good and secure firescreen. If you have any doubt, douse the coals with water before a stray wind blows up new danger. Never put your combustible anti-draft board on the fireplace until all is cool the next morning.

FIRE PRECAUTIONS

Cottagers should never underestimate the importance of fire precautions. You know that the cottage itself is probably much more flammable than your city residence, and it is certainly farther from professional help. Even if you have no danger from cigarette smoking, you can imagine many other sources of trouble, such as wiring, forgotten food on the stove, coals from the woodstove or fireplace, spontaneous combustion from chemical-soaked rags and grassfires edging toward the cottage, not to mention lightning. But cheer up: disaster rarely strikes, and the risk to people and property can be much reduced with thought and planning.

Equipment

Before you spend a single night in the cottage, ensure that you have the means to fight fire and control it. Your first purchase should be smoke detectors; if you don't know how many you should have, roughly sketch a floor plan of your building and ask for advice from a reputable salesperson.

Next are the fire extinguishers. You can buy fancy equipment with halon, which makes no mess. These models are great for spraying your computer or audio-visual equipment, but they cost several times as much as the standard extinguishers. You should purchase one or two A.5 B.C. U.L.C. listed fire extinguishers. Keep one in the kitchen and the other near any heating appliance that you may have. This extinguisher is suitable for fires of classes A (wood), B (oil and grease) and C (electrical). You may be horrified by the cost (around $75 each with little difference in price or quality between recognized brands), but consider the stakes. Each one, when discharged at full throttle, will last less than half a minute. Once you have discharged a fire extinguisher you are without protection from it until you can find a technician in town to refill it. Two, therefore, is the absolute minimum number to keep on hand, and more will give you increased peace of mind and safety. You might also have smaller models mounted near obvious hazards like the stoves and fireplaces, but not so near that you would find it hard to reach them through flames. You can use water pump models, but you will have to remember to empty them before freeze-up, and they are generally useless in winter. Also, they are good only for wood, paper or cloth — not oil or electricity. Snow is excellent for smothering small fires, but in the warmer seasons you may not be able to wait for it. Don't overlook the value of simple buckets. If you have a lot of them — and know always where they are — they could be especially useful for an outside fire near the lake.

Chimney fires are terrifying, but they need not be dangerous if handled calmly and promptly. If your chimneys are kept clean, such a fire is unlikely to start. As a further precaution, buy three or four of the chemical sticks made especially for chimney fires (about $10 each). You just close the draft, throw one in, and they use up the oxygen the fire needs to stay alight.

The next piece of equipment is inexpensive and easily acquired. It is a garden hose, which should always be kept attached and ready for service. It has its limitations, notably if a fire cuts off power to your pump, but if it is used promptly inside or out, it might forestall disaster. If you have a large cottage, have the plumber install a threaded tap to which a hose can be attached under your kitchen sink and possibly your bathroom sink. (A good idea for the city, too.) If you want to be extra careful, leave at least a short hose coiled up underneath it in the cupboard.

Don't forget also that your garden tank sprayer filled with clean water can be a ready fire-extinguisher: you might want to keep it that way. Another common example of household equipment that may be valuable in an emergency is the blanket. Ideally, blankets should be fireproof, but such blankets are very costly. An ordinary blanket soaked with water is an excellent fast answer to a small fire that you can smother, and if a nearby bushfire is spreading embers your way in a high wind, wet blankets on the roof may be good protection. Of course, the blanket will never be the same again.

From the livelier households, there have been tales of beer used to douse small fires. Apparently the foam helps cut off oxygen, as every drinker knows. (The fire department continues to prefer water, however.) Our standing offer to experiment with champagne has not been taken up. If Coke or Pepsi were significantly better for firefighting than water, we think that one of those companies would have mentioned it.

Next on our list of important equipment is ladders. See that your extension ladder (you have one, haven't you?) is kept permanently up the side of your house to reach the roof, or at least alongside it — and not somewhere down at the beach or over at the neighbor's. (Lock your upper windows to discourage burglars.) You might need it when you want to douse sparks from a chimney or extinguish a fire caused by radiation from a chimney fire. If your cottage has two floors, with bedrooms above, you might want some device to let occupants out safely — ordinary ladders, a fixed ladder you make yourself, a chain-type ladder sold for the purpose, or a stout knotted rope.

Consider buying or making a simple triangle of ³/₄-inch steel, with sides about 30 cm long; the ends do not have to be welded together. It can be painted red, with a sign on it saying, "Fire Only". Hang a straight piece of the same steel, also about 30 cm long, with it, by a flexible wire which is never detached. That must be recognized by family and neighbors as your fire alarm to bring people running, and it *must never be used for any other purpose*, except drill.

Finally, even if no one in your family smokes, provide jars with sand to serve as ashtrays at strategic places outside. Make and post rules about where one can smoke outside (for example, never when walking through the woods, but allowed by the beach or by the barbecue). It is difficult to ban all smoking by your guests. It should be possible, however, to control smoking with a few reasonable rules. Fire from a burning cottage or woods is definitely more injurious to mental health.

Drill

You have wasted your time and money on fire-fighting equipment unless all members of your family are trained to use it — and retrained annually. This calls for family conferences. One good time to schedule them is during the annual national fire prevention week, but since it is in autumn, it may be better for the city house than for the cottage. Try April conferences, or sessions on the first evening you are in the country. Children, as well as adults, must be taught what the hazards are, what to do when they spot a fire or smoke, what to do when someone else sounds the alarm, how to use all equipment, how to emerge from upstairs windows, how to get to the roof fast. Then practice *everything*, with the possible exception of discharging the chemical extinguishers. Part of this carefully-conceived plan is the assignment of responsibility for waking sleepers, calling neighbors, phoning the fire department, driving out to guide in the fire brigade, and bringing your own equipment to the fire itself. If you have persuaded your neighbors to be as careful as you, each of you will be able to command resources far greater than your own.

You would do well to write out your fire plan and leave at least one copy on the wall as a continuing reminder to yourselves, and as a guide to guests who may be there, with or without you.

Precautions

Good maintenance is the single best fire precaution. Wiring should be in first-rate shape, stoves and stove pipes must be kept in good order and checked annually for rusting. Keep your stove the designated distance from flammable walls, and clean the chimneys annually. Workshops should be kept tidy, with no oily rags left where they could ignite. (Innocent-looking boiled linseed oil on rags is a great way to give your insurance agent nightmares. If you must keep them, put them in an empty paint tin with the lid carefully secured.) Flammable liquids and gases should be stored thoughtfully — outside — and don't forget that some of your tools, like the chainsaw or lawnmower, have fuel which may vaporize. Bonfires should be built, tended and doused with great care. (See **Bonfires**.) Firewood and papers should be kept well away from lit stoves. Branches and parts of dead trees should not be near your incoming power lines. You need not worry much about lightning if you have nearby trees which are well above the highest point on your cottage: except that a tree struck by lightning may itself start a fire. If your cottage stands alone on high ground, it is imperative that you get advice from your electrician on lightning rods. (See **Lightning**.)

*F*IREWOOD

If you have a small lot with few trees, and a cottage that you want to heat often, the source of most of your firewood is likely to be your friendly dealer. Firewood is generally sold by the stove cord (equivalent to a pile of 16-inch logs 8 feet long and 4 feet high.) Unless your dealer has been warmly recommended by other clients, it would be a good idea to make your contract in person. Look at the wood to be delivered to you and consider the following:

Is it dry? (Lift a few pieces: if they are very heavy, they are probably also wet.)

Is it hardwood? (Even if you are no tree expert, you can probably tell the difference between hardwood and softwood. One is generally harder.)

Is it a reasonable size? (Not only is it no more than 16 inches long; is it split into reasonably small pieces — unless you have opted to get a lower price by splitting it yourself — which you may later regret.)

Does the price include stacking in a place of your choice, or just dumping it in the middle of your drive? It is a good idea always to have one year's supply of wood ahead, both to avoid being caught short when you most need it, and to let it dry even more.

Even if you buy your logs, you will still need kindling. You can surely find lots of dead branches during your walks, or your carpentry may yield a supply of scraps. Without kindling, you can start a fire with a Cape Cod lighter. It is a porous stone attached to a metal rod serving as a handle so that it can be kept in a metal jar of kerosene. The well-soaked stone is placed under light firewood and lit, without the need of paper or thin kindling. That sounds convenient, but sometimes the stone cracks, and people burn their hands by lifting it out of the fire when it is hot. The stone must be left to cool before being plunged anew into the pot of kerosene.

A variant of the lighter is a commercially made device of porous stone and cast iron which remains in the fireplace. Kerosene is poured onto it in preparation for lighting. It also works, but the presence of that, inflammable liquid by an open fire demands particular care.

On the other hand, you may have woods enough to maintain a steady supply of dead or pruned trees. Cut the wood in convenient lengths and stack it long before you need it. It is best to store wood for at least a year. If you try to burn green or damp wood, not only will you be frustrated when trying to keep the fire going, but it will give off less heat and a lot more creosote. When stacking green wood (loosely, of course), choose a place where the wind and sun can reach it. Stacking wood against the wall of the cottage is not as efficient, and it may lead to rot in the wall. Woodsheds are easy to build and rather picturesque, but if you are not that ambitious, keep the rain and snow from the top of the pile with a cover such as plastic or plywood, but don't run the plastic down the sides or it will not dry.

Before you stack, split. The wood will dry much faster, and you will be glad of a stove-ready supply some wet night when the room grows chilly. (See **Log Splitting**.)

If the wood is free, says our motto, use it. Some is far better than other, but all has some potential heat to warm your toes. Softwoods don't produce such long, even fires, and they will create more creosote in your stovepipe or chimney, although regular cleaning will prevent that problem. Hickory, oak, sugar maple and beech are best; they can have almost twice the heat value as the poorest softwoods. Birch, ash, elm and tamarack are your next best choices. If you are using much softwood, or plywood, or scrap wood with painted surfaces, check your pipes or chimney often for creosote buildup.

*F*IRST AID

Of course, the first step in first aid is to take precautions to avoid needing it. (See **Safety**.) Nevertheless, accidents will happen. There are two basic requirements for effective first aid: information and equipment.

Spend a few unhappy moments now considering what you would do in a major accident. When you are faced with a badly injured child you do not have time to start wondering if there is a hospital nearby. Find out now. Where is the nearest hospital? Where is the nearest clinic or doctor's office, and at what hours are they open? What is the fastest and most direct route to each? Is there a poison control centre within reach? What is the telephone number of each of these? Now, please write down this information in a way that is clear to anyone, and post it prominently.

Is at least one member of your family trained in Basic Cardiac Life Support? Find out now if a neighbor has completed the full course, or at least the training in cardiopulmonary resuscitation which forms part of it. Then list the name on your notice. Does everyone know how to perform Artificial Respiration? (See **Resuscitation**.)

Does your cottage library include a book on first aid and a medical dictionary for the layperson (available in a pocket book edition)? Does everyone know where these references are?

If you are at the cottage alone with younger members of the family, while the family car is away, do you know where you would go for emergency transportation?

Facing these questions now should give you a more comforting feeling of security. Next, the equipment.

First aid kits of varying scope and price are easily available from drug stores. You will have to go to the higher price range to be properly equipped, and it may well be that the cost will be higher than seeking out the necessary items separately. Whether you buy a kit, or make up you own, check it against this list.

- rubbing alcohol
- aspirin or stronger pain killer
- an ointment designed to reduce itch
- calamine lotion
- opthetic eye drops and eye patch
- laxative, antacid
- spares of all prescription medicines (in case the dog eats them)
- yellow (bar) laundry soap (for combatting poison ivy)
- many band aids in small and larger sizes
- cotton batten, sterile gauze, sterile cloth for bandages
- scissors (preferably blunt for bandages), large safety pins
- forceps or tweezers for removing slivers
- wide adhesive tape

You may note the omission of some common first aid items: iodine (soap and water, or clean water, is just as good); jelly for burns (use nothing except cold water — for example, immerse a burn in the lake — if you must have some covering en route to medical aid, use a wet towel only); and pressure dressings (if someone is bleeding heavily, pressure dressings are ineffective; one must apply direct pressure with hand or thumb.)

In compiling this relatively modest list, we assume that you could respond to an emergency with other equipment close at hand — such as a kettle to make sterile water, or slats of wood for temporary splints. If someone suffers a bad eye abrasion, say, from being hit by a branch, administer opthetic eye drops to freeze the surface of the cornea, and put on an eye patch for greater comfort en route to medical attention.

*F*ISH

What can one say of a pseudo-religion practiced by mystics incapable of self-expression? Can you fathom the lure of fishing if you sit for hours on a rock, watching the almost motionless occupant of the rowboat, hearing only occasionally the swish of a line cutting the air, and the little splat on the water? Is there any point, much later, asking how the fishing was, when you see only a person with an enigmatic smile, glazed eyes and no fish?

There must always be a gulf between fishers and normal people. To the first nothing can be said that is not already known. As for the second, we can only wonder whether you will attempt to bridge the gulf. We cannot persuade you to try fishing by citing the economic advantages of all that free food. Statistics prove that the cost per gram of the average angler's catch exceeds the price on the rarest of nightingale's tongues. There are social returns to be found in sharing the company of fellow zealots who are always ready to exchange tales. Also, near the angler's line, there are apparently to be found deep and hidden wells of inner peace. Do you want to look?

You will try fishing in the summer, we hope. Fishing through the ice seems to all outsiders to be a rare form of frigid torture in slow motion. It is to be indulged in only by the addict so desperate for a fix that any substitute drug will do. On the other hand, the opening of the fishing season is the promise of a new day at a time when the universe seems good to the peaceable kingdom of man and beast.

Fishing is a battle of wits with lightly armed opponents. Estimates of piscatorial brainpower vary with the source of your information, but it seems agreed that they tend to become wiser when and if they grow old. It is not for us to say if the same is true of the fishers. They are trying to fool the fish into impaling themselves on a hook by making it look like something natural to the fish scheme of things. Since no human has been known ever to have conversed seriously with a fish, centuries of angling lore are based on human guesses about what is on the mind, at any given time, of this animal of dubious intelligence.

The first step in a happy fishing career is to check out local regulations about what fish you are allowed to catch, when, and with what bait; and what permit you need to do it. If no fish and game office is handy, any reputable seller of fishing equipment should be able to point you in the right direction.

You may start out with a bamboo pole, some string, a pin and a worm: or maybe you already did, too long ago to remember. That has much to recommend it, because if a perverse Manager of All Things sends a fish to your line, you can smugly walk by all the empty-handed anglers with their computerized fishing reels and $20 lures. Conversely, if there are no fish that day, no one has the heart to blame your lack of angling skill.

But for most cottagers it is the rod and reel. On the end of the line, at least before it is incomprehensibly tangled, is a lure made from feathers, hair, metal, wood, cloth, plastic, "living" rubber, or the contents of your waste basket. It is cunningly — often secretly — designed to match your conclusion about what is on the fish's mind as it seeks food or carries on its appointed rounds. So help us, they even have perfume for fish, or at least scent which is calculated to attract those fish who suffer from poor eyesight. You can get computerized chart recorders which "pinpoint fish close up", and charts to keep you up with the phases of the moon and tables relating weather fronts and temperature to the mood of fish and their relative interest in the subtle colors of a thousand lures. There are endless publications to give the fisher some marginal advantage over the fish, including magazines featuring center-folds with fish posing in the nude. There is one secret you should know. The purpose of all this equipment is more to lure the fisher than the fish.

Or you could use live bait such as worms. The trick to attach-ing a worm to a line (according to some heartless practicers of the art) is to stretch the last hours of the tortured worm so that the fish will observe it squirming. This is done by impaling it once through the collar just below its head. Bigger night crawlers are more interesting to such large fish as bass and lake trout. Various insects, including grasshoppers and crickets, are favored by some fish in late summer. Minnow, frogs and crayfish also have their following.

Besides the rod, reel, lure and bait, some other equipment may be handy: a good pocket knife to cut a line or remove a hook from a fish, needle-nose pliers to pull a hook or fix a lure, an honest tapeline and honest scales to measure your catch.

Now there is the boat and related safety equipment. The stability of your craft is important to your enjoyment as well as to your safety, because you want to be able to give your whole attention to the sport without the worry of capsizing. This con-sideration generally eliminates anything but a rowboat with oars or small outboard motor. (See **Rowboats**.) You may want to use the motor for trolling, slowly dragging a line with lure or bait. Or if you do not mind admitting to being lazy, the motor will propel you to your special place. You must wear an authorized life jacket: a flotation device in the boat is not enough. (See **Lifejackets**.) Wearing safety glasses will lessen your chance of serious eye damage from that common accident with an untamed hook. As a beginner, you may be lucky enough to find a True Believer to accompany you. Your apprenticeship can then be much shorter, though possibly more painful.

Your expert friend will guide you to his or her favorite place. Where that will be may depend partly on the species that you wish to catch. Rock bass, not surprisingly, seem to like rocks, and may even favor the cribs you have made for your wharf when there are few people around. Most fish like sheltered places where they can get away from the weather, the sun, the current and even one another. Thus, stumps, rocks, weed beds and underwater ditches or rises are often good places to look.

Many fish, notably those with big eyes like the walleye, try to avoid sun because it hurts their eyes and makes it hard to find smaller fish to eat. Smaller fish do not like sun because it makes it easier for them to be seen by predators. Sun also tends to heat shallow water to a higher temperature than fish find ideal, though this is where they find most of their food. Therefore, the best time to catch fish is often the cool of early morning, during the evening or on overcast days.

If you are on your own, you should know that the first part of the art, after you cast the line, is to know what the fish is doing when it comes to investigate your lure. When it sees the lure, it may nibble rather tentatively. The instant it takes the bait is the time to sweep your rod dramatically upwards, and pray fast. Then you reel it in, which is no trick with most small fish. If it is large and hostile to your intentions, you must keep tension on the line so that the fish cannot throw the hook, but do not pull so hard that you tear the hook from its grasp.

Fly-casting, the Zen of fishing, is the cult of the upper hierarchy. At the end of your line is about 9 feet of ultra-lightweight material to which is attached either a dry fly, which floats on the water or a wet fly, which sinks. They are crafted to resemble insects or water creatures as humans think fish see them. The greatest challenge is to cast that line in a magnificent loop that does not immediately end the day in an utter tangle. But that's not all. A dry fly on the end must land gently on the water as flies are supposed to, that is, without 100 feet of line obviously attached to it. The fish may leap from the water to take the lure, or it may disappear just below the surface. Since a dry fly will not fool even a fish for long, you have to be pretty sharp about setting the hook at the right moment to catch the curious fish. The wet fly, typically, is used in moving water, where pulling it upstream gives the illusion of a swimming minnow or insect larvae.

For the really keen fisher, the season does not end with summer. To make ice-fishing slightly less masochistic, at least provide yourself with a shelter containing a stove. It might be a tent, or a small plywood structure with some insulation. Before you drag it out on the lake, be sure the ice is safe enough. As a beginner, you would be well advised to wait until some other ice huts appear. If you must make your own judgment on ice safety, do not trust anything less than 3 inches, but try to go for the added security of 4 inches minimum. By "minimum" we mean the thinnest ice within 6 feet of where you will be walking. Bear in mind that ice can vary greatly in thickness over a short distance because of currents, springs, rocks, reflection from overhanging rocks and so on.

Cut the hole through the ice with an ice chisel (or spud), an ice augur or an axe, in descending order of preference. If you are serious about catching a fish, you will make several holes. At each hole, measure the depth, and drop a monofilament line to about a foot from the bottom; it should be baited with minnow, meat or lure. Attach that line to a clever device of your own invention to signal a bite by sight or sound while you wait in the (comparative) warmth of the shelter. If you are lucky, northern pike or whitefish may nibble on your line.

In winter or in summer, fish should be prepared for cooking or freezing as soon as possible. Wash it in cold, salted water. These days, few people bother to scrape off the scales or remove the entrails; filleting is the preferred procedure. That just means cutting away the fillet from the rest of the fish. If that task is beyond you, ask for advice from an expert, or look up fish in a good cookbook. To fry, dip the fillet successively in milk, beaten eggs and bread crumbs before dropping it in the pan with a little fat, oil or salt pork. To broil, season with salt, pepper and herbs before placing the fish on a spit made of a metal rod or green stick. To poach, wrap the whole-dressed fish in wax paper, then in layers of wet newspaper; bury it in hot coals for about 20 minutes. To bake, wrap a slice of half-cooked bacon around the fish before placing it in heavy aluminum foil with a little butter; then wrap tightly and bury in hot coals for 4 or 5 minutes. To plank a fish, you need a smooth hardwood board about as long as the fish and twice as wide; split the fish down the back so that the

belly skin is whole, and tack or tie it to the heated plank, flesh side up. Prop the board in front of the fire, turn it occasionally, and baste and season.

Those are very brief forays into culinary adventures with fish. They assume that your catch is so limited, or your appetite so hearty, that you consume them immediately, without recourse to high-tech kitchen equipment. The main rule is: *Never overcook*. The approach to cooking depends in part on the species you have caught. Among the most popular warm weather fish in most parts of cottage country are bass, walleye, catfish, crappie, perch, pike and trout. They may be the most popular fish, but not necessarily the commonest catches, which are listed as branches, submerged logs, old tires and frequent colds.

*F*LAGS

It may or may not be the expression of a patriotic sentiment, but the presence of a flag rolling in the breeze down at the point adds a certain ambiance to cottage life. And it has its practical uses. It will indicate if the wind is right for sailboats or kites. The wind direction may give you a better clue to tomorrow's weather than the smooth-talking forecasters on the radio. Like the Queen, you may wish to use the flag to indicate that you are in official residence.

You, may, of course, be able to dig a hole and stick a pole in it, or if you are on bedrock, pile stones around the pole and pour a couple of buckets of wet cement to secure them. That method is simple, but if you have bad luck, the rope will tangle in the pulley the day after the cement hardens. We suggest a better system which invests a bit more work for a trouble-free future.

In addition to the flagpole, you will need two cedar posts. If you can dig, the posts should be set 4 feet into the ground, with 5 or 6 feet above. If you are on rock, they can be correspondingly shorter. You will also need 2 threaded steel rods, preferably 1 inch in diameter with 2 nuts and 2 steel washers for each; they

should be equal to the combined diameters of the 2 posts
and flagpole plus at least 3
inches; good quality flagpole
rope (not the braided kind,
which tangles) twice the length
of the flagpole; an eye and
galvanized pulley to fit the rope;
a cleat upon which to secure
the free end of the rope at the
bottom of the pole; and a flag.
The cedar posts and poles
should be de-barked before
starting.

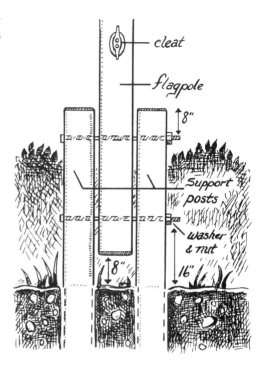

First, rig the flagpole with its
eye and pulley at the top, rope
threaded through and tied firmly
around the pole. Don't put on
the cleat until the end so that
you can judge a convenient
height for it.

Whether by digging or with rocks and cement, firmly install
the two posts absolutely vertical and parallel. The distance
between them is critical: equal to the diameter of the flagpole
at its lower end, plus a $1/2$ inch. If you are using concrete, pause
for two days to let it harden. Through one post, use a brace and
bit or a power drill to make two 1-inch holes, the lower about
16 inches from the ground, the upper about 8 inches from the
top. The threaded steel pipe should feed through the hole snugly: too tight to be pushed by hand, but easily tapped in with a
piece of wood, preferably with a nut loosely attached. (Don't
damage the thread by using a hammer on it.) Remove the rod.

Next muster your helpers to raise the flagpole. When it is precisely vertical with its base about 8 inches from the ground, and
centered between the posts, temporarily but firmly secure it
with blocks under its base and scraps of wood nailed across the
posts on both sides. If you are lucky enough to have a bit extension, drill through your existing holes, through the flagpole and
out the other post. Then insert the steel rods.

If your bit will not go this distance, drill a hole into the flagpole from each side of the post, lower the flagpole and finish drilling the hole through the pole itself. Then shift the pole so that the lower holes on the posts and pole are lined up. In inserting the steel rods, have two washers at each side of the flagpole, and one at each outer end of the rod. Put a bit of oil on the end threads of the rods. Hand-tighten the nuts. Raise the flagpole to the vertical and repeat the action with the upper rod. Tighten the four nuts with a wrench. That's it.

If you ever wish to lower the pole to put preservative on it, or to fix a tangle at the pulley, leave the lower rod intact. Put a rope around the pole as high as you can safely reach with a ladder, with one end of the rope on each side of the flagpole. With helpers keeping tension on both ends of the rope, tap out the top steel rod with a scrap of steel of smaller diameter. After a meeting to arrive at a unanimous decision on which direction to lower the pole, let it come gently to the ground. Simple.

There are some rules to follow in the flying of a flag, at least if you are flying the flag of Canada (or the U.S.A.) rather than a house pennant. Though normally flags are flown from dawn to dusk, there is nothing wrong with displaying them at night when they are illuminated — like the one dramatically flying on the Peace Tower in Ottawa. What is considered doubtful form is just leaving the national flag permanently up because no one has got around to lowering it. Flying a flag that is all faded and torn also is not done.

The flag of Canada must never have any other flag or pennant above it. If you are ambitious enough to have two poles, the Canadian flag must be on the left as spectators normally see it; if there are three poles, the Canadian flag must be in the center. If you are ceremoniously raising and lowering these flags, the Canadian flag must be raised first and lowered last. If you are flying a flag at half-mast, the center of the flag should be in the center of the flagpole. Again, if you are being ceremonious, you first raise the flag to the top, then lower it to the half-mast position; the converse at the end of the day.

If heads of state or chefs de protocol ever visit your cottage, perhaps you could ask them what to do.

FOOD STORAGE

The way you store food depends largely on the scale of luxury you have adopted for your cottage. For example, if you have a refrigerator, you might consider buying another for the shed to keep the drinks cold. You can probably get a second-hand model cheap. Its exterior may be somewhat battered, but if the workings are not damaged it could serve for years as your supplementary cooler.

If you are in that dwindling minority still dependent on blocks of ice, by now you have probably found all sorts of neat ways to make this method work most efficiently. You might have a small ice house insulated in the old-fashioned way with sawdust or more modernly with rigid insulation. You might have a pit or cellar cooled with ice. You might even have a real icebox which has not yet been converted into a bar or record cabinet.

The hazard you may not have thought much about in the city is animals. Especially towards the end of the summer, the mice start looking for well-equipped winter premises, and they are more intrepid than you might think. Earlier in the summer you may have been invaded by ants. (See **Ants, Mice.**) Through the winter, start saving metal containers for food you would customarily leave in cardboard boxes in the city. Do not count on plastic containers as proof against mice. They chew soft plastic as an aperitif, and are not stopped by the harder variety. If you want to be decorative, you can find — for a price — metal containers from antique stores and country auctions, for our ancestors knew more about food storage than we do. If you want to spend less, in junk stores you may find metal trunks or empty ammunition boxes for vulnerable foodstuffs.

If you are far more organized than most people, you may find extra space in your refrigerator as a refuge from ants and mice, but that is no use during your absence, when the refrigerator door should be left ajar. Then you turn to the oven where you put foodstuffs, soap and candles. (You also put a large sign on the oven door to warn enthusiastic cooks about turning on the oven.)

For convenience in any season, a mouse-proof cupboard is a great luxury, and it is not hard to make. Either take an existing well-built cupboard with tight-fitting doors, or make one. Then line it with galvanized fly screen (not fibreglass). If the cupboard is below the floor or in a damp place where even galvanized screen will rust, you should move up to the expensive bronze screen, but this is rarely necessary. You must cover the doors and all the interior, and see that all joins in the screen overlap generously. Use many tacks. If you are constructing anew, you can install the screen underneath the plywood, plasterboard, or other lining material to make the cupboard easier to clean and the screen harder for the mice to manipulate. It is conceivable that a voracious beast will eventually get into this cupboard, but it is unlikely; we claim a ninety percent success rate. But do not underestimate the ability of a mouse to enter through a minuscule crack around an ill-fitting door that has no baffle strips behind it. To further protect your cupboard, against squirrels or chipmunks, for example, reinforce the screen with $1/2$-inch hardware cloth.

Screened cupboards do not stop ants. While you are waiting for the deadly poison to take its effect, remember that ants do not swim very well. (Neither — perish the thought — can cockroaches.) For temporary protection, you can put a container in the centre of a pie plate with water. Or you can put edibles on a table or bed whose four legs are resting in containers of water. Too bad you can't do that for the winter: ants are handy at walking on ice.

G

GAMES: ON THE WAY

What may be the worst hour of the summer is not necessarily when the water pump coughs into extinction as the boss and family arrive for dinner: it is that middle hour of the long drive with a carful of young children. Some pre-planning may make the trip easier.

Before you leave, visit the local library and lead each child to the section on children's crafts. Let them choose one book on one craft — ensure that it is a craft more suited to the car than the bathtub. The child can then pack the materials needed and hand them over to mother or father, who is not to forget to pack them.

For the very young, playdough and silly putty are fine, but they require advance manufacture. Here is a recipe to make enough playdough for one child to mess up one car.

2 teaspoons of cooking oil

2 teaspoons of cream of tartar

1 cup of flour

$1/2$ cup of salt

Mix all thoroughly. Pour in water to which some exotic food coloring has been added. Stir over medium heat until the mess feels like dough. Cool and knead. Store in an airtight container. For silly putty, mix two parts of white glue well with one part of liquid starch. Slightly dry until it is workable. Store in an airtight container.

With younger children, especially, surprise is a vital element of success. Make up little packages for parents to dole out at reasonable intervals, or for older children, label them: "Open at Mud River", "Open at Joe's Gas Station". Packaging can be usable (facial tissue and elastic band) and contents simple:

a few raisins, peanuts, a voucher for an ice cream cone; a small tin of juice and a straw; a ribbon, string, buttons and odds and ends for sorting or stringing; colored pipe cleaners for artistic creations; bits of old gift wrapping, scotch tape and child's scissors; thin wood or cardboard punched with holes to practice sewing; paper plates and cups and string to make into telephones or crazy creatures; a zippered pencil case with crayons, blunt-end scissors, tape, paper clips; cardboard shapes to color and fit into weird shapes or mobiles; finger puppets or hand puppets.

Put the packages in a stout bag which can be closed. If your child becomes bored with any project put it back for possible re-issue later. For snacks, you could pack small containers of dry cereals or crackers that are much healthier for the car than messy candies.

If you have a young family, provide each member with a tray. Baking sheets covered with vinyl work well if they have edges to reduce spills. They lend themselves not only to meals but to play, providing a surface for playing with playdough, building sets, coloring books, note pads, and small puzzles. You could make your own draw-by-numbers with familiar cottage scenes. Magic sketch pads which erase their images with a flick are particularly good for road journeys. Whatever you bring, let it be new for the journey, or long out of circulation.

As the children grow older, origami — paper folding — is a creative and absorbing art in the ten to mid-teen age group. Also of interest are hand-held puzzles, such as shifting tiles in a box, tiny balls that slide into holes, tic-tac-toe, hi-q or such old stand-bys as Battleship and Hangman.

Then there are oral games. Before they start, build up expectations (and a semblance of order) by having everything else first stowed away. For the toddlers there are songs and nursery rhymes; if your own repertoire is quickly exhausted, a tape cassette could come to the rescue. Encourage the composition of original songs or rhyming words. At higher ages, singing rounds will entertain for minutes on end.

With older children, parents can entertain by singing songs from their courtship (and other Elizabethan madrigals) in return for which the teenagers must render their favorite songs.

If that sort of cultural exchange is still a few years away for your family, try "I spy with my little eye something...blue", or "something that begins with C". Then there is "I packed my grandmother's suitcase with... a word beginning with a, b, and so on. Or get them to pick up everything that has dropped on the floor, put it on a tray, allow everyone to see it for 30 seconds, cover it, and require all to list the items.

Why not turn to short stories? Each participant writes a sentence across the top of a page in response to the leader's question: "Where did it happen?" The sentence is folded over to conceal the writing and the page is passed along. In sequence, each participant answers "Where did it happen?", "Who was there?", "What did they do?" and so on, folding and passing the paper after each answer. After a dozen sentences, the papers are unfolded and the results read out.

When you recognize the symptoms of youthful fascination with cars, you can make up your own competitions based on brand recognition, license plates, year of origin, and so on. If you want to risk it, you can even embark on mathematical games. Find the number of hydro poles in one kilometer or mile, then calculate the speed of the car by counting them against a watch. Or just guess the number of minutes till you pass the next route marker, anti-littering sign, Hog Gulch, or whatever.

If you are not following a familiar route, introduce the children to map-reading, and have them announce the next community before you arrive. When they are older, give them large-scale maps from the federal Surveys and Mapping Branch which will allow them to tell you when you will pass a transmission line or a marsh on the right.

At some point you will have to stop the car. Apart from the obvious needs, vigorous activity is important. Have a ball or skipping rope hidden away so that the children do not first use it for mutual strangulation. Ten minutes of running races or jogging may help induce in children that state of sleepiness which drivers find so healthful.

GAMES: AT THE COTTAGE

A visit to the toy department of any local store will, of course, yield a bewildering variety of recreational equipment. A pocket book on games, indoor and outdoor, is a valuable part of any cottage library. Since the range of indoor entertainment for all ages and tastes is so infinite, we here confine ourselves to a few ideas for the great outdoors.

Net games like badminton and volleyball are a usual early choice because they do not need tailored lawns and can happily occupy people in groups ranging from two to a multitude. Don't try to play volleyball with a badminton net; it won't last through even one hard-fought game. If you cannot dig posts well into the ground, and then support them with ropes attached to trees or big rocks, you can make an easy portable post with 2-inch used iron pipe, two disposable plastic buckets (or the cardboard tubes sold for the purpose), and two bags of ready-mix cement. Posts with these cement bases can be used for any net games, if supported by guy ropes.

Tetherball, for which you have to buy the equipment, is a great outlet for wild physical spirits of all ages, but you have to be able to dig in the post very solidly indeed. If you haven't enough soil to dig in, do your best, and build up the post with heavy rocks secured with mucky cement poured over them — but don't let the rocks spread out so far from the post that a player could trip over them.

For those of more sedate athletic ambitions — from age four to ninety — don't overlook croquet. It is perhaps the quintessential cottage sport which is social, leisurely and equally interesting to the great expert and the totally incompetent.

One of the greatest — and most overlooked — of cottage games is popular in Québec and Europe where it is known as *pétanques* or *bocci*. The set consists of four heavy stainless steel balls about the size of tennis balls (but a lot more expensive) and a small wooden ball, known as a pig. The object of each player is to get two steel balls closer to the pig than the opponent can, by bowling, throwing or hitting away the opponent's ball. The advantage is that it can be played on a smooth court, on a beach, on a dirt road or rough ground, and all of the equipment can be carried in one hand. If you haven't bought *pétanques* yet, you can play roll ball by driving a stake in the ground and have the players, each with three balls, stand up to 60 feet away. The winner is the one whose ball rests closest to the stick.

Cottage ground is not usually much good for basketball, but you can have competitions by shooting for a hoop with its top 10 feet off the ground on a flat wall, although you don't even need that equipment. With two bushel baskets (remember them?) or round plastic laundry baskets on the ground 60 feet apart you can play bucketball — like basketball, except that you don't score if the basket falls over.

Horseshoes is a great game for the country. If you get the equipment from a local barn, look for shoes sized according to the ages of your family. Only two short pieces of pipe are needed — place them 40 feet apart — but if you become keen you will want to dig a sandpit around the stakes.

Tug-of-war needs only a strong rope and a lot of energy. Rolling target requires any old tire, which is rolled down the field while opposing young players try to throw a ball, bean bag or potato through it. Figure out your own scoring.

In the shallow water you can organize treasure dives by having a competitor from each of two teams dive simultaneously for a (reasonably) valuable object put on the bottom. Cork retrieve starts with a lot of corks or woodscraps scattered on the water so that two competitors can race to see who brings back more. The water poison game is not as lethal as it seems: the poison is a small float encircled by small fry holding hands. They try to pull and push their friends in to touch the poison without doing so themselves. Water log has one player floating like a log between two marked points about 60 feet apart; the other swimmers encircle the log until it suddenly rolls over and gives chase to reach the nearest goal point first. The tagged swimmer then becomes the log.

None of these amusements is very sophisticated, yet simplicity may be their greatest novelty and virtue. You can go on all summer by inventing your own variants. If you run out of ideas, the library or bookstore will help.

GARBAGE

Even if your cottage is in an area of such civilization (and high taxes) that you have regular garbage collection, there is one precaution to bear in mind. Your garbage must be much more securely stowed than in the city, or you will encourage visits from unwanted animals ranging from roaming dogs to bears. Galvanized pails with securely locking lids are worth the effort and expense. If you have raccoons about, be especially careful. They are so intrepid that they have been accused of stealing keys to padlocks and combinations to the safe. The alternative to metal pails is to construct a very strong garbage bin or hut which will allow you to use plastic pails or even garbage bags. Perhaps no such hut is proof against large bears, but it should be strong enough for security against all lesser mammals.

If you are disposing of your own garbage, sort it. The object is to reduce the quantity requiring special treatment because of the potential smell or attraction to animals. In one box put all combustibles like paper — except for paper soiled by perishable goods, which may take on a scent of its own. You can save that for autumn heat, for a bonfire, compost pile (see **Bonfires, Compost**) or for a pile in the woods which needs only light, cosmetic covering.

In another box, put metal, glass and plastic. (If there is a recycling program in the area, these items will have to be separated.) You will save trouble later, and avoid the problem of finding landfill sites, if you reduce this garbage down to its smallest volume. That means cutting both ends from tins, and squashing them flat with your foot before throwing them in the box. It really is a good idea to rinse them too, to eliminate their interest for animals. To break non-recyclable bottles, be sure to put a heavy cover of sacking or newspaper over them before smashing them with a hammer. By these techniques you can reduce the bulk to less than a quarter of its original size. When your box is full, its contents need only light covering in a pit.

The perishable garbage will have to be kept secure until you are ready for final disposal. This garbage, too, can be divided advantageously, with vegetable scraps (for compost) in one pail, and the rest in another. You will already have dug as deep and wide a pit as cirucmstances permit, leaving lots of loose earth in a pile by the side. As soon as you dump the perishable garbage, cover it thoroughly with earth. The more secure your garbage pails, the less frequent will be these burials, and the longer your pit will last.

In the unlikely event that, with this simple technique, you still attract unwanted animals, you may have to put strong chain-link fencing around the pit. Of course, when one pit is exhausted, the metal fence can be moved next season, for by then the contents will be decomposed enough to be less than tasty. The fence will not stop rodents like rats (which are also unlikely). If you see any signs of such disturbance, take prompt remedial measures , for once you bring them to your area, they will drift inside without invitation.

With all your care, you may drop the odd bit of garbage around the pit, and at least flies will be attracted. Therefore, put the installation as far as practicable from the house. And do a little forward planning. Don't ever use an old garbage site for a new guest cabin, or you will regret it the day construction starts.

GARDENING

The natural greenery of cottage country might seem to make gardening unnecessary. Nevertheless, you may want to control the growth, or perhaps you have been considering where to improve modestly upon nature by some planting of your own. You may want to watch it, or eat it.

Ornamental

Let's assume that you do not want this operation to be excessively labor intensive or costly. Your object may be simply to add some greenery to the cottage grounds, or you may want to cut your own flowers for the house. If you seek more privacy, you will be interested in trees. (See **Trees**.)

Landscaping is a marvellously creative pastime, for you are using living things to express your imagination. There is a wealth of literature to consult for ideas to adapt and material to use. If you tend to get carried away, remember that your objective is to enhance the natural environment, not to replace it. A suburban-style garden that is primly manicured sitting on the edge of the bush or rock seems like a bit of an unnecessary war with nature.

It makes sense to have a lawn where you can sit without being attacked by bugs and where family of all ages can play, but let it blend as unobtrusively as possible with the surroundings. The perfect lawn merges gradually into more natural ground cover, into pruned and open woods, into the bush itself: it does not end with a sudden break. It is more practical for upkeep that way and, we think, more pleasing.

If you don't favor the sound and fury of lawnmowers, but want a clearing, the solution is easy: just grade it to minimize the risk of broken ankles. But what do you do when the natural groundcover of low weeds grows intimidatingly tall with mullens, brambles or milkweed? Frankly, the easiest way to control the growth so the space will be useable is — a lawnmower. You can set it very high, and the cutting will take a fraction of the time with better results in appearance and usability than hand cutting.

Around that open space you may want gardens. Why not start with plantings you can find locally so that your garden looks friendly with the wilds? If there are loose rocks around, you can make rockeries. Try to arrange them casually enough that they might have been dropped by a passing ice age. In flat gardens or rockeries you can transplant wildflowers before they have buds. There is not much point in transplanting after they have bloomed, for so many of them are self-seeding annuals. You can more effectively collect their seeds in late summer and sprinkle them in their new home. Some seed houses offer packages of wildflower seeds for those who have not collected them.

Before embarking on this transplanting, it is well to arm yourself with some knowledge of wildflowers from a book or periodical such as *Century Home* or *Harrowsmith*, so that you will know what to look for. You needn't be an expert; common sense will lead you to move plants from shady places to shady places (like ferns or the low-growing wildflowers of the woods); and plants from sunny places to sunny places (like daisies, goldenrod, buttercup, brown-eyed susans). These can be planted in your rockeries, in conventional gardens of imaginative contours, or in a vernacular garden.

Ah, the vernacular garden! That's just a garden that preserves a calm conscience though you never weed it. (See **Weeds**.) It can be spectacular, satisfying, and very labor-saving. Successful vernaculars are often crowded into a defined space, edged by logs, for example, where wild and tame plants are tucked together to provide continuing bloom over the season. You can also improve on nature with varying color: if the wildflowers/weeds are mostly yellow, add some blue veronica and let it go native.

Some of those so-called weeds, like goldenrod, are regarded in western Europe as exotic plants. Look at them again to enjoy the many shapes and varieties, and even bring them in the house, unless you have allergies in the family. A book on weeds will indicate which are attractive, hardy, decorative and either self-seeding or perennial. Spikes of purple loosestrife, lost in the ditches of eastern Canada and the northeastern United States every July, can be a prize in the cottage garden, and they will easily spread. So too with deep purple vervaine. Queen Anne's lace, not to be confused with the coarser yarrow, can be spectacular. Seeds collected from the flat white head will germinate the next summer.

And don't forget the water plants. You can have your own pussy willows, marsh marigold and even water lillies by scanning the roadside instead of writing cheques. Just be sure to carry with you on any trip your handy trowel, plastic bag and pruning shears. Wild flags (dwarf iris) may be hiding by the water's edge. You can transplant bullrushes, but when you do, stand back: if they take at all, they multiply alarmingly.

If your retreat is accessible in early spring, you can transplant early flowers successfully by giving them a moist home similar to their native heath. Never pick a trillium, but you can transplant them with care by digging a generous clump of soil. There are more varieties and colors of violet than you may have imagined. Columbine is easy to spot with its harlequin blossom and fernlike foliage. Bloodroot, a favorite of the early settlers, is one of the first flowers of the northern spring.

These indigenous plantings do not exclude the possibility of adding some annuals grown from seed in the city, or bought from the local market: petunias, marigold, portulaca, snap-dragon, and so on. You can mix them with the local plants, but if you prefer not to, window boxes are a pleasant summer project which may enhance your architecture, improve the view, and provide cut flowers for the dining room table.

Is there any ground cover to substitute for grass? If you want to use the space, grass is probably the best. There are lots of low ground covers which are nice to look at, but none that stand the test of badminton or heated arguments in lawn chairs. Pachysandra (Japanese spurge), silver leaf, lily-of-the-valley and periwinkle look great in shadier areas where you will not walk much. Don't overlook the possibility of vines like virginia creeper which grows wild in many parts of Canada and the U.S.A. It can be trained to grow vertically to hide some unworthy object, or even to flourish on a dead tree, but it can also be used as ground cover in places you are not planning to walk. It turns a splendid red in autumn. If the area in question is wide open to the sun, try getting some packets of easy flowers — nasturtium, portulaca, candy tuft, viola or campanala (bluebell flower) — and mix them with light soil to broadcast over the whole space.

For shadier areas, remember the plantain lily, not really a lily at all, but foolproof in borders and bare spots. Its foliage is plain green or striped, and it produces a spiky mauve blossom in July. A perennial, it spreads quickly.

If your property has extensive woods, you can enhance the flower growth even without transplanting. It is largely a matter of clean-up — removing the underbrush and matted leaves that choke out growth, and possibly thinning trees, or their branches, to let in more sunlight. For example, if you are lucky enough to have a few trilliums, they will spread in a spectacular way if the ground is made a bit more inviting for them. It will take a year to harvest the rewards of your labors, but they will be impressive.

For lower visual barriers than trees provide, you may be considering bushes. Since you are unlikely to find any satisfactory bushes growing wild, it may be necessary to visit your friendly nursery. In many areas of Canada and the northern U.S.A., one of the first bushes planted by pioneers was lilac, and many a lonely lilac clump on the horizon is the only trace of where an early family once lived. If you see such a clump along the roadside, with a sharp spade you can cut the roots to bring home the small shoots that have spread out (called volunteers), without damaging the original. It will take a few years until they bloom (epsom salts, of all things, are a folk fertilizer to encourage blossoms), but they will soon provide a leafy barrier. You can also buy lilac bushes. Honeysuckle is another traditional bush so common that it seems almost native. It produces red berries in the fall, but the leaves are prone to insects.

In your passion to introduce ornamental planting, don't forget the opposite process. Pull out wild brambles with enthusiasm; they flourish in newly cleared land, give nasty scratches to passers-by, and choke out what you want to keep. You may want to eliminate plants which cause you or your friends medical problems: ragweed above all, and maybe goldenrod. Remove as well poison ivy, poison oak and even sumac, if any member of your family is known to come out in welts upon touching it. It is also a good idea to get rid of wild gooseberry which is dangerous to your white pines.

Vegetable Gardens

Are you planning a vegetable garden because you love growing vegetables, or cherish eating produce just minutes old? If so, you will find great enjoyment in a cottage vegetable garden. If you are thinking of vegetable gardens as an economy for the cottager, you are courting disappointment unless you estimate your labor to be worth no more than 25 cents an hour.

While ornamental gradens relate to the cottage environment, vegetable gardens are a project which require much the same knowledge and effort at the cottage as anywhere else. The single special limitation may be the length of time you are at the cottage. You may well be there early enough for spring planting, but will you be present for constant watering for that unexpected June drought which happens every year? Or will you be there early enough in the season to keep up your offensive on predatory animal life? And will you sadly have to leave the cottage when the tomatoes are still rich green and the corn is not quite big enough to pick?

The last of these problems calls for the selection of varieties that, above all, mature quickly. For watering in your absence, there are now high-tech devices, for a price, that measure the moisture of your soil and turn on the water when needed. But do you really trust, not just that equipment, but your whole water system when you are far away? If you do, at least install a low-pressure cut-off on your pump so that you do not return to a fried motor. (See **Water**.) You may be able to carry on the war against groundhogs, rabbits, tomato worms, cornborers or bugs by weekend forays. Keeping out the larger animals will probably require eternal vigilance, and a secure fence around the plot. It is said that raccoons will stay away if you leave on a radio; if it is tuned to a heavy metal station, it will probably drive them mad.

Some vegetables produce in glory while you are still in the city, such as rhubarb or asparagus (which takes years to produce anyway), so you may want to avoid them at the cottage. Beans, peas, carrots, green onions, spinach, and lettuce are among the easiest for the beginner, and they are with you all season. You could also add to North America's overcrowded zucchini population. Squash and pumpkins are certainly simple; they won't be ready by Labor Day, but if you are up at Thanksgiving, they should still be there for the taking. If you plant them on a hillock they will take off as a decorative vine with cuplike blossoms to cover unattractive barren ground. Herbs are ony a mild challenge, which make them a good choice for the new or recreational gardener. Dill and summer savory come near the top of the list because they are attractive and save money. Others, such as oregano, parsley (it's agonizingly slow starting from seed) and basil, also add a dimension of scent to your cottage garden in the long summer evenings.

It's fun all right, but so is visiting the farmer's market.

GENERATORS

With the spread of rural electricity, the need to generate your own may have dwindled — but not disappeared. Cottages are now opening up on ever more distant frontiers. It may happen that you want to build before the power arrives. A portable generator can come in handy if you ever contemplate supplementary construction beyond the reach of power lines. And it is also possible that the vagaries of power in your area make a back-up system a good idea, so that you are not waterless and dark just when the company arrives. Those are the rationalizations for an investment of around $1,000 plus any wiring.

In addition to cost, the other disadvantage of generators is the noise of the internal combustion motor while you are using power. It is comparable to a chain saw. You can reduce it considerably by building a well-insulated shed, but since you still need an exhaust system, you will always hear that motor.

There are sources of electricity other than the power company and the gasoline motor. A windmill which charges storage batteries, for example: quiet, relatively expensive, and with one huge disadvantage. Unless you have a 110/220 volt alternating current system, no ordinary appliance will work on this system. There will be endless trouble and expense in adapting appliances, and if utility lines later reach you, the storage battery system will be a write-off. That is why they are less common than they used to be.

Back to the generator. A 3000-watt generator (it takes two strong people, or one very strong person, to carry it) will handle everything you need except an electric range and electric heating. Since it will take care of the electric kettle, toaster and frying pan, you will not starve. If you are building anew, and expecting the utility company in a year or two, and then plan to use the generator as a back-up, you can do yourself a favor by planning ahead. Have your whole cottage wired as if you had normal service: it's much less expensive to do it while you are building than later when the hydro people come along. But here is the trick: ask the electrician to plan the circuits, under your close supervision, so that future emergency circuits can be isolated to work off the generator. This means having at least one light and one outlet in every room on a separate circuit, a circuit for kitchen appliances like the frying pan or kettle, a circuit for the water pump, and any other special circuits which your special appliances need. Let's assume that for these purposes you need five circuits. A line will then be brought from them to the generator, so that, years hence when all your neighbours have a power blackout, you can rev up the generator, flick a switch from hydro to generator, and carry on in reasonable comfort. If that idea appeals to you, do it while you are building, because it will be a big job to untangle the circuits later. Before the utility lines arrive, you can use the generator on all circuits (except stove and heating), but you must be careful not to overload by trying to use a total of more than about 2500 watts at a time.

If you are considering a generator for a cottage already served with electricity, it will probably be too much trouble to re-wire emergency circuits. You can get along with the generator and heavy extension cords. Ensure that your water pump is not connected permanently into house wiring, but has a plug and its own socket, either 110 or 220 volts; when normal power fails and you call on the generator, all you have to do is unplug the pump from the wall, and connect it with its own heavy extension cord to the generator.

Most generators start with the familiar rope. More expensive ones have a battery start. With a sympathetic technician, you can sometimes adapt an ordinary generator to a battery start at much less cost than to buy the luxury model. The generator is no harder to start than a lawnmower, unless it is winter, when you are less likely to use it. The battery start is therefore a frill, but one which makes it possible for any member of the family to turn on emergency power with the flick of two switches.

Maintenance of a generator takes about the same effort as any small motor, with appropriate oil changes being the main point to remember. It should be run for a few minutes once a month to keep it in shape, with a log to show usage. If you have the battery start, plug in the small charger for a day at the same time, just to be sure the battery is fully charged when you need it.

With these precautions you can laugh at the generation gap.

GUESTS

The best training to become a perfect guest is first to be a cottage host, and vice-versa. If you are lucky, you will have more memories of pleasant gestures than of thoughtlessness.

Let's start by dealing with unwanted guests. They may be bosom friends, but if they arrive without warning, they risk shattering both cottage peace and life-long friendship. No guest should arrive without earnest attempts to warn the host and learn if the time is convenient, even if there is a standing "drop in anytime" invitation.

The host, faced with such thoughtlessness and bad manners, has a problem which should be dealt with forthrightly. One precaution to avoid the problem is to issue that general invitation in writing, with a map if appropriate, but accompany it with a warning about phoning or writing in advance "because we are sometimes away or are caught up in family plans". If it is neighbors who have developed the habit, perhaps you could invite them to a picnic or other simple entertainment to show your friendship and hospitality, and make clear in the invitation that this seems a better idea than casual visits which may cause interruptions in plans.

The happy visiting experience starts with precise arrangements. "We'll drive over early in July" is just not good enough; the host may be needlessly sweeping the floors or laying in perishable food for days. The day and the hour must be set in advance. Equally important is the length of the visit. This can be established by the invitation, which should not be vague, as in "Visit us for the weekend" but clear, as in "We hope you will come up Friday evening and stay until after breakfast on Sunday".

A good guest never arrives empty-handed. If the guests ask what to bring, it is not kind to say "Just yourselves", for it will not help their problem. And they may resort to flowers (coals to Newcastle) or chocolates (wrecking your diet). It is better to suggest a pocketbook about snakes, or "whatever you like to drink", or even the steaks for Saturday's barbecue.

The guests deserve precise directions to your cottage. (See **Maps**.) If you are to meet them at the bus stop in town, be sure that the time and place is exact, and provide back-up phone numbers. ("If by any chance you miss that bus, please leave a message at Irma's Grocery, 555-6789, and if anything happens to us, we'll leave a message there for you.")

The host's first duty is an orientation tour, with clear instruction as to cottage dos and don'ts. Make a list of things to mention, such as washroom facilities (including warnings about what not to put in a toilet serviced by a septic tank), fire precautions, safety precautions in boats and at the water, smoking regulations, who sleeps where, the comings and goings of the family, the normal meal and rest habits, access to food, bug repellents, briefings on neighbors they are likely to meet, recreation facilities, and so on. This may sound tedious, but it is the fastest way to make the guest feel comfortable and at home.

The first requirement of the guests is to respect the briefing, and to disturb routines as little as possible. The second is to pitch in without fuss — quietly picking up a dish towel or grabbing a broom — but only if it does not give the impression that you think the floor is a mess which needs your immediate attention. That guests make their own beds and tidy the bedroom before anyone else has a chance goes without saying. Like air travellers, they also wipe out the washroom basin with a paper towel after using it. If guests are travelling by car, they may want to bring their own towels to save the drain on the cottage supply.

The sensitive guest will soon move the conversation onto cottage life and how the owners spend their time. From this may emerge pleasant little tasks which will please and not embarrass the hosts. ("I just love weeding gardens, but yours is so immaculate that I don't know if I can find any..." "If you really want that dead oak felled, I'd love to do it because I was once a forester in British Columbia.") The best contributing tasks may be special projects ("Let me repair that pier, remove those rocks from the road, mend that tapestry, stain the outhouse.") at which the guest's ideas and work habits are less likely to clash with your routine maintenance.

The ideal guest will respect the family's routine but not be such a slave to it that the family feels uncomfortable. How often have guest and host lain motionless in their beds waiting for the first sound of life from the other? Guests who like to rise early can show how much they feel at home by silently emerging and going for a long walk, paddle or swim while the family rests and gets organized for the day. If the stay is to be longer than a day or two, the best guests find an excuse to go away for a few hours, leaving the family some privacy to do the little things in which they don't want to involve the guest (like sweeping the dirt under the rug, or fixing the sewer, or phoning their creditors).

The sensitive guest will express appreciation of the cottage as it is and not try to reform it. "What you should do with that dock is..."; "Why don't you move that window..."; "It would be a lot more convenient if you just..." are all expressions which should not pass the lips of the ideal guest. The average cottager is not short of ideas for improvement, but merely lacks the will to move from hammock to action.

After departure, the prompt conventional thank-you note is something which no guest should overlook. It need not be Shakespearean in style, but it should be more than a couple of generalized expressions; mention some incident or aspect of the visit that was particularly appreciated. It might be accompanied by a small gift which relates to the observed needs of the cottage — for example, a book or a kitchen gadget.

After this happy encounter, guest and host alike will be scanning next summer's calendar for the date of a return visit.

H

*H*AMMOCKS

The hammock is probably the most instantly recognizable symbol of cottage life.

It is true that in many cottages, the hammock may sway lonely in the gentle breeze while the family hammers nails, cuts pipes, moves rocks or saws firewood. It is there as a symbol of hope that the family's work will one day be done, and they will be rewarded by an unaccustomed study of lazily passing clouds. In other cottages, the hammock is worn out more quickly than the garden rake.

Either way, a cottage should have a hammock, and we hope you will place it where it best satisfies your romantic notions. A favored spot is between trees at the edge of the woods. After all, the hammock is meant for relaxing in the shade. Even the arduous work of sunbathing should be done elsewhere.

You might choose a canvas hammock because it is tough and will give little trouble in maintenance. Just don't leave it out so that the rain will form puddles in it and hasten its decay. Canvas also has disadvantages. It is hotter than a net or an open weave fabric, and on humid days perspiring bodies will stain it and may make it smell less than sweet. You may even have to wash it — by throwing it in the lake.

A hammock made of soft material of a relatively open weave that lets some air through will not last as long and it, too, needs washing from time to time. It is likely to be more comfortable as well as less costly, and if it has old-fashioned fringe it will add to your décor.

A net is coolest of all and is really the classic cottage hammock. It also folds up quickly and very compactly. There is a trade-off between durability and comfort, for if the cord is hard enough to wear well, it may be a little uncomfortable for sensitive skin. Softer cord will feel better, but it may not hold up under weightier guests.

If you enjoy crafts, you may want to make your own hammock. A book from the library will explain the knots in detail in a way that any nuclear engineer can understand. It is a matter of acquiring three 2-pound cones of 30-ply non-scratch butcher's twine, making a net, 2 supports for hanging (called clews) and attaching rings.

Whether homemade or store-bought, the hammock must be mounted with an eye to safety. That obviously means solid trees; if the right ones are too far apart, you can add rope to the hammock ring. It also means not putting the hammock higher from the ground than needed for comfort in entry and exit. Finally, it means ensuring that, in case of disaster, the ground below is free of any rocks, stumps or sticks which would wreak physical or psychological harm to a plunging Aunt Hattie.

Harmful Plants

Your family will not encounter many plants that are really dangerous, but they should be persuaded not to eat anything they do not clearly recognize. It is all very well to go back to nature by surviving on the berries of the woods, but some of them can cause severe stomach upsets or worse. Many roots and leaves are dangerous, too (as cattle-owning farmers know), but we trust the chances of your young ones eating them are slim. Other plants can cause severe troubles with just a touch.

Of the latter variety, the most famous are poison oak and poison ivy. Just as there are no snakes in Ireland, there is no poison ivy in Newfoundland, but it is everywhere else. Get a colored picture of it and ensure that everyone can identify its three shiny dark green leaves. By the same token, they should be taught not to panic at the sight of every three-leaved plant in the woods, for there are an awful lot of harmless ones.

The fresh or dried juices of the poison ivy can be carried by clothing, tools, other plants in a refuse pile, the fur on your pet, or even smoke. At the first indication that you may have been exposed — before the rash breaks out, if possible — wash the skin with yellow bar soap or rubbing alcohol to remove the oily substance, being very careful about what you touch with your towel. A natural antidote is the flower of the jewel weed, a feathery, watery bush whose little orange blooms can be rubbed on the affected areas. Needless to say, you should try to eliminate poison ivy and poison oak from areas frequented by your family; buy a preparation from your garden store, and assume that you will have to use it more than once, and check again in the same places at the start of the next season.

Nightshade is a woody climber with deep purple flowers and bright red fruit attractive to children. Do not let them touch it: it is poisonous.

Other plants cause stings when touched, notably the stinging nettle. The rash it produces can give acute discomfort for hours and, for some people, much longer. It can grow to about 7 or 8 feet in height, often by the roadside. Fortunately, it has shallow roots and is easily pulled out if you wear gloves. If you do not, you can still eradicate it by grasping it from the bottom while avoiding the hairs on the stem.

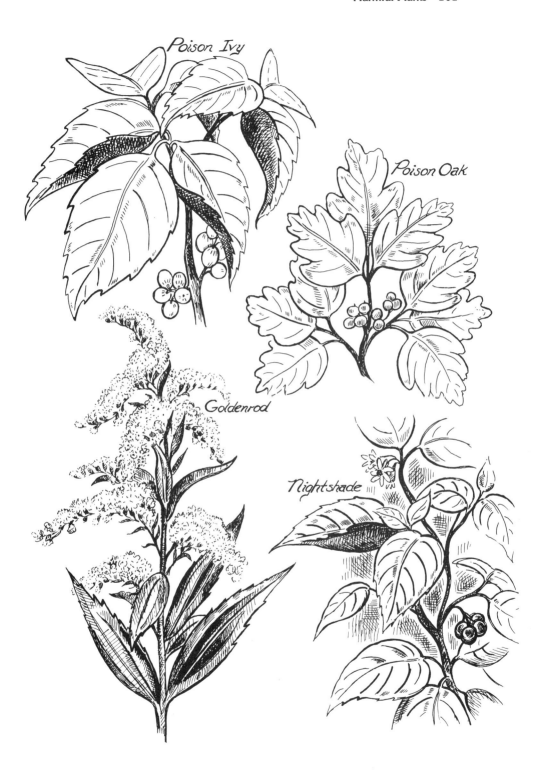

Poison Ivy

Poison Oak

Goldenrod

Nightshade

There are many thorny bushes which tend to grow quickly by an incredible network of roots after trees have been cleared. They do not cause itchy rashes but they are so sharp that the slightest touch may produce welts on young skin. If you keep yanking them out when they are young they will gradually become discouraged. The thorny wild gooseberry may seem a good plant for lovers of gooseberry jam, but it is deadly to the white pine because it carries the spores of blister rust. If you value your pines, get rid of it. (See **Trees**.)

Some plants create bad problems for people with allergies. The innocent sumac, which may be a bush or a tree 15 or 20 feet high, can trigger an allergic reaction in a few unfortunate people who have only to touch it. Ragweed and goldenrod are bad news for many hay fever sufferers, which is a pity because the goldenrod is a colorful plant. Ragweed, being less attractive, should be eradicated within range of the cottage, but the less threatening goldenrod might be left alone until you suspect problems.

Beyond these few, which are widespread across the continent (save for the deep South) there may be local hazards about which it is well to enquire. When you have noted your own harmful plants, get a book or agricultural pamphlet which identifies them clearly with colored pictures and text, and insist that your family pass a small course in plant identification. Comfort yourself that, on the whole, nature has given cottagers relatively few plants to worry about.

HEAT

This is about getting rid of it. If you would prefer a little more heat, please see **Cold**. Today we are too hot, and in doing something about it, we shall start with the big things.

The first is the cottage site, if you have a choice in the matter. Since the trees are your best ally in preventing heat build-up, don't touch a leaf of any that may later give you shade, and encourage the smaller ones that have potential. You do that by pruning and fertilizing them annually and, in the case of cedars, by giving them lots of water throughout the season. (See **Trees**.) At the same time, don't let thick bush growing close to your windows block the precious breeze. Drastic pruning may be an alternative to removal.

When you are choosing a site for the cottage, the main factor is likely to be the view. If you have any choice left after that, bear in mind which windows will be hit by the hot afternoon sun. If there were any thought of this being a winterized home one day, you would be thinking of the value of passive solar heat, but if this is to be always a summer cottage, you do just the opposite. If you can conveniently put most of your window glass on the north and east walls, you will avoid some of the heat problems.

The next measure is insulation, with highest priority to the roof and to the west and south walls. Just for keeping cool, you can forget about insulation in the floor, and certainly double-glazed windows would be an unwarranted expense. If you have a flat ceiling underneath a conventional gable or hip roof, you lay fibreglass in rolls or batts, or lay loose fill as thickly as you wish. Energy conservationists now recommend up to R-40, but R-28 will serve your summer needs well. If you are building anew or haven't yet lined the interior, install a plastic vapor barrier (6 mm polyethylene; rolls 10 feet wide with about 500 square feet is a convenient size) across the bottom of the joists before nailing on the plasterboard, plywood or whatever. If the cottage is already there, it may still be worth the trouble to put in that vapor barrier because of its value in cool seasons. Since you will have to lay it from the top side of the ceiling, it will loop up and down each joist, which takes more plastic. Then fit in or drop the insulation carefully so that there are no gaps, right to the outer walls. If you are choosing new or replacement shingles, you will ease your problem a little by avoiding black or dark colors.

It will probably not be worth the effort to insulate the walls unless you are building or installing new interior wall covering. The amount of insulation depends on the width of your studs; the insulation will lose its value if it is too tight or squashed down. If you are building anew, use 2 x 6s to give more room for insulation.

Before you leave the space under the roof, see that it is well ventilated. This means a cross draft swooshing through vents whose total open area is at least one square foot for 1500 square feet of ceiling space. More is better. In addition, you can eliminate the heat up there before it ever radiates down to you by installing a fan. (See **Fans**.)

If you have a so-called cathedral ceiling — open to the roof — you will have interior heat build-up unless you take preventative measures. With trouble and expense you could put rigid insulation underneath the roof, and cover it with wood or other decorative material or you could get an insulating product that goes on top of the roof, under the shingles. An easier and less expensive method is to install large windows at the highest possible points. You should be able to open and close them easily with a rope from the floor below. The windows up there can, of course, be made of simple wood construction, with screens instead of glass, since they will be open most of the time in fine warm weather.

Now we are down to ordinary windows. By far the most effective form of heat protection is the old-fashioned awning, which bounces back the hot sun before it gets inside the building. Conventional awnings are undoubtedly expensive, but you can make — or have made — a less elaborate version which will not have the finicky triangular end pieces.

You will need some $1/2$-inch iron rod, canvas, eyes, rope, a cleat on which to tie the rope and some brackets which only an awning store is likely to have. Cut the canvas so that one dimension is the same as the movable part of your window, and the other is about half the height of your window. Pockets, with the 2 rows of stitching 2 inches apart, are sewn along the 2 sides (that is, the side which will go across the top of your window and the one opposite it).

The cloth is ready. Now reach for the rod. Measure the distance from the window to where you will want the outer edge of the awning; assuming the awning will be about 45 degrees, a little mathematics should give you that measurement. Bend a right angle in that iron rod at that distance; the next straight section in the rod is, of course, the width of your canvas; then bend the second right angle and cut the rod so that the 2 side pieces are equal. Drill about $1/8$-inch holes close to each end of the rod. The metal work is done.

The next step is installation. Slide the finely crafted iron into the pocket in the canvas. The awning store's mounting clips hold the upper rod to the wall: they come with two hooks where pulleys can be attached. Screw these clips into the top of the window frame and clamp the top of the awning to them. If the window is no more than about 4 feet wide, one rope from each outer corner of the rod up to the top will probably suffice. If it is longer, you will also need a middle support, which requires a hole in the canvas at the middle of the lower rod, as well as a third clip in the wall.

Finally, the pulleys: in a typical installation you will need one single pulley at the top left, one double pulley in the middle, and a single and a double at the right. (If you have only two ropes, a single pulley and a double pulley will do.) The left rope goes from the end of your bar to the single pulley, through a middle pulley (to prevent sagging), through a right pulley, and down to the cleat which you have screwed on the side of the window frame to tie the rope. The middle rope goes up from the lower rod through the center pulley, over to a right pulley and down to the cleat. The right rope just goes up to the right pulley and down to the cleat.

Now all you need do is attach the ends of that u-shaped iron rod to your window frame so that it will be absolutely horizontal when the awning is down. A wire through the hole in the rod and through a screw eye on the wall will let the assembly move freely when you raise or lower the awning. Like tying your shoelaces, awning-making is easier in practice than on paper. It is much less costly than buying conventional awnings and the comfort produced is well worth the effort.

If you have several awnings of exactly the same size, rotate them each season to even out the wear from sun and rain. When one has to be replaced, you need only take the cloth to your friendly awning maker to have it duplicated. Each autumn you will, of course, have to take down the awning, including the rope and bars, but not the clips and cleat.

With awnings, there is less need for curtains and blinds. For ease of installation and low cost, the best buys are matchstick curtains or blinds. On awningless windows facing south or west, roll-down vinyl blinds with white exteriors are the most efficient in keeping out heat, but they won't improve the view.

Especially for bedrooms, the most efficient windows are double hung, rather than hinged. To get ventilation without excessive light, you can make a simple baffle for the bottom. Cut a piece of $1/2$-inch plywood just long enough to fit across the window frame and about 8 inches wide; mount it in place with two strips of 1 x 1 or less at an angle. The bottom will be almost against the window and the top slanting towards the room at about 30 degrees. You can then have the window and its opaque blind down to about 6 inches from the bottom with a minimum of light. To be really effective, you can paint the outer side of the plywood with a dark, non reflective paint. Instead of nailing the plywood to its strips, you can dado a slot or use hooks so that the plywood can be removed when every whisper of breeze is a more important consideration than unwanted light or drafts.

Managing the air supply takes a little thought. While the air remains relatively cool all night and early morning you will want to get the interior to that low temperature by having every window open. Later, when the hot breeze will only heat the cottage, it is better to close windows, except for the one which lets the breeze blow across you. A hot breeze by itself will only heat up the interior, but as it caresses your body it may cool you a little through evaporation, and it helps psychologically. Of course you can induce the breeze by using fans (see **Fans**), but remember their limitation. They are moving hot air — and even heating it with their motors — but the evaporation of perspiration helps. Therefore, use an ordinary fan only when someone is there — otherwise, it is just helping to heat up the cottage. (The exception, of course, is an exhaust fan which may be extracting overheated air from the stove.)

Don't forget the non-human members of your family on hot days. Be particularly mindful of a pet's need for fresh drinking water; it is more important than for people. And remember the motors, such as the one in the refrigerator, which may heat up unmercifully. At the least, see that the refrigerator is far enough out from the wall to allow circulation, and that the coils, usually at the bottom of the machine, are kept free of dust by reaching across them with a long brush or bottle cleaner. Persuade the family to open the refrigerator door just as little as possible. At best, let the fan blow on the motor occasionally.

If you have a classic heat wave with scorching sun, and a limitless supply of tap water from the lake, you can spray the sunny walls and roof. It may do a little good, and it will keep the youngsters occupied. They may as well dampen the ground immediately around the building, for heat is reflected back from it.

We retreat from the controversies about what to drink to get cool. There are those who insist on nothing but iced drinks, and they have dozens of recipes to make their case. Others swear that hot tea is much the best. And yet another school is prepared to demonstrate that, despite the fact that alcohol does heat one up, the best solution is to drink to oblivion.

Then there is always the lake.

I

*I*NSECTS

Ants

The biological textbooks are all wrong about the habitat of ants. Their true home is your summer cottage. For practical purposes you need divide the world's population of ants into only two classes: those which eat your food and those which eat your buildings.

Those which eat your food usually can be dispatched by commercial products. Ant traps have the advantage of being neat and no hazard to the family. Faster is a more lethal poison placed in small quantities in little dishes, but *not* where authorized inhabitants of the cottage can lick them. If you discover ants in your bag of sugar or other granular food, if you can't possibly get to the store to replace it, and if you are not squeamish, the solution is easy. Just spread it out thinly on the table or on a board in the sun, and they will all run away with extraordinary speed. And no one need ever know. If the ants are really persistent, you may consider complementing these measures with a spraying of chlordane around the wooden foundations or any other obvious route of entry — but not inside the building. It will certainly give them a bad headache at the least, and may solve your problems for a season. Chlordane is poisonous and to be treated with respect, but in our view it is not a hazard to humans when sensibly used.

The building-eating ants are a more serious problem, especially in older structures. It will take a long time until your home falls about your ears, but meanwhile it is unnerving to hear them in the silence of the night as they crunch away at your possessions, clean their teeth, and leave piles of sawdust as memories of their evening meal. Those little piles are the clue. You must soak the tiny entrance holes beside them with a solution of chlordane. Don't spray it inside the house, but soak the wood with a paint brush or rag that has been dipped in the solution, or squirt it in with an eyedropper. If you are able to trace their route to their repast, either drill holes, or make some with a large nail and soak the chlordane solution in. You are unlikely to get rid of carpenter ants with one attack. Keep the chlordane handy in a safely sealed container and be ready to use it in all seasons.

Blackflies

It is little comfort to know that there are 110 different species of blackfly in Canada, that they are not necessarily black, or that it is the female of the species that causes all the trouble. Since they favor wooded regions, they are a curse to many cottagers. Lumber companies often carry out blackfly spraying programs so that loggers can work in some comfort and productivity, but in most cottaging country that kind of professional attack is unlikely. Therefore, the only practical defences are the retreat to the cottage whose window screens are in perfect repair, the lavish use of insect repellent, and the wearing of garments which cover practically every square centimetre of skin (blackflies particularly enjoy biting behind the ears around the hairline). They live for only three weeks, and if you are lucky the worst onslaught may be over by the end of June — or it may not end until Christmas. Blackflies are hard to predict.

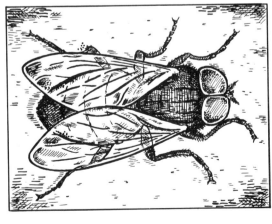

If you have plenty of land on which to build, the presence of blackflies may affect site selection. First, find out from the locals just how bad they are and how long they last. A windswept open space is less prone to blackfly attacks than a picturesque hideaway sheltered in the woods. (The same is true of mosquitos.) If you are lucky enough to have only a short season, beware of stirring up the turf, especially in the woods, later in the summer. That can awaken a whole new generation, though in such a small space of infestation, spraying with an insecticide can be effective. But if you are in blackfly country, spraying your own small plot to deflect the mass attacks is a wasted effort.

Good luck.

Earwigs

Earwigs can be a nuisance as they emerge each night to chomp the leaves of such plants as clematis, dahlia and gladiolus at any time from late spring to early autumn. They frequent old drainpipes or crawl under pots or pieces of wood wherever it is dark and damp. Sometimes there will be a mysterious and sudden plague of earwigs in a fairly defined area as they hit the top of a cycle. At the onset of a real scourge, the press and your neighborhood are full of absolutely foolproof ideas to deal with them, like putting out saucers of beer so they will die of drowning or alcoholism. The standard approved

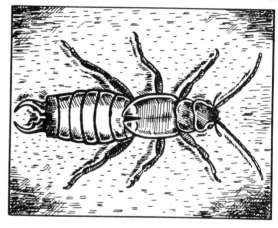

weapons are liquid spray or dust of carbaryl, Diazinon or malathion. Or, in the morning you may discover earwigs under debris and despatch them by mechanical means. The best preventative measure is to rake up old leaves, grass and debris. The myth that earwigs crawl into the ears of sleeping people — a story that apparently gave them their name — is mercifully untrue.

Houseflies

Just because houseflies do not bite people as often as mosquitoes or blackflies, do not underestimate their importance. They are notorious carriers of disease and may be responsible for sickness that could be avoided.

Outside, do not encourage the brutes. See that all edible garbage is kept in secure containers or covered with earth. (See **Garbage.**) Rake around your barbecue to cover up grease, crumbs or scraps. An old-time outhouse is a source of fly-carried disease unless it is made completely flyproof — meaning not just screens, but no spaces between the boards, a tight-fitting door and tight-fitting seat covers. (See **Outhouses**.) You certainly cannot remove all animal defecation in the woods, but get rid of any that family pets have left around the grounds; at best, your cottage will then be no more attractive to flies than elsewhere in the wilderness.

Life will be happier and healthier if there are screens on all the windows and doors. As a temporary measure until time and pocketbook allow otherwise, you can make do with fibreglass screen stapled to the window frames. Discipline the family about not holding doors open unnecessarily.

Inside, don't leave food exposed for flies, and be strict about cleaning up crumbs. Crumbs are not a source of disease, but they will attract flies that have been in dubious places. Don't leave the food dish of the cat or dog out for longer than neces-sary, either inside or outside.

The most effective, and ghastliest looking, weapon against flies is the old-fashioned sticky strip. If you can stand looking at the fly corpses, use these strips generously. You can even make your own if you would care to mix equal parts of melted resin and castor oil, then spread it over stiff strips of paper with a hot knife. Or mix an egg yolk with one tablespoon of molasses and a tablespoon of black pepper; put this delicacy in a saucer and it will knock them dead. Train the young people to be skilled with fly swatters; you could offer rewards for deceased speci-mens. If you can train your dog or cat to catch flies, good luck.

If you have a crib-aged child, don't trust to all these measures, but drape mosquito-netting as added protection; the very young may suffer from fly-carried disease more than older chil-dren or adults do.

Mosquitoes

You may as well start with the assumption that no high tech-nology is worth the money or trouble: not vapors, lamps or any other devices to attract and destroy insects, not even transmitters that emit inaudible hums. Outside, you will have to repel them or live with them. Inside you try to keep them away.

Commercial insect repellents are generally effective, and you can make your own if you happen to have some feverview, an ounce of which you add to $2^1/_2$ cups of boiling water. Wait till it's cool before rubbing it on, or you will have to look up the remedy for scalds. Besides using the repellent, you would do well to wear light-colored clothing. If you are really susceptible, buy or make one of those funny hats with mosquito netting hanging down from it, and wear gloves.

Many people can build up a tolerance for mosquitoes, and ignore repellents. The first few in spring may bother them, but later they hardly notice casual bites. No one, though, is immune to massed attacks from hordes of mosquitoes living hungrily by a marsh.

The environment of the cottage will affect the mosquito nuisance level. Since even a slight wind may keep them away, a cottage on a hill without many trees around is in an enviable situation. They may be deterred by running a strong fan. They certainly do not like smoke, which is why few pipe smokers die of malaria or encephalitis. Everyone at some time tries a smudge (a very smoky fire) which is guaranteed to get into the eyes of the maker, while the mosquitoes dance around laughing.

Can we control the source? Not likely, despite the relatively short range of the average mosquito. If there is one identifiable place with stagnant water which is the obvious main breeding ground, you can either drain it, or spray it. What you spray it with is terrifyingly controversial. A mixture of coal oil and insecticide is sometimes used, but that could be bad for the ecology. Just coal oil, or any light oil, spread sparingly on stagnant water or moist soil will choke a few million of the little monsters, if that makes any noticeable difference, but legitimate animals do not like oil either. If female mosquitoes don't get a meal of blood, they can't lay eggs, so the less they bite you and other animals the better. Probably more effective and less risky than spray are the mosquito's natural predators: frogs, toads, snakes, dragonflies and birds — especially purple martins. Just about all animals eat mosquitoes, but not enough of them.

Inside, your flyscreens are invaluable. An insecticide on a wax bar hung about the house is undoubtedly effective. There have been suggestions that insecticide vapors in a tightly enclosed space are dangerous, especially for infants, but no official warnings have been issued.

Sometimes it is a matter of weighing risks. The bar may pose a slight risk in certain conditions, but the mosquito can be a serious hazard in some areas at some times as a carrier of serious diseases. It may also cause bad reactions in people with certain allergies. The mosquito is responsible for the dread heartworm in dogs. (Heartworm is preventable: a visit to the vet is a must for your dog before going to mosquito country.)

Moths

There are about 7000 species of moth in North America. They all go through the stages of egg, larva (caterpillar), pupa (cocoon) and adult. A generation or two ago, the moths that struck the most terror in human hearts were the tiny ones that consumed clothing and wool, generally while the owners were at the cottage. Synthetic fibers have practically eliminated that problem, and the smell of mothballs in closets is almost forgotten.

Some moths damage gardens. Leopard moths affect many small trees, including apple, pear, cherry, birch. You can kill the caterpillars by spraying endosulfan or lindane on the trunks and branches. An alternative, as with any nesting caterpillars, is to burn out the nests when they form in spring. Be careful of fire, for burning embers could light unsuspected dry grass and leaves to start a major conflagration; it is best done between showers, with either a stick wrapped with oil-soaked rag (old method) or with a blow torch (faster, better control). Codling moths, mainly interested in apple, pear and wild fruit trees, must be destroyed before the caterpillars enter the fruit. Recommended chemicals are carbaryl, malathion or methoxychlor. Cornborers, cankerworms and tent caterpillars are also moths. Just about all 7,000 species are some nuisance because they eat foliage you want to enjoy. Unless you are faced by a real scourge or an attack on a particularly precious tree, we suggest that you just leave things to the balance of nature.

Spiders

We know that, technically, spiders are not insects, but you may wonder what to do about them. The answer is "Not much". There are about 50,000 species of spider, and the only place to escape them is Antarctica; even Ellesmere Island in the High Arctic has eight different kinds.

All spiders are poisonous to some degree. The black widow's venom is 200 times as poisonous as that of a rattlesnake; its distinctive hourglass pattern of red on its black back may be spotted from southern Ontario to British Columbia and throughout the U.S.A. Since spiders can ingest only liquids, they suck blood, exude enzymes into their prey to change tissues into soup, then drink that. The good news is that they help control other insect pests.

Most spiders in cottage country tend to be shy with people. The best idea is to keep out of their way when you see them. You may occasionally get a bite, which may be a little sore or itchy for a day or two, but it is rarely serious. Only in the cottage itself would we suggest you consider any open warfare with the use of chlordane or other insecticide. In most places outside, or even around docks and boathouses, you are unlikely to affect their numbers significantly, and if you do you will only be adding to your troubles from other insects. The old legends about the bad consequences of killing a spider probably were based on the wisdom that, despite their unlovable appearance, they are important to human welfare. If you have not already done so, please introduce yourself and your children to E.B. White's *Charlotte's Web*. Your attitude to spiders will never be the same again.

Termites

Termites are somewhat similar to ants, but not quite. If you have a long meeting with a termite, you will notice that its sides are straight, while the ant has a wasp waist, and that the termite's four wings are about the same size, while the ant's hind wings are shorter.

Termites eat cellulose. They will eat it year-round if they can, but they can last 10 months without it. They like damp places. They can approach your cottage by subterranean passages where you will never see them, then eat your wood undetected, and even go outside for a drink if your place is dry — all unbeknownst to you — until you see the damage they have caused.

Apart from consumed wood, the evidence of their presence may be found in large numbers of discarded wings in spring or early summer, indicating a new colony nearby. Tunnels, from a $1/4$ to a $1/2$ inch in diameter, may indicate the presence of termites, especially in damp places, near the foundations and where underground pipes go through the walls. Apparent rot, or hidden colonies in scrap wood left long on the ground, in posts or trellises, are also signs of termites.

In the unlikely event that you have termites inside the living space of your cottage, the prudent move is to call in an exterminator. If that is out of the question because of remoteness, ask a city exterminator (that's not someone who bombs cities) to give you advice and guidance in using chemicals, probably fluoridated silica aerogel, which is non-poisonous. If termites are in the exterior timber around your foundations, the treatment is chlordane, a poisonous chemical to be used in a water solution strictly according to directions. Spraying all wood within reach may help, but you should also poison the soil around the foundations or any wood touching the soil. To do this, dig shallow trenches and pour the solution with a watering can or pail. One such treatment will probably be effective, but keep a close and constant watch to see if you need to repeat the treatment. At the same time, clean up any wood scraps or refuse on the ground near the house, and if you ever find buried scraps dating from construction, remove them. Environmental hygiene, if you will pardon the expression, is always a sound measure in defenses against unwanted fauna and flora, especially of the termite kind.

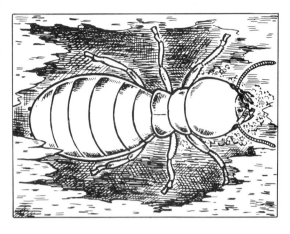

Wasps

Most of the time we can live in peaceful co-existence with wasps, but not always. A wasp circling over your food can spoil an outdoor meal. For some people, a single wasp bite can cause a serious allergic reaction. Especially for a small child, a swarm of predatory wasps on the attack is a major medical emergency.

For these reasons, most people want to eliminate nearby sources of wasps. There are two easy ways if you have no deep-felt principles against chemicals. One, taken from the traditional practice of farmers, is to spray chlordane outside on wood near where people sit, on the cottage walls beside the deck, or around outhouses. One spraying in early spring will generally discourage them, but you may need a refresher later in the summer.

The other method is to destroy their homes, especially if they have nested near your door, in your shed or around your woodpile. Using a commercial product in a pressurized tin is certainly the simplest. At night when all good wasps are asleep, blast a stream through the hole at the bottom of the nest, and have a pail with a little water right below, so that struggling wasps fall into it and shuffle off this mortal coil. In the absence of spray, there are several old techniques, all a little riskier even when done at night — the only time. With a pail containing a few inches of water in one hand, you use the other to scrape the whole nest off the board into the water, where they will drown. Or you can take a blow torch or tightly scrunched lighted newspaper, or oil-soaked rag on a pole to burn the nest, but these methods carry an obvious fire hazard. Also, the odd wasp with insomnia has been known to get away. To allay the consequences of that misfortune, have a buddy with a flashlight as backup, or cover yourself with mosquito netting.

The most terrifying wasps or hornets can be the ones that live under a rock in the ground. Inadvertently moving the stone may cause a whole swarm to attack the human. While treading well-used paths, therefore, watch for signs of ground wasps going to and from home. Then either mark the danger site or eliminate it at night. If it is in a place absolutely safe from the spread of fire, a splash of coal oil very promptly lit may well be the most effective, for liquid and heat reach right into the ground. The alternative is the chemical in the aerosol tin.

If wasps swarm on a person, especially a child, race into action. If it is a small child, it is probably advisable to pick him or her up and run fast for a couple of hundred yards beyond the normal range of the colony. If you have a towel or blanket handy, use it to wipe the wasps off as quickly as possible. If the ground is suitable, you may wish to roll the victim on the earth or sand, using your hands to wipe them off; you will also be stung. As soon as you are both clear of wasps, wrap the child in a towel or blanket and treat for shock. If there are many stings, race to the hospital and ask questions afterwards. If the hospital is too far, check your first aid book for shock, and try to phone for medical advice. In most cases the awful crisis will be over quickly and happily. Then consider a little psychotherapy so that the child does not develop a terribly inhibiting fear of insects.

K

KITES

If more than 80,000,000 kites are sold in North America each year, it would seem that a lot of people are flying them — or losing them. It is a sport that has been popular for well over 2,000 years since it was invented by the Chinese.

You can buy a kite for as little as a dollar (maybe less at a garage sale) or for as much as $1,000 if you want a hand-painted model with a long tail. If you are just starting, you may lean to the lower part of the cost spectrum. There are, of course, various shapes and sizes, but whatever you choose, there are some inevitable safety provisions:

- never fly it near power lines; or near a road where it could distract a driver;
- never fly it in a storm;
- do not use a metal frame or tail, or mylar in the construction;
- if you think this thing is really going to work, take along some gloves to make it easier to handle that sharp nylon line paying out at a furious rate.

The best time to fly your kite is after a storm when unstable clearing winds move in. Stand so that the wind is at your back, blowing equally on both ears. If there is a strong wind, just hold the kite aloft until it fills with wind, pay out a bit of string, and you are in business. If there is only light wind, walk the kite downwind a hundred paces, and have someone hold it up. When you feel the beginning of a breeze yell at your assistant to let go, pull in the string hand-over-hand and run backwards without falling. Drop the string on the ground to avoid tangling. When the kite goes high enough to leave those unpredictable ground gusts, you will feel a steadier pull signalling that it is ready for more string. If it drops, yank it to get it climbing. Don't let it climb at too sharp an angle overhead, or it may dive. If you have trouble getting it down again in a high wind, have a friend "walk down" the kite by strolling forward with the string under an arm, while you reel it in.

When you become adept at this art, you may want to experiment with different kinds of kites, or adjust the bridle attachment (the rig which connects to the line) by moving the attachment of the line up or down on it. Generally, in a light wind, you will have the attachment farther down, and in a strong wind, nearer the top of the bridle. You'll know if it is too low by the way it starts into wild lateral loops. If it is too high, it will tend just to flop lazily instead of taking full wind.

When you become attached to a kite — well, you know what we mean — you'll invent a reel to make it easier to wind in the string tangle-free. Any cylindrical tin will do, unless you want to pay a lot for a very large fishing reel. And you may want to try launching the kite with a rod and reel when the fishing isn't very good.

L

LADDERS

In our recurring theme of how to avoid disasters, ladders and scaffolds have their undoubted place, but they need not be hazardous. Safety starts with the trip to the hardware store.

The Canadian Standards Association certifies ladders with their CSA label in three grades. Type I is for construction. Type II is for farms and trades. Type III is for household use. We hope that you are going to buy a Type II aluminum extension ladder. Though more expensive than the other types, it is safer and longer-lasting than the bottom of the line. Unless you are very serious, you may find Type I too heavy as well as too expensive. Forget about wooden extension ladders. They are more rigid, but as they age they rot and have a tendency to break when you least want them to.

You cannot, of course, extend an extension ladder fully; for stability you need an overlap of about three rungs between the two parts. To decide which length to buy, calculate the highest point you want to reach, add twenty-five percent, then add another 3 feet.

The biggest safety step is in the set-up of a ladder. The approved way of erecting the ladder is to lay it on the ground with its rubber feet almost at the wall or tree. It is best to extend the ladder to the needed height before you raise it, but if this is not possible, extend it with the installed rope and pulley after the ladder is raised. Lift it to the vertical by picking up the far end and walking towards the wall underneath the ladder. Pull the bottom out from the wall a distance equal to a quarter of the length you will be using. In the likely event that this piece of ground is frustratingly uneven, don't rely on little wood shims. Take a piece of plywood and level it as a platform. If this is at a greater height than you normally like to fall, two other safety precautions are recommended. One is to tie the two sides of the ladder near its base to trees or large rocks so securely that it will not slip away. The other, after you climb the ladder, is to tie the top similarly, possibly to the window frames. If the ladder is against a window or door, warn your family that a sudden opening of it will cause you to say things you may later regret.

Whatever your high-level job, plan for it before going up the ladder. If it is painting, take a fastener to hook the tin conveniently instead of holding it. If it is carpentry, have your tools and supplies in belts and attached bags so that both hands are free while climbing and you do not wear yourself out running down for fallen objects. Some workers even attach tools such as hammers to their belts with a long string.

If you are working on a sloping roof, you can operate from a ladder flat on the slope, provided it is firmly attached by rope to something stable on the far side of the building. Don't try funny tricks, like using your only ladder for that work: leave your extension ladder safely in place against the wall, and find another ladder for the roof work. Have a buddy help raise it and stay within shouting distance until you come down — one way or another. If your work on the roof tempts you to leave the safety of the ladder rungs occasionally, another safety precaution is important. Tie a rope to an immovable object on the far side of the roof, and attach it around your waist, adjusting its length as you go up the roof. It's a nuisance, but not as inconvenient as lying for weeks in traction.

Other rules you will be glad you remembered are:

- Don't climb past the third rung from the top, or past the point at which the ladder rests against the wall;
- Don't reach too high: keep your beltbuckle between the side rails (while still wearing it, of course);
- Don't let a metal ladder near electric lines.

If you try, you can also damage yourself on a step ladder. Make sure the two sides are spread fully out. Don't stand on the top step.

If you are serious about construction, scaffolds are safe. Though they take time to assemble or construct, on a big job that will require less time than does the constant shifting of ladders. There are three approaches. You can make your own from 2 x 4s forming an H at each end with two cross braces joining them. You can rent metal scaffolding. As a compromise between the two, you can buy a neat device consisting of a pair of metal brackets into each of which two 2 x 4s can be quickly clamped as legs, with a 2 x 10 or 2 x 12 across the top as the platform. Not only are these quick to assemble and easy to store, but they adjust to the roughest ground or to stairs. If the legs are more than 3 feet off the ground, you must add cross-bracing from end to end to ensure stability. Between construction jobs you can adapt the assembly to a handy outdoor table.

No matter how confident you are of your scaffold, anchor the top with ropes tied to immovable objects if it is higher than 3 or 4 feet. Check the condition of the wood in your platform regularly, and be particularly wary of loose boards.

Keep up the good work!

LEAVES

Some fine autumn day when you are virtuously sweeping your grounds of leaves, a neighbor is likely to be seen leaning smugly on a tree and might finally be heard to say: "Why are you raking those leaves? They're Nature's fertilizer." You may feel like hitting him or her with your rake, rather than explaining the rationale. We recommend the latter.

Certainly leaves are one of nature's fertilizers, when there is nothing better around. If you are content to grow old waiting for nature to do a job that is not always very efficient, put away the rake and unroll the hammock for a final time.

Before leaves are naturally recycled into fertilizer, they smother the soil and make it difficult for other plant life to survive. Of course, some wildflowers survive, but not nearly as many as if you give them a chance to get the sun and air. The most obvious evidence of that truth is grass. If the leaves on your grass remain unraked, the once healthy lawn will die in great brown splotches, and no one will be happy. On the other hand, if you remove all the leaves from your lawn or woods, you must eventually provide some substitute to replace the soil nutrients that plants absorb.

Therefore, if you crave a lawn, you must rake the leaves in late autumn, and again in early spring (noting with frustration that the oaks and beeches just won't drop their leaves on schedule). In the more open part of the woods which you frequent or see from the cottage, an annual raking is in order, but it need not — should not — be nearly as thorough. Get rid of the dead brush and matted leaves which will smother wildflowers, but you can leave enough to convert eventually to soil. If it is just an edge of the woods by your lawn, you may wish to rake more thoroughly, partly to discourage leaves from blowing back. Distribute some dried sheep or cow manure around each spring, or sprinkle a chemical fertilizer if it is not against your principles. You will do a far better job than nature alone.

Pine needles are highly acid. They must be thoroughly removed from your lawn, and in a predominantly deciduous bush (which thrives on less acid soil) they are best cleaned up. Apart from their chemical quality, they can be even more smothering than leaves.

Then what to do with all those leaves? Burning them is no longer practical because of fire hazards and local regulations. If you are ambitious, you may recycle them yourself (see **Compost**.) A compromise is to pile them in some low dip in the landscape, and let them rot by themselves very slowly. Or you can throw them down a sand embankment to help prevent erosion and encourage weed growth.

Dry leaves can also be used for insulation on your perennial flowerbeds. Don't just stack leaves on flowerbeds, for they may become sodden and matted, with little insulating value. Spread small brush on the soil, and put the leaves on top to leave generous air spaces. Be warned, though, that you may be constructing condominiums for mice. Some people throw old plastic sheeting over these leaf piles to keep out rain and snow, but this also traps moisture which may rot plants before you remove it. Old pieces of plywood or equivalent to shed the rain are safer.

Some leaves perversely land on the water and sink onto your beautiful sand bottom. Raking these away is important if you wish to preserve the quality of swimming and discourage unwanted plant life. If you can do it in late autumn without getting hypothermia, you will find it easier when the water level is lower and the leaves are in better shape. You may want to do another light raking just before swimming starts.

If you have eavestroughs, be sure to remove the leaves twice a year if there are overhanging trees, or annually if there are not. That is important not only for the efficiency but for the preservation of your eavestroughs.

If you have ditches along your road, rake them out annually to pull out leaves and plant growth. Be sure to check that any culverts are not building up crippling dams of matted leaves.

LIFEJACKETS

Even if you have no boat, buying life jackets is important; in the course of a summer, neighbors may well invite members of your family to go out with them. All must be equipped with life jackets.

There is one unbreakable rule: always use a life jacket which is clearly marked with approval by Transport Canada or, in the United States, by a state authority. Don't take the salesperson's word for its safety. Do not rely on a life jacket you have bought abroad unless you are certain that it meets Transport Canada's standards.

Two approved types are common. Those filled with kapok can be damaged by rough treatment. If the vinyl inserts containing the kapok are damaged, water can seep in and make them useless. If a jacket feels heavy, throw it out. Life jackets made with foam are generally more durable, but they also should be treated gently. Foam tends to shrink with age, heat or sunlight. You can extend its life by stowing it out of the sun and heat whenever possible. When a life jacket is wet, dry it in a well-ventilated place. Don't try to clean it with harsh detergents, cleaning fluids or gasoline.

When you bring the new life jackets to the cottage, gather all the family and try them out in the water at the first opportunity. Children need special practice in getting used to them, for although a life jacket will keep a child afloat, it will not guarantee that the wearer can breathe. Children need to be trained to float or paddle with their faces clear of the water so that in an emergency they are less likely to panic. They should never be allowed to step into a boat before they have properly tied on a life jacket — jackets available under the seat are not good enough.

When putting on a keyhole-type life jacket, ensure that the straps are tied around the waist, not around the jacket. This lets the jacket pivot away from the

body to let the wearer assume an inclined floating backward position, with the mouth clear of the water. If you must swim while wearing the life jacket, use a backstroke or sidestroke.

A variant on life jackets is the Personal Flotation Device (PFD), which is intended to be worn constantly. PFDs are more comfortable than life jackets for long use, but they are less buoyant than approved life jackets, and the wearer may find it harder to maneuvre while wearing a PFD. One type has its own flotation material, and the other is inflated by compressed CO_2. Buy only PFDs with labels showing Transport Canada approval.

Lighting

Indoor

A special feature of cottages, not generally found in your city home, is the presence of moths circling your lamps. They are probably not nuisance enough to make you take action against them, unless the light is close enough to you that an occasional moth bangs into your face. In planning indoor lighting, therefore, bear in mind this occasional hazard, and place lights a convenient distance from the user. For example, don't have a bedlight within inches of your page, but use somewhat stronger illumination focussed from 2 or 3 feet away. In general, moths and other bugs are more likely to be attracted by a bare, exposed bulb than by a bullet-type opaque shade.

Outdoor

How effective are anti-bug lights? We refer not to bug-killing devices, but to those yellow bulbs which are said to repel flying things. We believe them effective enough to be worthwhile. If you have an ordinary white bulb and an anti-bug yellow one in use simultaneously outside, you can observe a difference in the insect world around your cottage. Besides, anti-bug lights do not harm the ecology. These bulbs are most effective when used in fixtures attached to the cottage near windows (so that bugs will not spend their time working through the screen), and in areas where you sit long after dark (for example, near the barbecue waiting for the chicken legs to cook). Anti-bug lights give a pleasant enough glow, but they are not good for reading.

If you have spacious grounds which tempt you to decorative (as opposed to area) lighting, consider a low voltage system. Around water, low voltage lights are a must. The savings in consumption may not cover the original cost, but low-voltage systems are safer than 110-volt lights. If you are on a limited budget, consider a less costly approach to lighting paths. This arrangement may not be something that inspectors will rejoice over, but it is just as safe as lighting on a construction site, or as any portable appliance used outdoors.

All you need is some extension cord, long and heavy enough for your needs, a plug, one pigtail socket (heavy plastic for outdoor use) for every lamp, one clay flower pot about 6 inches in diameter for every lamp, lots of scrap wire for hanging the fixtures, wire connectors, a roll of electrician's tape and a supply of one-inch staples. Across the path, at least 8 feet above the ground, string scrap wire (securely stapled to trees on both sides) at each point that you will want to put a light. Put a socket inside a flower pot, which will be your lampshade, and feed the pigtail wires through the drainage hole in the bottom of the pot. Secure the pot well with scrap wire and tape to the cross wires you have just installed. Feed in your extension cord, breaking it at each fixture to connect it to the pigtail; secure it with a wire connector, then generously wrap electrician's tape around it to keep the connection waterproof. Screw in 25-watt clear bulbs (they look far better than frosted), plug the extension cord into an outlet protected by a ground fault interrupter, and be enlightened by the result.

For security, or finding Uncle Mort's dentures after the party, you may want area lighting with 150-watt floodlight bulbs. (Be careful not to pick up spotlights, which look the same, by mistake.) Why not put them on dimmer switches that will enable you to create a more romantic glow? If you are interested in aesthetics, try putting lights on the ground (the source hidden from casual view) facing straight into the foliage. Your creative instincts may be further nourished by trying different-colored bulbs. In winter, blue light on the snow is dramatic. In autumn, you may want to enhance the natural colors using amber or even red lighting. Blue or green against leaves also works well. Of course, any colored bulb gives far less illumination than white.

Finally, a gesture in the direction of good neighborliness. Your outside floodlights may be a convenience and a security comfort, but they can be an unsuspected nuisance to neighbors who do not enjoy the glare. Such light may be irritating even across the water. You don't need to deprive yourself of floodlighting: use makeshift shades to ensure that it is lighting only you, and not the unspoiled wilderness. Just happen to mention your good works to your neighbors; you will get brownie points, and the idea may spread.

Lightning

As every schoolchild knows, lightning is an electrical discharge causing fast expansion and contraction of air, which in turn creates thunder. But did you remember the rough formula that, for every second's lapse between lightning and thunder the action is about one mile away? During a lively storm, you can usually hear it at least ten miles away, and do a rough calculation of its speed and direction before you panic. The legendary ability of animals to foretell storms, which they generally deplore, may be attributable to their ability to hear an oncoming disturbance 50 miles away. Don't underestimate the prescience of the family dog: it may be more accurate than your human forecaster. And don't believe the myth that lightning never strikes twice in the same place.

It's no wonder that people and animals are nervous about lightning. It can generate a billion volts of electricity, which is shocking. Sheet lightning, a reflection of a distant flash, is a harmless and free pyrotechnic display. Forked lightning can be dangerous. It starts with a faintly luminous leader stroke darting from side to side looking for the best path to earth, and is quickly followed by an intensely bright return stroke which carries most of the current. What you see as a slightly flickering single stroke is really a fast series of strokes.

That lightning is looking for the easiest place to touch ground, and you should make the effort to ensure it is not you or your buildings that it finds. Anything that rises alone and prominently above ground is a likely target. That could be a tall building, a tree or a human being, especially when that human is sticking above the surface of a broad body of water.

If you are lucky enough to have a high tower or high voltage transmission line very near, you can watch the worst of storms complacently. Those installations are grounded to attract the lightning, and keep it away from the transmission wires themselves. (That is what those two top wires, without insulators, are for.) If you have high trees near your cottage, the chances of the building being hit are low, but you cannot completely predict the erratic behavior of this powerful force. If the trees are more than several feet away, or not very much higher than your building, you could still be at some risk. If you have chosen to build your cottage alone on a hilltop, you must take defensive action before you occupy the premises.

This means installing lightning conductors — carefully. They will attract the lightning and guide it harmlessly into the ground, but if they are not installed and maintained well, they may merely guide it into your structure, causing instant fire, and perhaps worse. The metal rod should be firmly attached to each end of the building, with its point well above the chimney. A very

heavy copper wire, specified by your electrician, will lead from it to another metal rod buried deep in the ground some yards from the building. If you are on rock where it cannot be deeply buried, a long rod should be placed on the ground and covered with lots of compacted earth which you may have to bring in; the damper the place the better.

With this installation in place and checked annually, the cottage is probably the safest place to be if an electric storm passes over you. Stay away from the walls where the wire runs down from the roof — just in case. Closing the windows around that area may give you slight added protection. During a bad storm, don't touch metal plumbing fixtures which may be naturally grounded, or electrical appliances, all of which are — or should be — grounded. Turn those appliances off, except for any that may be equipped with an external surge protector. Don't use the phone unnecessarily. It may ring a little by itself with ground surges; just leave it alone.

But what if you are not at home? The first rule is to move away from any likely target, such as a tall tree; and stay away from wide open spaces where you may become the favored target. That is usually not very difficult, if you remain in scrub woods away from big trees, or even in a ditch or low depression. If you are in a car on the highway, conventional wisdom holds that you are safer than in the open, for the path of the surge will be through the car's metal frame to the ground. Even though lightning-struck cars are rare, we confess to some lack of enthusiasm about having 10,000 amps hitting that close to inflammable fuel. If a bad storm is really near, it might be safer to stop at the nearest available shelter even at the cost of getting wet.

If you hear an approaching electric storm while you are out on the water, you have an emergency. It is not the time to remember that no member of the family should be allowed on open water when there is any hint or likelihood of an electric storm. Your only possible action is to get to shore, any shore, fast. If that is clearly impossible, and the storm comes right overhead, the unenviable alternatives are to lie flat in the boat or, wearing life jackets and holding life preservers if available, to slip overboard and remain a few yards away from the boat with the lowest possible profile until danger has passed. A rope tied between the boat and you will ensure that you can regain your craft despite the probable high winds.

All this sounds pretty scary, but using good sense makes electrocution by lightning one of the unlikeliest of all life's worries.

*L*OCAL PEOPLE

When we talk and think about the cottage world, let's remember that it is not just a place of boats and pumps and insects. It is also a place of people: neighboring cottagers and permanent residents. Your enjoyment of the summer largely depends on how much you and they enjoy each other's company.

Getting along with neighboring cottagers may be the easier part, for chances are that, as common refugees from city life, you share background and objectives with them. For good relations you need only good will and the kind of toleration that makes good neighborhoods anywhere.

There can be an added negative dimension in relations with permanent residents. They may live with a legacy of distrust of city people, because of some real or imagined problem in the past, or just because of a cultural difference. They may think of city people as rich (because they have two homes, which country people do not), as stingy (because they don't want to expend as much of their wealth locally as may be expected of them), demanding (because they want to change local rules to suit their convenience), arrogant (because they seem only to talk to one another and don't bother with the community), and so on. City people have their own suspicions about the way they are being exploited and cold-shouldered.

There is no easy answer, except effort on both sides. It really is worth being patient and forgiving in the hope of breaking down prejudices and making new and different kinds of friends. Elsewhere (see **Newspapers**) we have suggested taking the time to know what is happening locally by reading the press. Making yourself known to shopkeepers, and then patronizing them as often as possible will certainly improve relations with the merchants and produce friends who can be of practical help when you urgently need advice, labor, or some special order.

Attending local functions is almost a must. If you go to the local strawberry festival, pioneer days, church picnic, summer fete, or whatever the event may be, make a point of meeting and talking to some of the volunteers running it so that they can appreciate your expression of appreciation. Maybe you can invite some of them to drop by your cottage for a drink or a sail one day: give them a map to your place to show you mean it.

Perhaps there is a local farm family to whom your property once belonged. They would probably respond warmly if you took the trouble to call, introduce yourselves, and make a point of visiting at least once a summer, whether or not they take advantage of your invitation to your cottage. Why not send them a Christmas card, possibly enclosing a local photo of interest which you have taken, or at least a few personal lines of warm greeting? And while you are at your Christmas list, perhaps there are a few others well worth the trouble of a card: a worker who has served well (and whom you may want again!), a shopkeeper who has been especially helpful, maybe the local police detachment, or someone you met at a local function.

These are not always easy cultural gaps to cross. Over-zealousness could be as damaging as appearing to be patronizing. Local people, partly because they are different, could be among your most interesting friends. Reaching out could make everyone's summer much happier.

LOCKS

There is no way to make your average cottage completely burglar-proof. If you install amazingly secure locks, thieves may come in through the windows or perhaps smash in the door. It seems pointless, therefore, to spend a lot of time and money on highly secure hardware. The object is to protect yourself against casual entry or vandals. Convenience is about as important as security.

If you have a conventional lock on the front door, it may be the spring type, meaning that you learn how to slam the door gently and it locks by itself. It could be a deadbolt, a lock that is mechanically held in place instead of being operated with a spring. The first one is easy for people of evil intentions to open with a credit card or equivalent, but would you rather the thief showed his skill on the lock or his brawn on the window? The deadbolt type is much better, though more of a nuisance. When you are inside, one deadbolt type can be locked with a key, and another can be locked by turning a knob. Before you conclude that the key is much safer (because the thief can come in through the window and easily unlock the front door when there is a knob), bear in mind that in a panic situation, such as a fire, there could be disaster if people rush the door and can't find the key.

Whatever the type of lock, you probably need only one door so equipped. Other doors can have a stout carriage bolt — but not so stout that a burglar will take away half your wall when using a crowbar on the lock.

Quantities of keys are a vexation. No matter how you resolve to color-code and mark them, you are bound to waste a lot of time finding the right key when you need it fast. Here is a tip to reduce the number. If you have more than one door fitted with conventional locks, remove the barrel of all but the first one and get your friendly locksmith to provide you with a new barrel so that one key fits all. For your many padlocks around the place, why not ask the locksmith to get you a quantity which all have the same key? As padlocks themselves cannot be changed, you will need all new padlocks, so make that decision early in your cottage life. Then all you ever need carry around is one key for the door, and one for all the padlocks. A further bounty is that since each padlock comes with two keys, you will have lots of spares to give members of the family.

You should also hide copies of the two vital keys in some place more imaginative than under the doormat, just in case... You can also lend one to a neighbor or a tradesperson without advertising that it will unlock all your treasures.

To avoid carrying even the one key, you can, of course, use combination locks. Unless you have the same combination on all of them, it will be a nuisance to remember which is which. And if you once give the combination to a tradesperson, your security is blown for all time. Besides, cheaper combination locks are less secure than comparable keyed padlocks.

With all this efficiency, you are still likely to accumulate odd keys which have come with various bits of portable equipment. If you are to avoid terrible frustration some day, we urge you to stow a well-labelled spare of each of these in a concealed place. (See also **Security.**)

LOG BUILDINGS

An old log building can make a superb summer cottage. It will require a lot of work, but the costs are relatively low and you can achieve a unique and distinguished home which, with care, will last the centuries through all seasons. Offering a detailed manual would occupy much of this book, but a fast trip through the restoration of a heritage log building may help you to judge if it would suit you.

The first time-consuming task is finding an abandoned log house or barn, not so beautiful that the owner will want a million dollars for it, not so decrepit that it is a dubious target for restoration. True conservationists do not believe in moving old log structures unless they cannot be saved where they stand, and they are also against butchering buildings just to get old pieces of wood to use in a new home. Don't be discouraged if an abandoned cabin looks down at heel, with windows and doors rotted, and the sill logs (on the ground) turned to mush. On almost any old log building you will have to discard those sill logs and build up a concrete foundation to replace them. You should also assume you will be replacing windows and doors anyway. As long as the main logs are reasonably sound, take a chance.

The next job is photographing the building from every conceivable angle, with close-ups of any peculiar joints where old windows or doors may have been changed or replaced. As you dismantle the structure, continue the photography, and make detailed notes of irregularities. Then mark every log with a spray can, using a different color for each wall, numbering from sill log — or the first salvageable log above it — up to the plate log, with the marking repeated on every log which is severed for a window or door. Mark the rafters with two other colors, one for each side, and write down whether you have numbered them from south to north, or whatever.

After deciding what is to be saved and what discarded, dismantle the interior and roof. If you want to save space and money on transportation, pay a gang of children to extract all nails from salvageable lumber before you leave the site. You have to take apart everything including the rafters, but not the wall logs with their chinking.

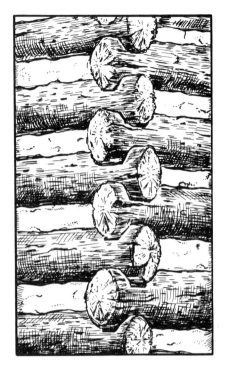

Then you contract for transportation. The best bet is a huge log-carrying truck of the kind that serves lumber camps; it will have a heavy crane to reach over and load the logs. If this is out of the question, try a truck which delivers cement blocks: it has a smaller crane. Failing these, you can use a forklift, which is likely to be more expensive and will have to be moved for unloading at the new site. Then you will need one or more other flatbed trucks onto which the logs will be loaded by the crane after they are plucked off the standing walls. The old chinking just falls away.

Meanwhile, back at the new site... you have cleared and levelled the area, stripping off the earth if it is on bedrock. And you have made foundations to the standard for any new house. Do yourself a favor by making the foundation high enough for a crawl space, providing a doorway for access; this will be useful for wiring and plumbing that you will wish to conceal, for better ventilation and for occasional inspection. Be sure you also have large ventilation ports in the foundations — at least the area of two cement blocks in two opposite walls.

You have a choice in the floor design: inside the log walls or to their outer edge. If the loss of the rotted sill logs makes the headroom on the ground floor skimpy, you can increase it by running the foundation higher than the floor, concealing it inside with baseboards and outside with backfill. This approach takes more time, but in addition to giving you flexibility in height, it leaves the floor independent of the walls, for long-term maintenance.

The next stage is the most soul-satisfying and — if all goes well — the fastest. Find the four bottom logs and start erecting like a child with building blocks — keeping the walls the same height as you go up. You may have to use scrap lumber, saplings, nails or wire to temporarily brace logs which have been severed for doors and windows.

When the walls are near shoulder height and are becoming difficult to lift into place, use a trick invented by the pioneers. Find your two long top logs and lay them on a wall as a ramp. Then you can roll each succeeding log easily into place. Those last two logs can be hoisted by people standing on the top with ropes. Then, your walls are finished.

Now is a good time to secure those openings for doors and windows by making solid frames (of rough, old unplaned 2-inch lumber if you can find it, about the same width as the logs) and nailing 6-inch spikes through them into the ends of the logs. Not only must those frames be absolutely level with perfect right angles, but they should be the right size for the windows and doors you have already decided on. You might find windows at a wrecker's where they are cheap — the old wood will fit the mood of the place. You can make a door easily yourself: vertical boards with batten strips on the outside, any thin plywood in the center to block drafts through old wood and to prevent sagging, and diagonal boards on the inner side.

Now that your walls are really secure, you can make a safe platform to work on the roof. You will usually find that there was no ridge board to which the rafters were nailed: leave it that way. If you have a large and good platform, you can nail each pair of rafters at the top, nail in a cross-tie from 2 x 3 or 1 x 6 (there probably was not one there already), and use two or three people to raise each pair of rafters gently to the vertical position. Temporarily secure them with ropes or scrap lumber, and nail in the bottoms. When all are in place, make them true and vertical before nailing a few temporary boards on the underside to keep them that way.

If you have salvaged the old roof boards and would like them to show from the interior, this is the time to install them.

Any insulation will have to go above them — you can accomplish the installation with a little ingenuity and the products made for the purpose. For authenticity and atmosphere, you may choose cedar shingles, which take several times as long to install as asphalt and cost considerably more. If you don't bash them with ice choppers, and if tree branches are kept away from them, they should last at least 15 years with minor maintenance.

It is best to leave the chinking until after this roof construction, in case the building vibrates. The pioneers laced their mortar with horsehair, which is not in good supply these days. Nifty formulae have been invented, but the simplest is ordinary mortar used with saplings, wire lath and bits of foam insulation to fill gaps. Trouble-free — but not cheap — is ready-mix mortar, to which you need add only water. Chink the entire exterior or interior first, and let it harden before tackling the other side of the logs. It is a pleasant job for willing helpers without discrimination as to age and sex. If you do the job well, it will last for years until your annual inspection shows the need for minor patching.

Now, let's go back inside. You have installed woodframe windows and doors. You can easily make your own screens out of rectangles of 1 x 2 with fiberglass — far cruder than you would like in a modern cottage — but fitting the mood. If you want to preserve the atmosphere with a plank floor on top of the plywood, try to get old pine from a wrecker. It can be dressed or undressed, and its strength does not matter because there is plywood underneath. Remove every trace of a nail, install the boards with countersunk nails, and rent a floor sander to smooth it out. That is a hard day's work. After you have thoroughly vacuumed and damp-mopped the boards, apply two coats of good quality matte-finish urethane-type finish within 48 hours of one another, wait at least another 48 hours and apply at least three or four coats of hard paste wax. It will look terrific and needs only occasional rewaxing in heavily trod spots to keep it that way.

We are tempted to go on with all the wonderful things you can now do with this living work of art, but we don't want to intrude on your imagination.

Or, you could build a cottage with new logs: undoubtedly attractive, more expensive, and not quite in the same class as an authentic survival of our frontier heritage.

LOG SPLITTING

There are many reasons to split logs, some of which have little to do with burning firewood. You may have a sudden urge for exercise or weight loss. You may wish to release your frustration and irritations against the government/your boss/your mate. (For government, we recommend splitting knotty rock elm.) These are legitimate reasons, but bear in mind also that when wood is split, it will dry more quickly, burn more satisfyingly, and cause less creosote build-up in the chimney.

When gathering wood, try to make on-the-spot decisions about what to split, then leave it in a separate pile for later action, while you stack the rest. (See **Firewood**.) If you are going to take the non-exercising mechanical route, you may even leave that splitting pile for a year or two until you bring in the equipment.

If you are going to split with the sweat of your brow, you will need an axe. They vary greatly in weight and quality. You can buy anything from a small hatchet to a normal axe with a head weighing from about 2 to 8 pounds. The choice for splitting depends largely on your physique: the heavier the axe, the more effective. You should be pretty confident of your muscles if you buy an axe heavier than 3½ pounds. For a few dollars more you can get an excellent splitting axe, which has on it cunning levers to split open the log as the blade is embedded. This axe is designed not only for faster work, but it just about eliminates that frustrating jamming when you strike a mighty blow, only to have the tool firmly embed itself in the log. These axes are not for small people. When you buy the axe, get a spare wooden handle and wedges to install it. That will not only avoid frustration if the original handle breaks, but save you carrying the axe head to the store to get a match.

If you are going to be serious about log splitting, you might also equip yourself with steel splitting wedges of two kinds: one pointed wedge, or two chisel-like wedges. To drive them you need a sledgehammer. You must also have steel-toed boots and safety glasses, and wearing a hard hat is never a bad idea. No matter how hot the day, wear your heavy jeans (no shorts, please) because lethal splinters may fly around.

If your logs are at all wet or green, the best time to split is on a crisp morning when the overnight temperature has been well below freezing. If you don't have much chance then, separate out the logs roughly according to their state, splitting the drier ones first, and leaving the rest to age a bit more.

Put the log vertically on a large and steady base log. If you are into hard wood that resists all your impressive muscle, turn to the wedges. The pointed wedge can be pounded into the end grain with the sledgehammer until something gives. You may find that the wedges with the chisel-type edge work better for you. To use these, place the log securely in a horizontal position and wham one wedge right into the grain about a third of the way from the end. Place the second wedge along the same split, and bash again in the hope that the log (only) will be severed. It is not a very fast production line.

If the thought of all this work gives you a splitting headache, you may opt to rent a power-driven log splitter and haul it behind your car to your cottage. (You do have a trailer hitch?) The electric ones are handier, but they may not be powerful enough if you are dealing with hard, twisted wood like elm. If you are using the electric type, be wary of long extension cords which, unless they are very heavy, will rob you of so much power that the splitter may be useless. The gas motors are more powerful, although, like all internal combustion engines, they can be trickier to operate. Besides power, their other big advantage is that they can be hauled to wherever the logs are, instead of to the power outlet. They don't require any human strength except for log lifting, and there is no particular trick to using them, beyond keeping your hands away from the machine's moving parts. The nuisance of hauling the splitter may tempt you to buy one. If you are not really in the firewood business, renting makes better economic sense, unless you are willing to pay handsomely for convenience.

The final option is to get someone else to split logs for you. The supply of sturdy young splitters anxious to wield an axe on your behalf seems to be drying up, but the number of people with mechanical splitters available for rental with an operator is increasing. Before your hire one, inquire about the rates, preferably after the operator has seen your log pile. Opt for a rate based on cords produced rather than on the hours worked. It is generally better for labor-management relations, and it gives you an interesting comparison with the cost of cordwood delivered.

M

MANUALS

If your vision of the cottage is a hammock swinging to the hum of cicadas, please don't balk at the suggestion of keeping a cottage manual. The whole idea is to save a lot of time by investing a little, and to make those summer days as carefree as possible.

The purpose of a cottage manual is to record every simple operation so that any stranger would know how to run everything with minimum hassle and damage to the premises. Consider the uses:

- If the chief maintainer becomes ill or must suddenly go away, the rest of the family will have instructions to follow;
- you may suddenly want or need to rent your cottage, and be unable to go there to explain how everything works;
- the manual is a cunning way to involve the other members of the family in summer chores;
- you might — perish the thought — forget just how the generator or other gear works after a winter in the city.

The time to start the manual is in winter when your mind is drifting to the lake and your hands are (relatively) idle. You finish your first draft to test on the first visit, then make notes all summer for the new, enlarged, revised edition for next season.

The manual should be in loose-leaf form or on large library cards to permit alphabetical organization and easy revision. The format depends on your circumstances. You may be obsessed with eliminating the porcupines from the outhouse before Uncle Fred sits on one, or you may be concerned with instructing the gardener, three maids and the butler about the first spring reception. Here are just a few examples.

Title Page

Since this may be your first and last book, why not make it professional? Include here the full postal, geographical and survey (township, lot) identification of your property. Add your full permanent address, and "in case of trouble, please notify...".

Maps

Here include a clear map from the nearest reputable town, together with a detailed verbal description. ("About 500 yards after the Moonbeam Café, there is a concealed crossroads; turn left and watch for the swamp by an abandoned barn about 3 miles on the right....")

Then, even if your estate is nearer one acre than 100, include a map of the property based on the survey map with your deed. It will help show the boundaries by indicating landmarks ("the northwest corner is marked by a red post 2 feet north of the outhouse"). Then any tenant will know the limits beyond which the blueberries will not (or will) be picked. Mark on the plan the cottage, outhouse, underground pipes or wires and any personal features such as the spot where you think you buried old Felix three years ago. You might even mark any precious plants which you don't want to see yanked away, or which someone may be trying to find after a hard winter.

Pictures

A section of photos will help make the rest of the manual meaningful to a stranger, and it may assist you next February when you are planning that great new addition. Start with the aerial photo you got from the federal government. (See **Photos**.) Comb the family photo archives, and note gaps which should be filled next spring.

Business Notes

This is the spot to record where precious documents are kept, and to list annual payments which must be made. It is not good news, for example, if you receive no tax bill; your failure to pay, for whatever reason, may lead to land seizure by the municipality and heart seizure by you. List the insurance agent and any annual tributes — to the local person whom you have hired for winter supervision, for example.

As a second subsection, you could list here the names of all tradespeople on whom a tenant might want to call: electrician, plumber, gravel supplier, woodcutter, septic tank emptier, general repair person and so on. It would be handy to list also the stores you prefer for different types of supplies, from croissants to chlordane.

Arrival

Note the choreography on arrival, particularly any gates which should be closed after you pass. Explain which key opens which door. Include your secret hiding places for spare keys only if you are not concerned that publication will compromise security. Explain the procedure for checking the premises. (See **Opening Up.**)

Equipment

This section must be detailed if it is to be useful. Don't say, "Start the pump". Explain to the stranger who is unfamiliar with your equipment that the pump is the green metal thing under the bench in the shed. Point out each of its important features, then describe precisely how to set up and operate it, step-by-step, with diagrams if necessary.

Think of all the other equipment which may need attention and explain the details of such procedures as checking the oil and fuelling the lawnmower and chain saw, attaching garden hoses, moving out the boat, re-assembling the dock, cleaning out and starting the refrigerator, and taking the cap off the chimney.

Fire

Even if you have complete fire instructions posted on the wall (see **Fire Precautions**), draw attention to them and add supplementary information, such as more detailed guidance on what to do if a fire breaks out. Include a copy of your fire instructions, in case the wall set has been lost.

Medical Aid

Where are the first-aid book and the medical manual kept? How do you reach the nearest doctor, nurse, ambulance, hospital, poison control center? Where is the nearest pharmacist? In an emergency, what is the best route for medical help?

Are there poisonous flora and fauna? How do you fight blackflies, mosquitoes, and wasps? (Be soothing in your explanations, or the prospective tenant may flee in terror.) How do you discourage plastic-eating porcupines and garbage-consuming raccoons? How do you wash dogs with tomato juice after a canine-skunk conflict?

Local Amenities

For strangers, some notes about local people, places and events could be helpful. Who are the neighbors and are they friendly? What are the (known) entertainments for teenagers? What nearby sights are worth a visit? Are there any social events not to be missed, like the annual picnic, strawberry social, Orange parade or local regatta?

Closing Up

This could be the most important section of all if you ever hope to visit your cottage again. (See **Closing Up**.) Write it in infinite detail.

There it is, your masterpiece. It but remains to negotiate movie rights, and maybe set it all to music.

Though as a class cottagers are splendid people, they have one almost universal failing that could be corrected. They do not tell you the directions to their cottages clearly and simply. As a consequence, they subject their invited friends to mental turmoil and wasted time, and put tradespeople in a mood to charge double for their services.

The ideal directions are on two sides of a single piece of paper. On the face is a hand-drawn road map showing the route from the nearest easily found town(s) or landmark. It does not have to take you all the way from the city if you live within reach of a sizeable town which is clearly shown on all provincial or state road maps. But bear in mind that most, but not all, visitors will come from the city. Friends may come from their own cottages, and tradespeople may come from almost anywhere, if at all. At least an indication of alternative starting points is therefore necessary.

The roads on your map should be marked with the provincial, state, or local route numbers and enough passing landmarks to cheer the traveller on. Exact distances can be marked either on the sketch or at the bottom of the sheet. Don't guess at them — they are easy to measure. It is especially important that the exact distance be marked near the object of the journey, possibly with the warning that if you see such-and-such you have gone too far. If the local lane has a closed gate, note it, possibly with an admonition to close it after passing.

On the back of the sheet should be a verbal description to reinforce the map and to guide those who cannot read maps. It will also list distances from the city or other major landmarks so that travellers will know whether to pause or press on to use your washroom. Warnings about bad roads or speed traps may be appreciated. The text should include your geographical address and the telephone number of your cottage or nearest message center. One of the uses of this verbal

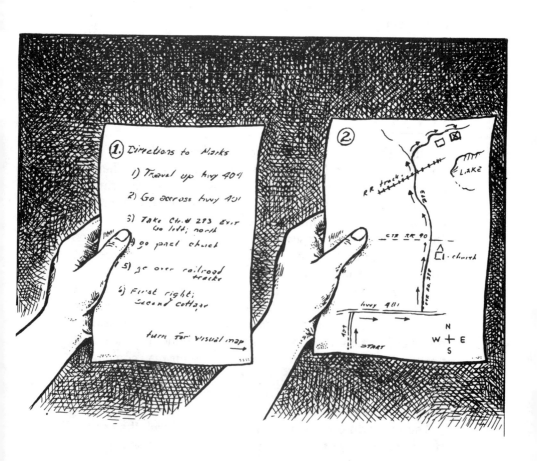

description is to have something to dictate quickly when you need to phone directions, so that the long-distance charges do not mount while you try to describe the route to your cottage.

You will consider your own policy for distributing the map. For expected visitors it is invaluable. If there are people you don't really want to invite but can't ignore, a general welcome accompanied by a map will ease your conscience and please the recipient. Your hopes that they will, or will not, come can then remain your secret.

Quite apart from these hand-drawn maps, you should provide yourself with excellent large-scale maps (1:50,000) made by the federal government. They will tell you a lot about what you can't see from the road or lake, and will be invaluable for hiking tours. They can also make highway travel more interesting. (See **Games**.) You can contact the nearest provincial office of the federal Department of Energy, Mines and Resources, or write to the Surveys and Mapping Branch, 615 Booth Street, Ottawa K1A 0E9. (Telephone: (613) 998-9900.) Ask for a free map index and inquire about current prices. (Including handling, they are about $5 plus provincial sales tax.) You will then send back the numbers shown on the index with your order and cheque.

MUSHROOMS

If you are an incipient mycologist, hours of pleasure may await you in gathering mushrooms from near your cottage, and consuming them as a fresh delicacy with your friends. Since you do not wish to die in the process, please take care.

The word mushroom is generally used to include any kind of fleshy fungus, including puffballs and morels. Many people talk about toadstools as though they were the poisonous version of mushrooms, but that is both scientifically inaccurate and misleading. Toadstool does not mean anything in particular — it is slang, if you like, for mushroom. Some mushrooms are very poisonous and many are not. The good and the bad are often very closely related botanically and seem to look — to the amateur — much alike.

There are many folk tales about the way to distinguish dangerous mushrooms from safe ones. "If it peels, it is good to eat." "A chemical test, like the blackening of silver, will set them apart." All of these tales are dangerous nonsense. There are only two ways to learn to make the vital distinction.

1. Go out in the company of an acknowledged expert.

2. Very carefully compare each mushrooms collected with pictures and descriptions of edible mushrooms. If the specimen leaves any doubt at all in your mind that it is one of the edible varieties described, discard it.

This process is not as difficult and risky as it may sound. A little experience in collecting will soon enable you to recognize the safe species, but keep referring back to that text with each new species until you are really skilled at spotting the vital characteristics.

To gather mushrooms, all you need is a sharp knife, some pieces of waxed or tissue paper and a container. To identify species now unknown to you, dig deeply into the ground to get the whole plant, because the base of the stem is an important recognition point. Wrap each specimen separately before putting it in the container. When you bring your collection back and open your reference book, you may be confused by the slight variations that occur in mushrooms, just as in people. Be cautious at first, and discard the deviants, even though later you may recognize them as safe.

After you are confident of the identification of the species, when you go to collect for dinner, cut the stem well above the ground to avoid dirt. Choose the younger variety and leave the overly mature. Cut them open to check that there are no larvae inside, nor tunnel-like pinholes.

Since some species need more cooking than others, prepare them separately. They should be washed and dried, but not necessarily peeled, unless the caps are sticky or scaly. You will learn by experience whether the stems are tough or desirable. When frying, go easy on the butter.

With this sort of care, you are unlikely to have any trouble. If you suspect that someone has eaten an inedible mushroom, empty the victim's stomach fast and call a doctor.

Thus, the most important step is to acquire that reference booklet on mushrooms from your library, bookseller or Department of Agriculture. Just be sure it lists and illustrates a variety of edible species. Good collecting!

N

NAMES

Up in the country where there are no street signs, you have at last the creative opportunity to choose your own name for the cottage, and then promote it with signs, letterhead and even singing commercials, if you wish.

Back in the city you might be pleased to have a street named after you, especialy if you live in a municipality which does not insist on its citizens being dead before being so honored. Many cottagers, their imagination exhausted, put up a sign reading, for example, "Smith", which is brutal in the simplicity of its message. Surveys prove that cottagers rarely name the cottage after themselves (Chalet Smith, Smith Acres). When they choose a name at all, it often verges on the touching, such as "Bide-a-Wee" or "Heart's Content." "Mon Repos" has a certain cosmopolitan bilingualism about it, but the days when it, too, was new and original have long since passed. There are also many alleged Indian names, all of which when translated seem to mean "place where the waters meet."

The naming of the cottage often precipitates a race for keen wit, but, alas, others have been there before. Whether copyright or not, "Offhand Manor," "Wit's End," "Last Resort" and "Rock Bottom" have all figured in literature. If you are searching for puns, you may be impressed by the bilingual wordplay of "Au pin d'or," which does have the slight disadvantage of requiring a long explanation to each newcomer.

Other signs noted in passing have been "Beside the Point," "Inflation Eyry," "Sun Dee Rest No," "Nomanisan Island," and "Dunworkin." In recognition of our beloved dog, we have been considering "Cri de cur."

The name does not have to be clever. Perhaps it will mean more if it is personal, relating to some event in family life, or some hope or dream. Possibly it comes from a precocious remark of the children which gains the aura of legend with the passing years.

There is no hurry about naming the cottage. Wait patiently for inspiration, but also let the family join in seeking it. You may achieve more than a name.

NEWSPAPERS

You may think of your cottage as an annex to your city home, but it is more than that. It is part of a world of its own. Both for your own protection, and for the enrichment of your cottage experience, it is worth learning about that world. That is why we recommend that you subscribe to the community newspaper, preferably year-round. The cost is not crippling, and it can pay dividends.

At first you may see it as a curious alternative to the sophisticated city press. It may be overladen with funny glitches which suggest that no proofreader has ever touched the copy. But be careful about fast judgements. The capitalization of community papers may be low, but the quality of their contents is often high.

You may start by looking for any news which could directly affect your property — the summary of the municipal budget, a restrictive by-law, the decision to improve some local roads, but not others. You have been warned, but more than that. As a taxpayer, you have the right to express your views. So few people have the initiative to write a letter that yours may well be influential.

If the issue is likely to affect you seriously — for example, a measure discriminating against temporary residents — you may want to get the support of neighbors to express a stronger view. Don't wait for someone else to do it. That's what everyone else is doing, and the others may not even know about the information you have found in the paper. Next summer you may want to participate in organizing a local residents' association.

The local press gradually offers other rewards. Purely local and seemingly trivial issues unfold week-by-week like a serial story. You begin to know some of the permanent residents from a distance, and, perhaps, eventually as friends. At least you have a basis of conversation. The local people appreciate the city people who care.

Both the display ads and the classifieds may be revealing. If local prices are nearly competitive with the city, it is strongly in your interest to patronize the nearby merchant. That is where you will take the machine that does not work, and where you will receive fast advice. It is the source of local wisdom on all sorts of subjects. The ads help you to know the local merchants better. The classified ads are often worth clipping for a file of tradespeople to hire in advance of the summer rush which usurps all their time. That is where you may find a bargain in used equipment and supplies. Many people would rather buy such things from a local family, which will always be there, than from an anonymous source in the city.

And if you need help, don't overlook the possibility of placing your own ad. They are one of the world's last bargains, whether you are looking for help with the chores, a babysitter or a second-hand stove. If you are looking for a cottage for yourself or for friends, start looking in the classifieds, for many are never put in the hands of agents.

The final dividend is seeing that local paper drop in the mail some February morning, to keep alive your hope that summer will come.

NORTHERN LIGHTS

Northern lights, or *aurora borealis* if you prefer to impress, are one of the pleasures reserved largely for cottagers. That is partly because cottagers are away from the city glow which dims the effect, and partly because cottage country tends to be farther north.

You may remember from schooldays that the northern lights are caused by protons and electrons shooting out from the sun at hundreds of thousands of miles a second and hitting the earth's upper atmosphere to release energy in the form of light. The earth's magnetic field tends to pull them towards the magnetic poles. That is why the display is so vivid in the north. (Australia and New Zealand share the southern lights.) As the particles collide with the atmosphere, they change their electric charge and glow like the inside of a fluorescent light tube. When a hundred million protons and electrons strike one square inch of the earth's atmosphere, the whole sky seems to be on fire.

The best time for viewing is generally March-April and September-October, but cottagers typically enjoy the northern lights in the clear nights of late August. The display they are seeing is about 75 miles (110 km) above the earth, and stretching as much as ten times that high. There are many different forms. Arcs of light may stretch for hundreds of miles. Long thin rays may form enormous curtains. They may dart in rays and crowns, spread like enormous erupting flowers, or shift like the colored arc-lights of a pageant. Though the aurora ranges the spectrum, the predominating color is bluish-green, caused by atomic oxygen. The red highlights are provided by molecular oxygen and hydrogen.

Northern lights are associated with magnetic storms. The best shows are seen when there is a lot of sunspot activity, at which time they tend to move farther south.

This awesome display, far beyond the craft of man, often will be a highlight of the cottage summer. It will be even more overpowering if you happen to be in the northern territories, where the whole world sometimes seems illuminated by them. Do they crackle? Northerners swear that they do, but scientific minds have replied that it is impossible. We'll just say that when the northern spectacle is at its height, *something* crackles.

O

*O*IL LAMPS

It is easy to see why the coming of electricity did violence to the market for oil lamps. They are too dim to be healthy for reading, and they need much more care than your average electric fixture. But they have their uses.

Every cottage should have a couple of oil lamps as a standby for the night when the power fails. If you are particular about your décor, you may want to buy them from the plentiful stocks at antique stores, so that they will remain an ornament in good times and bad. When

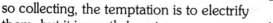

so collecting, the temptation is to electrify them, but it is worth keeping one or two in their natural state for use during emergencies.

If you are more interested in a practical lamp, the local hardware store probably can satisfy your needs. Consider buying at least one workmanlike model in a metal frame with handle. They are much safer to light your way when you are walking with them, and less likely to be disastrously knocked over when sitting on a shelf. For spots of illumination in rooms, the inexpensive glass and china models are fine. Neither is really good for reading. If you expect long and frequent power failures, you probably should consider the more sophisticated pressure-type lanterns, which give an intense off-white light. They are, however, more difficult to maintain and more dangerous.

For safety, the main precaution is to see that lighted lamps are carefully placed where there is minimum risk of their being knocked over. Remember that people today are not used to taking the instinctive care of our forebears when handling oil lamps. The family may also need a reminder that the glass chimney can become very hot, and should not be touched. The other precaution is to store the fuel safely outside, and to fill the lamps outside where spillage will not soak into a floor.

If the lamps are kept filled, the wick will burn very slowly and need only rare replacement. The wick may have to be turned up a little to make it easier to light, but then it should be quickly turned down, or the chimney will blacken with the smoke in seconds. The chimney will need cleaning after use. Instead of dirtying the sink with the greasy soot, first clean as much as you can with a newspaper, using warm water and detergent or soap only for the final polish.

Especially if you have pleasant-looking oil lamps, don't wait for an emergency to use them. They are an alternative to candles at dinner, or the final touch for a cool evening with family and friends by the fireplace. Their yellowish light casts a glow that is magical for people whose imaginations roam in the past.

OPENING UP

There is far more to opening up a cottage than turning the key in the lock. It is a time to survey and plan. If there is any damage from the winter, it is better to discover it all at once instead of risking continuing unhappy surprises. It is a time to notice jobs to be done and, equally important, to list supplies and tools to bring on the next trip.

As the car slows to a stop, have your pencil and notepaper ready. Ask the members of the family to report back to you on the state of the woods, the beach, the moorings for the dock, the outbuildings, and so on. This keeps the excited tourists occupied while you methodically check the inside alone.

First, walk around the cottage checking for any sign of a break-in. Look to see if there are broken windows, boards gnawed by porcupines, or if the roof has been struck by falling branches. When you check off this list of doleful but remote possibilities, your morale will begin to rise.

If there is evidence of a break-in, pursue that problem first. A thief's favorite targets are usually audio-visual equipment, binoculars, camera equipment, knives and tools. You must not touch anything before the police arrive for fingerprinting, but be warned that your average policeman will scorn your request as evidence of your undue exposure to TV whodunits. The police will generally be courteous in making reports of break-ins, and may be interested in any really peculiar identifying habits of the burglar, but unless you have lost the Topkapi jewels, don't expect the police to look for fingerprints or foot imprints in the mud. Before the family enters to confuse things, make the most complete possible list of missing or damaged items for the police and your insurance agent.

If you have not had a break-in, the interior search need not take long. Is there any evidence of leaks? Have any animals been living rent-free? You will want to remove the last mortal remains of a bird, for instance, before younger members of the family become emotional and demand a proper funeral. Give upholstery the once-over to see that squirrels or mice have not been consuming it. What is the extent of the clean-up needed to erase any signs of the legendary incontinence of mice? Are there any bottles or tins broken from the freezing of forgotten liquid contents? Is there any visible sign of split water pipes? The real test, of course, is when the pump starts.

Then turn on the electricity. Try out large and small appliances and lights to see that all circuits are working. Check out your electric-powered tools to ensure that rust has not put them on a list for city repair. Before you switch on the stove, remember to check the oven for those things you were concealing from the mice. If there is a phone, does it work? Do the smoke detectors or intercom (if any) need new batteries? Do the fire extinguishers need recharging? Is there oil for the lamps? How about pulling out the gasoline containers to get fresh refills? (The old gas may work, but it won't do your engines any good.)

By now the family may be bursting in the gates with their tales of fallen robins' nests and other horrors. By the time you have compared notes you may have gathered strength for the real test: starting up the water system. When it is working, and you have checked all the water lines, you might make sure that the chimneys are clear of unwanted blockages by burning a couple sheets of newspaper in stove or fireplace. Is there firewood ready for this evening? If you have decided that you are too exhausted to clean the chimney or stovepipe today, post a reminder on the wall so that this chore is not too long postponed.

Then you make your own tour of outbuildings and grounds. The old rowboat may need caulking: are supplies on hand? Varnish? Is the outhouse intact? Will the road need new gravel this spring, or will pick, shovel and rake restore it to passability? Has ice damaged any shore installations? In this tour, did you notice any dead animals which may have succumbed to rabies?

This survey may seem an invitation to complete depression, but more likely it will be the reverse. Especially if you start by psyching yourself to expect disaster everywhere, you will be agreeably surprised at how well the old place has weathered, and for the rest of the season things can only improve.

OUTHOUSES

Those cottagers who still possess an outhouse (or backhouse, or *bécosse* as Canada's other official language describes it) may be heartened to realize that these quaint buildings are now considered part of our architectural heritage, and have been the subject of learned papers and coffee-table books. If you have graduated to modern waste-disposal systems, perhaps you should preserve your system as a potential historic monument.

The privy is an honoured institution. (In government, there is even a Privy Council with a Cabinet Minister as President.) Its main drawback is not pollution, but inconvenience. Well made and maintained, it is as safe for the environment as any system. If you are building a new or replacement facility, you must be careful where you put it — find a nice compromise between convenience and perfection. It must be far enough away from the cottage that smells and insects congregating near it do not bother the family. It must be placed so that drainage, especially snowmelt and spring surface water, do not pick up waste products to leave on the ground or in waterways. You should line the pit with concrete to make it completely safe from seepage. Alternatively, you can make it semiportable so that eventually you can cover the nearly full pit with earth and plant sweet violets, while moving the structure to a new spot.

The outhouse should be given the same tender loving care as the North American bathroom. A scrubbing of the inside should be at least an annual ritual, and stain, paint or preservative should be applied before the signs of wear show. This is not just cosmetic cleanliness. It is a discouragement to pollution-carrying insects as well as an encouragement to patrons. In addition, it is well to spray it at least annually with a chlordane solution. The spray will tend to divert wasps, than which there are few more undesirable neighbors in an outhouse.

Of course, porcupines are not very good company either. Country folklore has it that the most popular commercial products for dumping in an outhouse also serve to put off porcupines; the chemicals do not harm them, but persuade them to go and find their own privy.

The ideal outhouse should be virtually bug-tight. Put a lining of thin plywood, fibreboard or equivalent inside the knotty boards with their thick gaps between. Be sure it is on walls, ceiling, door and floor. Since an almost airtight structure will not allow enough ventilation, you should have two window openings, which can be covered with tightly applied screen without window sash, and a screened vent pipe from the operational part of the establishment.

All this is easy to set up, and not very time-consuming. Where you may have trouble is in the dwindling supply of department store catalogues without which no heritage outhouse is complete.

P

No one wants to spend unnecessary time caring for the surfaces of a house. At the cottage it is even more important to find trouble-free solutions, for the season is short, help is not always easy to find, and the brief summer holiday offers pleasanter pastimes than painting.

Therefore, the first rule is to seek quality rather than low price in paint products and equipment. Do not take the all too common attitude that lower quality products are good enough for the cottage. The dollars you save on cheap material may end up being spent on more frequent applications or, worse, on time-consuming and expensive treatment of surfaces on which the paint has blistered or flaked and the wood has begun to rot. Price may be an indication of quality, but it is not a sure guide. You would be wise to consult *Canadian Consumer*, published by the Consumer's Association of Canada, or the *Consumer's Reports*, published by the Consumer's Union of the United States, Inc., about paint and other finishes for exterior and interior.

The time you have to spend on maintenance will be much reduced if you use as little paint as possible. On pine or cedar siding you have many choices. One preservative is boiled linseed oil thinned with turpentine or with a fungicide, but beware: if any trace of the mix remains on the surface it may turn gummy and black instead of penetrating the wood. The corrective measures are extremely labor intensive. It will also show different coloration according to where the sun and wind hit most.

You can also choose a commercial brand of colored stain according to your tastes, but be sure the quality is good. There is a cheaper alternative, and its preservative properties may well be superior. It is a 1:1 mixture of creosote and a clear (not green) fungicide with a pentachlorophenol base, (sold under commercial names which usually include "pent —").

There are some disadvantages to using this solution. Pentachlorophenol in concentration is dangerous to breathe (it is widely banned in the U.S.A.) It should not be used indoors, nor even on furniture which will be placed indoors, and neither it nor creosote should be used on any table surface indoors or out. To lessen the likelihood of inhaling the fumes, it is better to brush than to spray it. Some people find the mixture irritating if it comes into contact with the skin. Don't leave it — or any stain — on the skin. It comes off easily enough with petroleum paint thinner, followed by soap and warm water. The other limitation is that, while the mixture goes on almost black, it dries out to a shade of pleasant brown. You can make the brown lighter or darker according to the proportion of creosote in the mix, but if you really want the nuances of color available in commercial stains you have to add oil colors.

The theory behind the mix is that it gives you both an oily wood preservative (creosote) and a fungicide. Creosote alone can be gummy and stay on the surface of some wood, but thus thinned, it soaks in well. It is easy to touch up walls which have been bleached by sun, wind and rain. If, after a few years, one wall is darker because of less exposure, you can recoat it with a mix containing less creosote, or add more creosote when doing walls subject to more weathering. If you like this treatment, you may want to invest in 20L pails; they can be stored over winter for use when you need them. Most important, though, is the need to mix the creosote thoroughly before the elements are put together, and as you work. Otherwise, the heavy solids in the creosote will sink to the bottom and give you different shades of brown.

This same mix can be used for installations touching the ground, like posts or the underside of shed floors. Coat the boards before installing them and let the preservative soak in for an hour or two before handling them.

Although this preservative will work on most of your surfaces, you will probably wish to coat the windows and doors with a good paint. Since most people now have aluminum in the city, we may forget the importance of continuing attention to painted frames. When any sign of checking or flaking starts, scrape, coat and repaint promptly before rot has a chance to set in. Touch up windows and doors as soon as the need is evident — it will save a lot of time in the long run. If you have a rot problem with some frames, undercoat them with fungicide or aluminum paint before putting on the color paint of your choice.

When choosing paint for interior and exterior, you will avoid trouble for yourself if you have as few varieties as possible. Paint cannot be safely stored at the cottage over the winter, and it is a nuisance to bring it all to the city. Also, it is well to use ready-mixed colors rather than custom-made. The former will probably give an acceptable match for later repainting, and therefore, less paint has to be stored. But never underestimate the capacity of paint manufacturers to change colors for no reason except to irritate customers.

PARKING

Dreams of country beauty include such scenes as the sun flicking silver on the ripples of the lake, painted sunsets on the distant hills, or the silhouettes of whispering pines — but they rarely dwell on cars. Isn't it worth a little thought about what to do with them?

If you can drive to your very door, you may be tempted to leave the car there until the next trip out. It is convenient to be able to unload and load with minimum effort, but then it takes only a few seconds to move the car to its own little niche neatly curtained by trees and away from paint-fading sun. If, by any unlucky chance, you have porcupines about, it is easy in that spot to string some light chain-link fence to ensure that you still have a radiator hose when you go to start the car. This is also an out-of-sight area where you can stow things like empty gasoline containers or beer bottles to await the next trip out. Some day, when you have run out of projects, you can string some electric wiring and a plastic waterpipe to the parking spot so that, if you must, you can work on the vehicle there, out of harm's way.

While you are planning this magnificent landscaping, make space for a couple of visitors' cars as well, and mark it clearly with signs. Otherwise you can be sure that someday, some guest is going to drive aimlessly about your precious grounds, crushing all those priceless seedlings you planted last spring.

PHOTOS

A comprehensive collection of photographs can give you great pleasure in the dreary city months, make your friends envious, and help you plan new projects. Yet, possibly the first photo to think of is one which you do not take at all.

When it comes to aerial photography, Canadians are real achievers, perhaps because we have so much geography to photograph. Excellent, revealing and reasonably up-to-date photos exist of your property, and the National Air Photo Library is anxious to sell them to you. Take them up on it. The pictures will tell you much about the world around you, and they are unfailing as conversation pieces when framed on the living room wall.

There is a considerable array available in black and white, color and stereo. Relatively cheap contact prints in black and white and in color give you just what the airborne camera happened to include in one shot. That is unlikely to be what you want. Enlargements include the exact area you select. They are generally square, and range from 25 x 25 cm (10 x 10 inches) to 101 x 101 cm (40 x 40 inches) or 101 x 152 cm (40 x 60 inches). Since prices change, it is best to write or phone for a current list of prices and sizes. In relation to the quality and to the general cost of aerial photos, the tariffs are not unreasonable: from about $20 for the smaller black and white, and from about $50 for color. The address is 615 Booth Street, Ottawa K1A 0E9; telephone (613) 995-4560.

When you write, be sure to give the telephone number where you can be reached by day, and send along directions about what you want by enclosing a marked road map. They will phone you back (at their expense) to describe what is available there. If you are still not sure of the precise area you want, you may want to order a photo embracing a relatively large area. Then you can photocopy it and mark the precise location of which you would like an enlargement, and send it back to them.

In theory, you could specify a photo of just your cottage, but the Library guarantees enlargements of only five times the size of a contact print: greater enlargement can be just too vague and grainy. The contact prints are based on photos of a scale of 1:50,000. When you are speaking to the Library, ask them to tell you the date when your area was last photographed, and how often it is usually done. A few years later you can then get an up-to-date photo by sending in the present photo, or a copy of your present order.

Your own cottage photo collection may be largely for happy reminiscence of carefree holidays. But do include in it some record shots, including the cottage from every angle, inside and out, other buildings, the road in, a panorama of the property from a high tree (if that is practical) and even the view from the windows. You will be surprised how often those record shots may come in handy — even if you are not claiming a disastrous insurance loss. One of the pleasures they will give is a family showing 10 or 25 years later to see how it has all changed in your creative hands.

Also, if you want to elicit the respectful sympathy of family and friends, take before and after shots of your major improvements. That is the only way that they may half believe how hard you worked.

PLANNING

The best time to start is at the end of the season. That is when you should list all repairs and new projects for the next year — not on July 1. Those plans will do more than nourish dreams through the winter. In the case of equipment, having necessary repairs already in mind gives you time to read up on the qualities of different brands and types, to do some comparison shopping, and possibly to take advantage of sales, which generally occur in autumn. Sometimes, too, you will be rudely surprised by how long it takes to fill orders for special quantities of even ordinary materials — such as 20L tins of preservative — which you want for convenience and economy.

On that autumn list, write down more than just "new deck". Take time to get accurate measurements. If you haven't already taken detailed photos of your whole establishment, (see **Photos**), now is the time to get a picture of the area where the deck will go. In February your memory for the finer points of the cottage may be more uncertain than you expect. If you are equipped with detailed information, however, you can spend pleasant evenings working out designs, bills of materials, and even work plans. If building permits are necessary, the time to apply is early spring.

Your experience of cottage living may by now have told you what supplies you can find locally. If you have doubts about the availability of certain items, late summer is the time to find out, so that you will not be awaiting backorders next June. Also, check the inventories of your suppliers. Reduction in inventories is a notable cost-cutting step taken by modern retailers (unlike the old-timers, who always had sheds of stuff for all seasons, in all seasons). If you need 100 pounds of 3-inch nails next summer, be sure your only convenient store does not stock just 23 ounces of them, all in infuriating little plastic packages. Lining up adequate quantities of necessary items well in advance saves both frustration and money.

Labor, when you need it, may be as scarce as materials. If you haven't yet made contacts with reliable tradespeople, consider advertising locally for them in early spring. (See **Newspapers**.) If you already maintain good relations with such people, try to commit them to your jobs well in advance. They may let you down, but an advance agreement will give you arguing power if they don't show up.

On the grander scale of planning, you could try having a master plan for your property. For example, if you are building modestly with thoughts of later expansion, it could be worthwhile at the outset to finish all the excavation and even the foundations. If you decide now where a future boathouse, workshed or woodstack would go, you will not plant trees or create your most precious gardens in those places. Gradually over the winters you can make plans — an inexpensive form of recreation. Then you are ready if a sudden opportunity appears — a workcrew at your next-door neighbor's, for example, that is ready to give a good price for the extra work in the same month that you won the lottery.

When you build or add to the cottage, it is a good idea to have a working assumption about the years ahead. Is there any chance that you will ever want to use it for an all-season retreat, or even a year-round home? You may not want to go to the extra expense of the higher standards now, but some planning will help save you from future grief. For example, not burying your water pipes inside exterior walls may save you re-plumbing. Or, even if you don't want to insulate walls now, using 2 x 6 instead of 2 x 4 for studs will make it possible to use fibreglass later. Putting your cottage on a complete foundation instead of on piers (which some municipalities now require anyway) is far easier to do before there is a building there. Even if you are adding a wing to a cottage built to minimum standards, you should consider upgrading the new section.

Only a little less important than your own planning is a little forward planning among your neighbors. You might try to negotiate a Treaty of Friendship and Cooperation requiring all parties to notify the others whenever they are about to import special equipment or tradespeople. It is often time-consuming and expensive to get in a backhoe or bulldozer; if everyone near is able to make use of it, the individual cost will be reduced. It is pretty frustrating, when you have just spent three scorching days with crowbar, pick and shovel levelling out a sort of badminton court, to see a bulldozer ambling up the road. Planning and cooperation work well with tradespeople too. By keeping a list of small jobs, none worth bringing in an electrician from town, you can take advantage of one being next door — if your neighbor tells you.

PLUMBING

Those of you who are standing with cheque book in hand waiting for the plumber to arrive can ignore this note. We are having a small conversation with those creative adventurers who decide to try plumbing for themselves.

The first two vital questions are the source of the water and its disposal. The first is fairly easy. (See **Pumps**.) The second is not. (See **Biological Toilets; Septic Systems**.) If you decide on a septic system, no one will blame you if you contract with a local person to do the work, leaving a pipe ready to be connected. Perversely, water is harder to dispose of than to acquire. If you have a flush toilet, you should consider hiring a professional to connect up the drainage system throughout the house, for you need curious things such as vents, which would take too much space to explain here. If you have just sinks and a shower, you can do a workable job yourself, though it would be prudent not to boast about it to the local inspectors. If you are really keen, you can install the drainage system yourself, with a (waterproof) book from the library in one hand. Connecting the incoming water is far simpler.

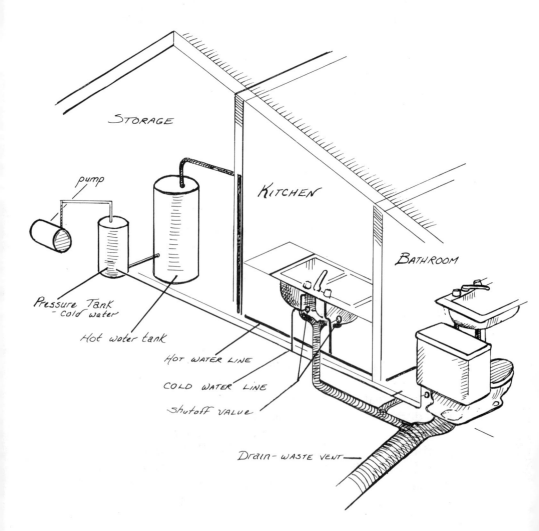

STORAGE

pump

KITCHEN

BATHROOM

Pressure Tank
- cold water

Hot water tank

HOT WATER LINE

COLD WATER LINE

Shutoff VALVE

Drain - WASTE VENT

Planning a plumbing system is within the capacity of any advanced mathematician. When you have decided on the pumping equipment, you select the spot for it — preferably not under the kitchen sink where it is hard to reach and where all the water you spill may be awkward to dry up. Besides, you may as well have it next to the hot water tank. This usually means that the nerve center of your plumbing will be in the annexed storage room, or in a cupboard built against the outside of the cottage. If the exterior walls of the cupboard are insulated and the interior is not, you can stretch the running water season past those first frosty nights.

If your only hot water is for a sink, a washroom basin and a not-too-frequently-used shower, you can probably manage with a 12-gallon tank, which uses only 120 volts. (It is about 20 inches in diameter and 21 inches high.) If you want a bathtub or a dishwasher, you probably should go beyond the 25-gallon to 40-gallons, which will need 240 volts. When you buy the tank, include a spare heating element; a plumber will rarely have the right size in his truck, and you can easily replace a faulty one yourself.

A plumbing diagram is obviously needed to calculate how much pipe to buy. For cold water, trace it from the pump tank to the hot water heater, and to each faucet inside and whatever outside taps you decide on. Don't be too skimpy on the outside taps, they don't cost much and could be a good fire precaution. For hot water, you need no longer use copper pipe, which requires careful soldering that is hard for the amateur to master; there are now plastic pipes made especially for carrying hot water. There is no point using them for cold water, for the traditional black plastic pipe is cheaper and quite acceptable. Never buy economy grade; number two pipe is quite satisfactory for the cottage, but expensive number one is even better. For all the difference in cost, you may as well use 3/4-inch pipe, even though 1/2-inch will do. Except for the toilet (which needs only cold water) your estimate of the length of the interior black plastic pipe needed is about the same as for the hot water pipe.

The qualities of genius are required when you calculate all the joints and clamps you need: T's, right angles, joiners, valves between lengths of plastic pipe, joiners to connect to taps, valves, drain cocks, faucets and teflon tape. If you are a total novice, look at the plumbing section of a catalogue that shows you all the kinds of fittings, then draw beautiful diagrams, with enlarged plans for each joint, suitably identified. Try to find a sympathetic plumbing retailer who is willing to go over your diagram and check out your calculations — and do not wait until the middle of the cottage season. When you are absolutely sure of everything you need, add twenty percent to cover mistakes and sudden new ideas. You can always return surplus unused fittings. Be especially lavish in the number of clamps you buy, for drips can sometimes be cured simply by double-clamping.

The fittings for the hot water pipes are of standard quality. For the cold water you can use galvanized connectors, nylon, or cheap plastic, although the latter have a tendency to snap when you strain mightily to move or disconnect a pipe.

When you have all that pipe and boxes of fittings, the fun starts. We are going to suggest more than the minimum your average plumber might put in, to make the system easier to drain or repair. Begin at the pump tank. Before you go anywhere, install a valve here so that you can prime or adjust your pump without water going farther than the pump tank. Run cold water pipe from this valve to a T-pipe, one arm of which will lead to your whole cold water system. Unless *both* the pump tank and the hot water tank are equipped with threaded drain cocks for emptying in autumn, in this section of pipe install a second T, to which you will attach a drain cock; in autumn you can put a garden hose on it and neatly empty both tanks in the great outdoors. Whenever you install a fitting, put a drop of oil on each clamp, especially when working in damp places: a year or two hence you will be glad you did. Before you go on to the hot water tank, install a valve so that you can cut off the whole hot water system when it needs repair. Just remember: pump tank, valve, T for cold water system, T for drain cock, valve, hot water tank.

Now continue to the first faucet, which may be the kitchen sink. You can secure the floppy plastic piping to walls with either large staples and short screws (not nails), or lengths of metal strapping and screws. You need to install a T before going on to the bathroom. The taps in both bathroom and kitchen are probably equipped — or should be — with about a foot of thin brass tubing from each faucet. Ask your retailer to specify the connection you will need to feed these into the plastic pipe; there is quite a choice as to how you can connect. If you don't mind spending a few extra dollars, put a valve under each faucet so that if you need to make repairs you can shut it off and leave the rest of the system operational. This is especially recommended to procrastinators who are really not anxious to fix the bathroom tap tonight.

Driving force and pure logic will carry you easily through the cold-water connections. The hot water follows the same general pattern, but techniques vary with the kind of hot water pipes you buy. There is one trick to remember. You must drain both systems completely in the autumn, a complication city dwellers need not face. To make that easier, add T-pipes in low spots, with either a drain cock or a simple plug or cap to empty the line. Bear in mind that if you are using $3/4$-inch plastic pipe, by a wonderful coincidence, $1/2$-inch galvanized pipe can be secured to it with clamps neatly inserted. Thus, you can make a T with 3 short $1/2$-inch galvanized nipples fitted into a galvanized T; then screw a cap on the end of one nipple with no other fitting needed. Whenever you do connect metal to metal, be sure that you wind one thickness of teflon tape onto the threads before screwing together the pieces. Not only will this precaution produce a leak-proof joint, but it will also be much easier to detach.

If you have the minimum of plumbing, with no flush toilet, and you have decided to put in the drains yourself, you can manage with $1^1/2$-inch plastic pipe of lower quality. You should still use a trap under the sink, so that you can more easily find your wedding ring when it drops down the drain. A trap also will discourage wiggly things from wandering up the pipe into the sink. You may find it simpler to lead one pipe straight out from the kitchen sink trap and another straight out from the bathroom into pits with porous fill; the separate outlets will give a faster flow when you have no venting, and save a lot of pipe. This so-called grey water from a sink or shower is illegal in many jurisdictions, so check before going ahead with your plans. Many people say that it is no more unsanitary than washing in a bowl and throwing the slops outside, and it is not going to create any visual or olfactory pollution if it is draining into sandy soil.

Let us suppose, then, that your water system is complete — and even working — either by your own labor or someone else's. What about maintenance? For the drainage end, a good quality rubber plunger is a necessity for any system, from primitive to conventional. Smear a little petroleum jelly on the bottom, block the sink vent (if there is one) with a wet cloth, and, with a few inches of water in the sink or bowl, plunge like crazy. By unscrewing the black plastic plug in the bottom of the trap, you can clear the trouble if it happens to be in that area. (Remember to put a pan under it to catch the water.) If the plunger does not work, you can try the augur which you thoughtfully bought. If your home equipment does not include one, you can make an augur out of a wire coat hanger; it may work, but amateurs often find that it does not augur well. The third line of attack is a chemical drain cleaner. If you have a conventional system, you may be able to forestall all of these operations by using a powerful chemical cleaner, strictly according to directions, every month or two. (That is a good precaution in the city as well.) Another important precaution is a prominent sign over the toilet urging guests not to use it as a garbage disposal unit, as they might in the city. Tobacco is particularly bad for the septic system. Some country people with septic tanks provide a closed metal container for all used paper, and thus prolong the active life of systems between emptyings. A final precaution you may easily forget is to prevent any tree from growing within 10 feet of your septic tank and drainage field. If you have willows about, keep them even farther away.

For maintenance of the water intake system, keep spares of all fittings, especially clamps. You must have two large pipe wrenches to undo difficult metal fittings, a good adjustable wrench and a slot screwdriver. To tighten or retighten clamps, a vise-grip type wrench is much more powerful than a screwdriver. If you are also installing a system, it is worthwhile to equip yourself with a socket wrench to fit the screwclamps, and you will appreciate it for maintenance. You should have an assortment of washers including one to repair any dripping faucet. There are many different types of faucet, but the disassembly and washer replacement should prove fairly straightforward no matter which type you use. When you take the faucet apart and find that washer underneath that brass screw, do not be downcast if you do not have an exact match. You can sand down a larger one to fit snugly. You will also need plastic pipe joiners of the appropriate diameter, so that you can hacksaw through the pipe to remove the splits caused by ice or porcupine teeth and rejoin the pieces.

The autumn rite of draining is a bit of a bore, but it pays to be patient and careful. When the water and the electricity connected to the hot water tank are off, open every faucet and drain cock or plug in the system, including the ones on the hot water tank and on the pump. To finish the job, buy a few feet of stretchable rubber tubing (not garden hose or vinyl) with a sufficient diameter to fit tightly over the end of each faucet. Set it up, then blow hard. An alternative is to invent a fitting that will enable your shop-type vacuum to do the job. And don't forget to loosen the plug in each trap to drain the water out of it. For the toilet, empty the tank and bail out all possible water from the bowl. Draining alone is not enough for safety: be sure to pour a small amount of anti-freeze (not alcohol, which evaporates) into the bowl before you leave it for the winter. A product is sold for this purpose, and car anti-freeze also works well.

Your main plumbing problem at the cottage is likely to be leaks in the plastic pipe. As noted, they are easy to fix by cutting out the leaky section and rejoining, or replacing, it with plastic joiners and clamps. For a temporary repair, you may be able to get away with just tightening a clamp or two over the leak. But be sure to do a proper job tomorrow morning. First thing.

*P*OLITICS

The political history of cottage country varies enormously, but there are some fairly common threads. At first, cottagers are welcomed as a boost to an economy whose local and geographical resources are often relatively thin. They may become the area's largest cash industry. Political power, however, tends to rest with the permanent residents whose sensitivity to the interests of summer people may not be keen. Even if the local authority is eminently fair, it is a situation in which suspicions can easily grow that the city folk are being exploited unmercifully.

If you are the owner of cottage property, you have a major investment in the community. Such an investment warrants consideration of the political environment, for it will certainly affect your asset. The first approach to that self-education is a subscription to the local newspaper. (See **Newspapers**.)

The normal danger signals for which you will watch are large local expenditures, especially those needing heavy borrowing, for which you will be paying in steeper taxes with no personal benefit. Does the village really need a million dollar town hall or a limousine for the mayor? Are strict new building regulations designed as a boon to the local contracting industry or as a genuine benefit to the quality of cottage life? Is money for local roads being fairly distributed to the benefit of all taxpayers, or is it mostly for the townspeople?

If you have anxieties, what can you do about them? You can write letters to the mayor and council. They may not be immediately persuasive, but so few people write letters that yours are bound to have some effect. You can seek out elected representatives in person during the cottage season, or even phone them from the city. You can write to the newspaper to let everyone know that cottagers are aroused and informed.

Organization is more effective than isolated effort. If there is any association of cottagers, you should support it. It may seem feckless and a waste of time, but perhaps you can improve it. If there is a province-wide federation of cottage-owner societies, it too should be supported, for sometimes you will benefit from a strong provincial voice. If there is no local organization, someone should start it: why not you?

If there is a tension between permanent people and cottagers, a strong card in the hands of the former is distance. Municipal regulations may provide that authorization to borrow can be delayed for a referendum if a certain number of taxpayers sign a petition: but how many will journey from the city to sign a petition? One long-term objective of an association could be to provide that such protests be registered between June and September. An even stronger weapon could be a change in voting laws to provide that municipal elections are conducted in summer when most property owners can exercise their franchise. With the uniformity of municipal elections in most provinces, that could be difficult, but meanwhile cottage associations could rent buses to bring in members to vote. City dwellers would not necessarily run for office — regular attendance at council meetings would be difficult — but candidates would be obliged to hear cottager's needs. It is also worth the trouble to attend meetings of development companies with plans for the cottage area.

Organization is the first step toward ensuring a fair political environment. Bear in mind also that the local council is not the only possible target of representations. On far-reaching issues, provincial or state departments should not be overlooked. Municipal Affairs is an obvious pressure point, but for some questions Finance or Environment may be key players. And of course there are questions, such as acid rain, in which the federal government is involved.

The main point is not to ignore politics even when things seem to be going well. This is, after all, a democracy, and owning a cottage gives you a new opportunity and responsibility to play your part in it.

Pollution

Cottagers may seem more likely to be the victims of than the cause of pollution. They are probably more acutely aware than city dwellers of the tragedy of acid rain. Even if your lake and your woods have not yet been affected by acid rain, it could happen next year. Cottagers generally feel a special and personal responsibility to make their voices heard in urging that the scourge of air pollution from uncontrolled smokestacks and leaded gasoline in vehicles become a higher priority among our national problems.

At the same time, we should look to our own pollution. The most common damage caused by cottagers comes from disposal of sewage. Most jurisdictions have now become rightly strict about specifications for disposal systems, notably septic tanks and their drainage fields. Generally speaking, those municipal inspectors, who sometimes seem so annoyingly meticulous in passing each stage of construction of a septic field, are on the cottager's side and deserve our cooperation when contractors look for corners to cut. Even if new sytems are well-installed, there are countless old ones dating from times when standards were more casual. Almost no official has time to worry about those unless there is a complaint about seepage.

Any action that pollutes precious recreational water is of serious concern to all cottagers. If you have a long-established system, you might ask your local municipal office for a copy of today's requirements, so that you can judge how well you conform. If you seem to be below standard, it may be a risk not only to the environment but to the efficient working of your own system. Therefore, ask a reliable septic tank installer for advice, including an estimate, which should cost you nothing. Then you can make a sensible decision on whether to let it go for a few years, or to do some early upgrading. For example, if your system is under capacity, it might be feasible, as a temporary measure, to divert some grey water (from sinks or shower) from the tank to a sandy disposal pit.

Some environmentally sensitive jurisdictions forbid the dumping of any material in a waterway, including sand for your beach. (See **Beaches**.) The problem is that the fill may contain pollutants, including oil. Even if there are not strict laws where you live, be wary of such fill. You should really inspect its source before ordering it, and watch each truckload very carefully. If polluted fill is dumped on your land, you are in for great trouble, and you may even end up with the horrendous job of removing it from the water.

Since present regulations generally require that a septic field be more than 100 feet from a waterway or well, that is a safe distance to keep clear of any other potential source of pollution. For example, park your car at least that distance from the lake or well. Don't throw any refuse where surface water might carry elements of it into the lake. And, obviously, be extremely careful about spilling oil or gas around the motorboat, and check it often for leaks.

The smoke you create may not be a great hazard in the infinity of the universe, but an outdoor fire (see **Bonfires**) may give your neighbors high blood pressure. In the long dry season, any sniff of woodsmoke may create fears of bushfires in the area. If you must have a bonfire, at least tell your neighbors in advance. In the height of summer, outdoor fires are an especially bad idea.

Perhaps the commonest form of pollution of which cottagers are guilty is noise. We all underestimate the carrying capacity of sound over water, and we sometimes forget that near neighbors had hoped to make their retreats havens of peace. Teenagers with ghetto blasters, especially, must be reminded of the need for consideration for the human race. In landscape planning, consider the sound absorbtive capacity of thick foliage growing between you and your neighbors to help create mutual peace. Cedars are a good supplement to deciduous trees, whose foliage starts higher from the ground.

What about power boats and water-skiers? The cottage world is divided between those who consider speeding across the lake an expression of freedom and release, and those who look on it as thoughtless ruination of country peace. Rare jurisdictions control the size of motors, but for the most part cottage country is free of such regulation. If you have any kind of cottagers' association, you may wish to develop some rules pertaining to the use of power boats. It may be imprudent to try to restrict the size of motors, which would eliminate water-skiing entirely, but it is surely reasonable to set times for the use of all boats above a certain horsepower, with particular emphasis on their early morning and evening use. The lonely loon should never have to compete with the internal combustion engine.

Not all noise pollution is from the ghetto blaster or the lake. Cottagers may rightly rebel against over-regulation in the country, but an association can encourage people to do their chain-sawing and even grass-mowing on weekdays and Saturdays before the cocktail hour. It is prudent to suggest such measures before the beginning of specific complaints which tend to personalize and embitter rational discussion.

Another small point on sound pollution: many cottagers have security and fire systems with sirens that should be tested occasionally. The annoyance and mental turmoil which such tests may cause can be minimized if it is agreed that they should take place at one specific time — such as noon on any Saturday or Sunday. Then all will know that the sirens do not signal crisis, but prudent maintenance which will soon be finished.

*P*OWER BOATS

You may detect in these pages a small prejudice that power boats, and much power equipment, is justified only when it is a necessary means to an end. The down side is that any internal combustion engine can be extremely irritating to innocent hearers, destroying the hard-won peace of the country and even causing health problems. The irritation caused is related not only to the number of decibels emitted by the machine, but to what it may be doing. A chain saw may whine miserably, but one assumes that the operator runs it through necessity, and is suffering from the noise pollution as much as anyone else. On the other hand, a boater who roars his machine in pointless circles around the lake to fulfill some adolescent urge is probably the area's public enemy number one, and something should be done about it. Even the social costs of water skiing, itself no doubt a worthy sport, should be weighed against the damage a 35 horsepower outboard does to the summer peace of others; perhaps it should be confined in time and place.

Since power boats are the only water craft which harm the peaceful enjoyment of summer, we hope you will consider carefully any decision to buy one. There are two general kinds: inboard and outboard. The inboard powerboat is driven by a stationary engine mounted in the hull, with a drive shaft connecting the propeller at the rear. The outboard boat is propelled by one or more detachable motors with the propellers built into them: they normally clamp on the stern. Big motorboats with a sleeping cabin, galley, and plumbing are called cruisers, but there is no firmly defined line between motorboat and cruiser, or cruiser and yacht. Most popular outboards are from 10 to 18 feet long. Real yachts are usually at least 70 feet, and they may run as large as the Royal Yacht *Britannia*.

The inboard motors have one big advantage for the peace of the neighborhood: per unit of horsepower, they are much quieter than outboards. They are also far more expensive both to buy and to maintain.

If you can reach your cottage only by water, you will probably need a power boat. In that case your requirements will be very special, and you may consider it necessary to have a vessel that will carry everything from the day's milk to a refrigerator to keep it in. Or you may be eyeing one of those remarkable craft that skims just above any water in liquid form, and over land as well.

For the average cottager, a small power boat is a means to go over to the fishing spots or to visit the neighbors at the far end of the lake without excessive exertion. Surely time that is passed gliding along the picturesque lake is not wasted, and speed is therefore a low priority. You could start with an aluminum or fiberglass boat (see **Rowboats**) and add a motor to it. A 1^1/$_2$ horsepower will get you there without even interrupting conversation aboard, and if you want more speed, you can go as high as 9¹/₂ horsepower with these small punts.

If your motor is 10 horsepower or higher you must have a Ministry of Transport licence and a plate defining the load and engine power; the latter will cost you one dollar from any Customs or Ship Safety Office, or Coast Guard headquarters in Ottawa. Regulations in the United States vary from state to state, so it is best to contact your local authority for information. The law also requires that every boat carry a lifejacket or life-saving cushion for each person aboard, two oars or two paddles and a bailer. Be sure to have a rope for both bow and stern, and a short chain to secure your motor.

If you have opted for a small motorboat, you have a choice of an electric or a gasoline motor. The former has a relatively low speed and limited range before its battery must be recharged. On the other hand, it is much quieter, lighter, far easier to start and simpler to maintain. (Compare, by analogy, an electric and a gas lawnmower.) If you expect to use the boat only for relatively short runs at a leisurely pace, the electric motor could be an attractive option.

Over 12 million motorboats use North American waterways each summer, and most of these have outboard motors. They cost much less than inboards, and they are flexible in use. You can slip them onto a variety of small boats, made of wood, flat or molded plywood, aluminum or fiberglass. As need be, you can replace either boat or motor alone. For maintenance you can lift the motor into your workshop or put it in the trunk of the car to go to the expert. It is enormously easier than towing an incapacitated inboard motor to the nearest marina that has repair facilities. For winter you can either do your own standard seasonal maintenance on a portable outboard motor, or leave it with the technician. You and one friend can drag or carry the motorless boat to winter safety. If you have to scrape, sand or paint, you can manage easily indoors or out. Maintenance on the hull of the inboard motorboat is much harder because it is usually larger and always more awkward to handle. Unless you are leaving it at a marina, you also have the problem of removing it from the water, and transporting it by trailer to a suitable winter resting place.

Logic, however, should not necessarily interfere with the pleasures of summer, as long as they do not harm others. If you have money to spend on a motorboat of one kind or another, and if it gives more satisfaction than any other self-indulgence, let no one dissuade you. But don't forget safety. In addition to the safety equipment needed for any boat (see **Boating Safety**), be sure you have a fire extinguisher wherever you have gasoline or diesel fuel. Also, be very strict with young people: in any boat they risk harm to themselves, but in a motorboat, not only is the danger of self-inflicted injury high, but they may maim or kill other innocent people.

There are no universal rules comparable to driving regulations for land vehicles. There are no age limits for drivers, nor any form of licensing of pleasure boat operators. Many jurisdictions are clamping down hard on drinking boaters, for it is illegal to operate a boat while impaired. Many organizations, such as the Power Squadrons and the Red Cross, offer training courses which greatly contribute to safety on the water.

Whether or not you take a course, you should be equipped with basic boating regulations, which include rules for the lights that must be carried from sunset to sunrise on either power boats or sailboats. Briefly, you must have a red light to port, green to starboard, and white light adequate for the driver to see other boats or obstacles. The *Boating Safety Guide* also includes rules for steering and respecting right-of-way, whistle signals and the meanings of buoys, and much other safety information. For a free copy, write to Transport Canada, Ottawa K1A 0N5.

PUMPS

There are at least four sources of running water for the cottage.
1. **Rain water** It can be collected in a wooden barrel or clean 40-gallon drum from gutters on the roof. The water can then be moved inside by a hand-operated, old-fashioned pump beside the kitchen sink. Advantages: cheap, picturesque, independent of power supply, soft water. Disadvantages: limited and sometimes dubious supply, not drinkable. Cost: could be as low as $100.
2. **The lake** (or river) Unless you are more than 20 feet above the river, the water can be moved by a shallow well pump.

Advantages: inexhaustible supply, relatively simple and inexpensive system. Disadvantages: not drinkable, vulnerable to early frost. Cost: excluding labor, could be around $500.

3. **Shallow dug well** Advantages: less pipe line to install and maintain, relatively simple and inexpensive system, may be drinkable, but test it first. Disadvantages: depending on water table, supply may not be adequate all summer; some risk of later pollution; finding and digging the well may be quite a chore. Cost: excluding labor, about the same as for the lake.

4. **Deep drilled well** Advantages: safest supply for quality and quantity (if it is drilled deep enough); with insulation on pipe, can be run into cold season; a permanent source if you ever contemplate year-round cottage use. Disadvantages: cost of drilling and of pump is high; most likely to need professional help for repair. Cost: upwards of $12 a foot to drill. (It's a gamble — maybe 100 feet, maybe 500 — the level of the lake has no relevance to the depth of the well.) Then, for a submersible pump installed and connected, expect to pay about $1000.

If you go for the drilled well and it produces a good flow (at least 200 gallons an hour), you need nothing else. If you are worried about its capacity and want added fire protection, you could have a deep well and use the lake; or combine a shallow well for drinkable water with a lake-water system. Rainwater is of limited use as a supplement, because if a shallow well goes dry, chances are so will the rain barrel. If you consider a shallow well, do not be cynical about asking a water diviner to find a source for you. These people do not advertise in the yellow pages, but diligent local questioning may put you on their track. Whatever your opinions about country folklore, water diviners have an astonishing record of success.

Since most cottagers depend on the lake, since deep well systems are generally under the tender care of a friendly plumber, and since the technology of a shallow well is just about the same as for a lake, we will dwell briefly on the lake system for the do-it-yourselfer who is starting out.

Before buying the equipment, the first thing you must know is the exact vertical height between the surface of the water source and the top of the water pump in its final installation. You can work out that distance with your own makeshift survey equipment. Find one 5-foot piece of straight scrap lumber of any dimension, one longer (6 to 10 feet) piece of straight lumber of any dimension, a spirit level, a short stake and a buddy. Put the short piece vertically at the actual shoreline and the longer piece absolutely horizontal (with the spirit level) on top of it, so that you can sight along the slope towards the cottage. At the point on the ground, or on the cottage wall, that you see as you sight along the horizontal board, have your buddy put in the stake. If you are not yet up to the cottage, move your gear up to the stake, and do it again until you reach it. Now add up those 5-foot units and the bit at the end, and add another couple of feet to allow for the summer drop in lake level. If the cottage is more than 20 feet above the river, you will still want to know roughly the vertical lift, but accuracy is not critical. Roughly estimate the length of pipe from the lake to the pump. With the aid of a chart, which should be free, the dealer will recommend the pump and motor you need.

If your height is over 20 feet, you will need a deep well pump, which is a bit trickier to prime and maintain than a shallow well, plus double pipe from the source to the pump. You can put the pump part way down the hill so that the pump is drawing from a shorter height, but that is rarely a good idea. You will lose pressure in the system (about half a pound for each vertical foot of push) and it is often a nuisance to have the pump far from the cottage. The two pipes from the pump to the lake are of different sizes; if you have a very long horizontal distance, you can reduce the resistance somewhat by using an adapter to step up the smaller pipe so they are both the same, then stepping it down again at the pump. We hope you are consulting a reputable supply dealer who will give you good free advice on your specific situation. Don't step up the pipe unless you are so advised. If you do, your first task on fitting it will be to spray-paint an identifying mark on both ends so that you do not confuse the two identical pipes and misconnect them at the pump.

With all the equipment unloaded from the car, you can start down at the lake. The intake must always be below the surface, no matter how low the water level drops in the summer, yet it must not be too near the bottom, where sand may be picked up. The best installation point is, therefore, a buoy (see **Buoys**) with the intake hooked just under it. From the foot valve you will have either one or two pipes, depending on whether it is a shallow or deep well. Be sure that the foot valve is well secured with at least two tight clamps. There is a lot of pressure there, and that is the one place where you cannot spot a leak.

Just above the point that the pipe leaves the lake, we recommend that you cut the pipe or pipes and insert a valve or valves ($1^1/_2$- or $1^1/_4$-inch). Ordinarily they will remain open at all times, but if you have trouble with the foot valve out in the lake, you can close the valve(s) and fix the foot valve without draining the whole system. That trick will cut your tedious priming time by about eighty percent.

Go straight to the pump. Although covering the pipe with earth will protect it from the sun and porcupines, which are not the best things for plastic, you will also find it harder to detect leaks when it is underground. Do not bury the pipe until you are sure the system is working well. Ideally, you will have no dips where water can freeze in winter and split the pipe. Also, the nearer you come to a perfectly level line without dips, the easier will be the priming. Take some time with pick and shovel to even off the high places and fill in the low. By this time you will be sweating with tension and much else, and porcupines love the salt in sweat; if you have any porcupines, we recommend that you always handle your outdoor pipe with clean gloves. Now you can connect the one or two lines to the pump.

You can save yourself trouble when priming if, just before the pipe reaches the pump, you insert a T-clamp to which you attach a vertical galvanized pipe from 8 to 12 inches long, equipped with a cap. If you attach that outlet pipe with the valve to the tank, you can test the system even before the plumbing in the cottage has been done. (See **Plumbing**.)

To prime, undo the cap on the vertical pipe you have just installed, and pour water into it with a funnel. If the lake is far away, and if you have two pipes, this process requires much patience (unless you have a secondary system such as a rain barrel or shallow well to feed it). When the obscene burping seems to stop and the water rests at the top of your vertical pipe, cap it by hand-turning (a wrench is unnecessary until the pressure builds up), and turn it on. Don't expect the needle on the dial to jump obediently the first time — there is probably more air to clear. When nothing seems to be happening for about 30 seconds, switch off, and pour in more water. Your pump may be equipped with an adjustable screw which governs the size of the intake — just follow the directions in the manual. Close it down at first, and open it to get maximum flow without losing pressure. If the needle keeps trembling violently, you still have air in the pipe. You may be able to clear this small amount by leaving the pump running, and easing off the cap until water and air spit out of it. When the needle is steady within its proper limits, tighten the cap with a pipe wrench. There is an art to it, which the keen student will soon master.

The pump switch is probably set so that it will cut off when it reaches about 40 pounds pressure, and turn on when it drops to 25. Leave it that way unless you need extra pressure to go up a hill, for higher pressure is an invitation to leaks. If you must change the pressure, do it by adjusting the two screws in the switch box.

With luck, you will not have to touch that pump again until you drain it in autumn. When cold weather comes, thorough draining is your protection against costly repairs. Open the drain cock for the tank to empty and detach the incoming line(s). Look for a small drain cock at the bottom of the pump, and open it. Run the pump dry for just a few seconds. Remove the line from the lake, detach the foot valve assembly, take it apart, clean and dry it thoroughly for winter storage. Try to get rid of all water in the line, if necessary by lifting it where it still lies in low places.

If the pump ceases to produce water in mid-season, the most likely faults are a leak in the line or sand in the foot valve. If you suspect a leak, before disaster strikes close the valve leading to the cottage so that no water is being used, and turn off the electricity for an hour. If you lose pressure, remedial action is called for.

First, inspect the whole line for signs of a leak. If you find none, close the valve or valves you thoughtfully installed by the water's edge, and pull the pipe and foot valve out of the lake. Take off the screen and thoroughly clean the diaphragm and spring with a small brush and a pail of clean water. Place the valve on a board (not in the sand) on the dry beach, and open the valve(s). When the water rushes down to the foot valve it should not leak out. If there is still a dribble, check the tightness of the clamps on the line, and possibly add new ones. When that is in order, put the pipe and foot valve back in the lake, and prime again. Chances are very high that you will now get water. If you don't, it is a case for the pump expert.

R

R_{AFTS}

For sunbathing and unspectacular diving, the best kind of raft is a cedar frame on floats. It is easily built, light to carry or propel, long-lasting with minimum maintenance, and reasonably stable. Those advantages usually justify the cost of the materials.

Eight feet by four feet is a size which will carry four adults easily without being too monstrous to handle. You will need two styrofoam floatation units (96 × 20 × 7 inches) the cost of which may horrify you (about $45 each); three pieces of 2 × 6 cedar 8 feet long, about 108 feet of 1 × 4 cedar (or 144 feet of 1 × 3) in lengths of 8, 12 or 16 feet, a pound of galvanized 2-inch nails; less than a pound of galvanized 3¹/₂-inch nails; a galvanized steel ring with a screw for wood; and whatever length of ¹/₄-inch polypropylene rope strikes your fancy. Avoid substitution. Any wood other than cedar, unless it is pressure treated, will rot too quickly, and pressure-treated wood is heavier than cedar.

You make the frame with two 8-foot pieces of 2 × 8 on the sides and two 42-inch long pieces nailed inside at the ends. That means the sides, from outer edge to outer edge, are 45 inches apart. Saw just enough off the ends of the floats to let them fit snugly in the frame. Put 4-foot 1 × 4 (or 1 × 3) slats diagonally across each corner on the bottom to hold in the floats, to keep the frame a true rectangle, and to save wear when the raft is dragged over ground. Turn it upside down, check that the corners are still at right angles, and nail down the 4-foot 1 × 4 slats with 1 inch between each; they can extend 1¹/₂ inches beyond the 2 × 8s. See that the nails are well set in, with a nail set if necessary, for in the blazing sun a protruding nail head can feel distinctly hot. Now you can screw in the eye at one end, attach the rope, and you are ready to announce your triumph. If building the raft takes more than part of an afternoon, something is wrong. To fix it in place, make an anchor from either an angular rock or a cement block (8-inch or larger) on a piece of stouter rope or light chain attached to the eye. You can also attach the raft to a buoy. (See **Buoys**.)

There are all sorts of alternatives to the cedar raft. The old-fashioned kind is built with three or four logs or old railway ties that are 6 to 8 feet long. Don't cut down a tree and expect the logs from it to float well; the wood should be well dried, and allowed to redry by pulling the raft clear of the water in the non-swimming season. Stabilize the logs by driving 6-inch spikes through cross pieces made of saplings or 2×4s, and put boards or saplings on top. It is picturesque and cheap, but it is very heavy to propel or to lift onto the beach, and it will tip or sink down at the edges far more easily than the kind with flotation devices.

You can make a more spectacular design from watertight 40-gallon drums, with a diving board or even a diving tower on top. The main problem is to secure the drums tightly to a frame with heavy stranded wire and proper U-fasteners. It is not enough to wire each drum to the frame; the drums must be tightly secured to one another with wire or with a wooden frame. Because of the height, you cannot make a small raft that will be stable. We suggest six barrels supporting a

frame 8 feet by 12 feet. That should take a diving board. As for a diving tower, only testing the raft and weighing the divers will tell how high a tower can go without risk of capsizing the raft. If you were thinking of half-measures — using half-size drums or 20L tins — consider whether you would not be just as well advised to buy the stable and unsinkable flotation material described in the first raft model.

If you crave sophistication, a winter project that will keep you home most nights is one stage up from a raft: a pedal boat. The airtight platform is made from marine plywood glued to a frame. The motive power comes from pieces in the bicycle repair shop. We once had a design from a library book, modified by examination of a factory-made bicycle boat. What we best remember about that design were those 560 brass screws that whiled away many winter evenings. The extraordinary thing about that homemade boat was that it worked, and it never leaked a drop of water until it was retired.

RAINY DAYS

For adults at least, the first rainy day may provide a welcome rest. It cools the air, gives nourishment to thirsty flora, cuts the dust and puts a new twist on the art of relaxing. Successive rainy days can be trying.

You may want to spend the rainy daylight hours catching up on your reading. If your conscience requires that part of the time be devoted to something productive on your long agenda, you could consider:
- catching up on the preparation or amendment of that manual of cottage living you always intended to prepare. (See **Manuals**.)
- making lists. They are a great moral excuse for labor. Lists of things you want to buy on the next trip to town, and the next time you win the lottery. Check out all supplies from sugar to nails and screws;
- reviewing with the family all safety precautions, including fire, boating, and first aid;
- cleaning and maintaining small motors;
- oiling all door and window hinges (bet you never thought of that);

- making that tight window or door fit properly;
- caulking, which keeps out both cold and mosquitoes;
- preparing detailed plans for the next big carpentry project;
- repainting the rusty barbecue;
- any job you've been awaiting a rainy day to finish.

That should get you through the monsoon season. When you start looking for less physically active pursuits, you can turn to cards, or consult that book of adult games you thoughtfully brought. You could, finally, take up the painting of brilliant canvases, except that you probably did not bring materials. But lack of materials gives no excuse for not launching a career in writing. If you feel self-conscious about penning a great short story, persuade other members of the family to join in friendly competition, with the results to be read aloud. As a less taxing alternative, a series of limericks will enrich cottage cultural life, especially when sung to the accompaniment of tinkling glasses. We have not forgotten to mention television, but your own inventions for active intellectual sports are bound to pass the time more agreeably and memorably than passive spectating.

Of course, the children present an entirely different challenge. To the board games you have brought, the new games you have discovered in the games book, you can add some of the pastimes you leaned on during the trip up.

If you really do get steady rain for two or three days, don't stretch interior ingenuity too far. It is time to get in the car, go to town, or visit a neighbor similarly suffering. Cabin fever is one disease your local clinic cannot treat.

RENTING

When You are the Owner

The care and handling of tenants at the cottage may require more thought than in the city. If your tenants were found by advertisement, they may turn out to be precious folk who will maintain the place to standards you never dreamed of, or they may be the type who enliven their parties by burning the furniture. Even decent, well-meaning people could leave a trail of disaster behind them. Invidious as it may seem, you should ask for the names and addresses of previous landlords, and follow up on the information. If it is not illegal in your jurisdiction, you may also want to consider requesting from the tenants a damage deposit.

In fairness to yourself and to them, there should be a minimum of surprises. If they have not seen the cottage, show them pictures, warn them of local hazards (rattlesnakes or the Quimsby-Joneses), and tell them what maintenance and other operations they are expected to handle — all *before* signing the lease. If you oversell, you are asking for trouble. The well-being of your property depends not only on the right people occupying it, but also on keeping those people in a cooperative, friendly frame of mind throughout.

Whether you are renting to friends or strangers, you must resign yourself to spending some time on paperwork that will guide your tenants in the operation of your cottage. If you have already prepared a manual (see **Manuals**), you are off to a flying start. If you do not have a manual, now is the time to write one.

Even the best manuals will require some supplement to be useful to tenants. You might want to list the items that you are leaving for the tenants, for example, and what they should remember to bring with them. You should also make clear any elements of maintenance which they can ignore. For example, you should certainly count on going to the cottage at the end of the season to check up, and then you can do the autumn shut-down yourself. Ideally, you should accompany the tenants at the beginning of the season, which also relieves them of the opening-up chores.

Perhaps the manual should also be supplemented by notes on the current condition of some equipment. ("The boat needs refinishing, but it will be all right this season." "If the chain saw is hard to start, take it into the hardware store, for I did not have a chance to tune it up last autumn." "Please bring in the sails and the badminton net to a dry place whenever they are not in use. There are racquets, but you may need more birds.")

Making an inventory is a boring task, but it is less trying and less time-consuming than arguing with the tenants later, or holding grudges against them. As you do the inventory, you may think of precious mementoes that should be packed away to relieve tenants of responsibility for them. On your list, include not only each article, but a column for notes on any deficiencies ("broken rung", "cigarette burn on top"). List the articles in a way that makes it easy for the stranger to find and identify them. (Not "spindleback chair", but "living room: antique solid pine chair with six round spindles.") It is obviously best if you review the list together, but at least give the tenants a copy and ask them to report back within a week if they find any problems with it.

If you expect the tenants to replace consumables they use, say so. Firewood is the main item, but it could also be annoying if you return to seek in vain the basic non-perishable food-stuffs you always expect to be there. If they do not replace these items, at least insist that they list those that you will have to replace.

Problems with mechanical equipment will be minimized if you can appoint a local agent, whether a neighbor or a tradesperson, to help the tenant. If the pump breaks down, you do not want the tenants to be without water, but neither do you want them to run up a $100 charge for someone to turn a valve or change a fuse. If at all possible, ask the tenant to call in your agent before expensive help is summoned from elsewhere.

If the information is not already in your manual, list for the tenants the names of friends and neighbors on whom they can call for help or just company. Don't make your briefing look like a shorter version of the Criminal Code, but convince the tenants that you are trying to help them have a good summer.

If You are a Tenant

Unfortunately, you may not always be dealing with the kind of thoughtful owner described above. Your irreplaceable summer should be worth a fast visit to the property before you sign up. You are at a disadvantage in not being able to seek references, for even if you know any of the neighbors, they cannot be counted upon to give a stranger frank and objective advice which may seem critical of their friend. If you make the visit and talk to the local people, you may get an impression of what life at the cottage will be like. If you rent through a local agent rather than through a newspaper advertisement, you may feel that you are taking less risk.

You have a moral right to ask the landlord for some type of list or manual of operation, for you don't want to spend the summer wondering where things are, how they function and where to get help. You must be furnished with a list of tradespeople you can call on, or an agent to call them for you. You should define clearly the kind of maintenance that you will pay for, and the kind that should be charged to the owner. Try to arrange for authorized kinds of bills to be sent directly from the tradesperson to the owner.

If you have not yet been to the cottage, think of all the equipment you will need, from brandy snifters to sheets and towels. Ask the owner what items will be available for your use. If you plan to extend your stay into the cool seasons, remember to inquire about such creature comforts as electric blankets. How is firewood to be replaced? Is the power already on, and who pays for it? Is the telephone to be switched to your name? In case of dire emergency, where can the owner be reached throughout the season? Are there any local people familiar with the property whom you could employ to help with clean-up and maintenance? Is there any objection to subletting for a week if you decide to travel?

If your stay goes really well, take time to drop a note to the owner. It will help you to secure a return engagement if you want it and will provide you with a reference for other rental projects. Most of all, a thank-you note will make both of you feel good.

RESUSCITATION

There are several means of resuscitating someone who has stopped breathing, but the most important to the cottager are those which can be administered without mechanical aids, but with some knowledge of techniques. Can anything be more important than learning those techniques if there is even one chance in a thousand that you can save a life? Autumn is a good time to ask in the city about a Basic Life Support (BCLS) course, which will show you how to handle a range of life-threatening emergencies. Your doctor, medical clinic or hospital, Red Cross, St. John's Ambulance or YM/YWCA will be able to advise you. At least one member of every family should be a graduate, but why not have adult members take it together? Meanwhile, here is brief guidance on two life-saving techniques. Please practice them with family members.

1. Café Cardiac

The victim, in the middle of a normal meal, is suddenly silent and perhaps unable to cry out or even breathe, because of a food blockage. The situation is life-threatening unless a companion moves in seconds.

Pull the victim to a standing position, with his or her back towards you. Hit the victim hard with an open hand between the shoulder blades to try to dislodge the food blockage. If breathing does not start, wait only a few seconds before repeating. If a third effort fails, grasp the victim from behind around his or her waist with both arms; with great firmness (but not hard enough to crack a rib) squeeze the victim's abdomen in a series of rapid tensing motions until the passage is cleared. Pressure must be applied to the lower sternum by having your thumb and closed fist of one hand in contact with the victim's sternum, while your other hand is placed on top. The increasingly firm pressure should clear the passage.

The crisis could happen anywhere, but with this simple technique, the chances are that in a couple of minutes the victim will have completely recovered and enjoy the rest of the meal.

2. Artificial Respiration

Everyone must know how to do mouth-to-mouth artificial respiration, and have practiced it. Here are the six steps as outlined by the International Red Cross Society.

1. Use rescue breathing when persons have stopped breathing as a result of: drowning, choking, suffocation, excessive drugs, electric shock, heart attack, gas poisoning, smoke inhalation.
2. START IMMEDIATELY. The sooner you start, the greater the chance of success. Apply rescue breathing anywhere: on a dock, on the beach, in a boat, from a boat, standing in water, kneeling in water, on the ground, in a car, on a hydro pole, in a chair, on a bed, on the street. Send someone for medical aid.

3. Open the victim's airway by lifting the neck with one hand and tilting the head back with the other hand.
4. Pinch nostrils to prevent air leakage. Maintain open airway by keeping the neck elevated.
5. Seal your mouth tightly around the victim's mouth and blow in. The victim's chest should rise.
6. Remove mouth. Release nostrils. Listen for air escaping from the lungs. Watch for the chest to fall.

Repeat last three steps 12 to 15 times a minute. Continue until medical help arrives or breathing is restored.

Please remember: these directions could save a life in an emergency, but they are no substitute for enrolment in a BCLS course. Don't take a chance.

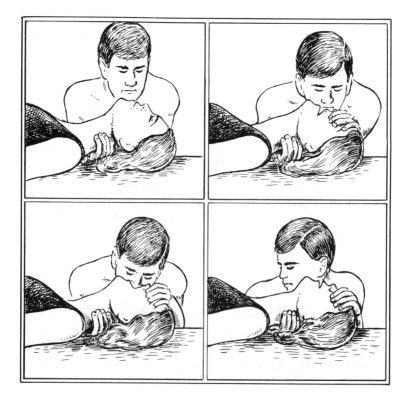

Roads

The condition of the average road into the average cottage is saddening. We don't mean the provincial or county road — which can be improved only by pressuring the local authorities — but the private lane which leads you and your visitors to the cottage itself. Of course, it takes time and some money to improve your road, but the benefits are real:

- In the long run, good maintenance will save money. Not only will you have to spend less on major repairs to the road, but there will be less wear and tear on the vehicles that use it most — namely, yours;
- Delivery people are sensitive to bad cottage roads; they may inquire about their condition, and refuse to use yours unless you can prove that there are no deep ruts or potholes;
- Good roads improve the disposition of new arrivals, both guests and tradespeople.

Some of the work you need may call for heavy equipment but, with luck, such repairs will be necessary only once. Annual maintenance can generally be done painlessly with a grader and gravel truck; or with more pain and less money by pick, shovel, rake and a makeshift scraper which you can make yourself.

You really should start by examining critically the grade of the road. No part of it should be low enough to allow run-off to cross it or flow down it with all your expensive gravel. At the risk of looking foolish, take a walk down your road with an umbrella during the heaviest downpour of the season to see what is happening. Your road should not have sharp dips, large rocks, or sudden crests. It should have a shallow ditch on each side.

To achieve these objectives you may have to install an occasional culvert to carry surface water harmlessly from one side to the other. Although digging the trench for it may seem an extreme form of exercise, that may cause you less trouble and expense than bringing in a backhoe. You do not have to reach Department of Highways standards. An 8- or 10-inch diameter culvert is enough. You have three choices:

- a wooden culvert, which is not hard to make. For the sides and bottom, you may be lucky enough to have readily available cedar logs; otherwise, use 2-inch pressure-treated lumber. The same boards go on top, with a span of no more than 1 foot;
- a galvanized steel culvert, which has a long life when the ground is not permanently damp. It is far lighter to transport than concrete, and you may be able to bring it on the roof rack of your car;
- concrete culverts, which are very permanent and extremely heavy (nearly 400 pounds for each 10-inch diameter piece). The cost difference between steel and concrete is not great. One advantage of concrete is that, since it comes in short lengths (usually about 3 feet), you can easily add to them later when you move up to a four-lane speedway.

If you have not laid a culvert before, remember three points: make it deep enough to allow a minimum of 8 inches of fill on top — preferably more; use a level to see that it slopes in the right direction, and make it long enough. If it comes near the edge of the road, you not only have no scope for widening, but the culvert can itself be a hazard.

If possible, remove sharp crests in the road. If they are caused by huge boulders or bedrock, level out the slope as much as possible. For this purpose, or for filling dips, use the cheapest fill available and be lavish with it. Depending on nearby resources, that could be sand. On top of it put a thick layer — a minimum of 6 inches — of heavier fill such as "pit run", a mixture of stones and gravel which varies in quality according to the pit. Ideally, it should have some clay, but not solid clay. Then top off the whole road with a finishing coat of acceptable crushed gravel.

For any major road rehabilitation, it is certainly worth bringing in a spreader or bulldozer to spread the layers and compact them. This requires coordination of a trucker and a heavy equipment operator, which is not always easy, unless one of the two arranges for the other. The crush run flows easily from the truck when it is not too wet, and a good driver can spread it so that only a modest amount of handwork is needed to even it out when you don't want to contract for a blade. Whether you are using heavy equipment or hand tools, it is important to maintain a crown down the center of the road to throw water into the ditch before it gathers steam and washes out your precious gravel.

When your road is in good basic shape like this, annual maintenance is not hard. Some years you may want to add more top gravel as it disperses to the sides or gets crushed into the lower levels. The main point is never to leave an incipient rut or pothole unattended. Water collects in such holes, the material becomes soft, and deterioration of the road is rapid. Shovelling a bit of loose gravel from the sides into the depressions will fix it. Then run over the whole thing with the grader.

Here are two of the many ways to make a grader. Lay out three old railway ties or heavy (hardwood) logs about 6 feet long so that the outer two logs are about 4 feet apart. Squared lumber is better than round logs. Secure them well with heavy flexible wire or light chain stapled in. Across the top, staple to all three ties a single piece of old chain link fence. Attach to one of the outer logs a piece of chain with a hook at the free end. The length of the chain depends on the vehicle that will tow the device; the grader should end up close to the rear bumper, but you will be attaching it to the frame of the vehicle or to the trailer hitch if there happens to be one. Now turn the whole device upside down, attach it to the vehicle (truck or big car), and you are in business.

Use this grader only after the road has been somewhat softened by rain. For greater effect, you can ask a couple of large but nimble volunteers to stand on the forward log while holding onto the vehicle; this gives a little more pressure. The helper(s) can also aid you in moving the device around when you come to the end of the road.

If you want to be fancier, you can get a local ironworker to make up the same kind of device from scrap steel beams and chain welded to them, omitting the fencing. They are much heavier and keep a relatively sharp edge to dislodge semi-embedded stones.

When your own road is smoothed to perfection with three or four runs, you can make a fortune by hiring yourself out to the local authorities.

ROCKS

The removal of rocks often presents a sort of primitive challenge that may exceed the bounds of reason. Nevertheless, there are many occasions when it is desirable to combine human muscle and brains to remove that stony object before another foot is bashed or car spring broken.

Here we exclude all thought of removing by blasting, strong though the temptation may be. In virtually all jurisdictions, the laws on who can blast and where are rightly strict. Forget it, unless you want to call in a licensed blaster.

For ordinary small rocks apparently weighing only a few tons, the indispensable tools are two long steel bars (properly called 16-pound chisels, if that is the size you select), a 2,000-pound-test winch (commonly called a come-along dolly), some chain or very strong rope, and an old tire.

With all this equipment, almost anything that can be wiggled even slightly with a bar can be moved. First, dig around the object so that you can apply the bar to the lower part. Wasn't it Archimedes who said that if he had a bar long enough he could lift the world? He would have to place a small rock under it to provide leverage, and a buddy to slip a rock into the little gap created as the rock lifts from its resting place. If it is a huge rock, this is where two bars in the hands of two people will help.

If you need even more pressure, bring out the come-along. Loop a chain tightly around some protrusion of the rock to prevent slipping. Attach one end of the come-along to the chain and the other end to a strong tree or even larger rock, and lever up the come-along until it is taking as much pressure as it and you can stand. If that does not dislodge the rock, it will make levering with bars easier. When the rock begins to come out of the ground, the come-along should pull it away with less time and effort than the crowbars need.

What's the tire for? If you want to get the rock right out of the way, or to use it as a buttress beside an eroding road, roll it into the tire, and attach a chain to the tire and to a vehicle. It will drag much more easily and harmlessly than if it is gouging into the ground on its final passage.

Underwater rocks are a tougher problem, despite the seemingly lighter weight of rocks when submerged. The main trouble is that the bottom is likely to be so soft that it is difficult or impossible to place rocks for effective leverage of the bar. Try to scoop out the sand around the rock so that you can get a chain firmly fixed to it, and use the come-along dolly. Of course, the absence of nearby trees may require a very long chain or very strong rope attached to the nearest immovable object, which can serve as an anchor for the come-along. If the rock is simply immovable, you may just have to mark the obstruction with a buoy.

There is one other somewhat bizarre trick which can occasionally work on land. If the offending rock is surrounded by other rock, you may be able to find or make space to insert a strong hydraulic jack, if you have one. As the rock rises, you inset stones until you can move the jack for the next stage, until finally the come-along can take over.

If you must remove that rock, and all hand methods fail, there is still one possible solution short of blasting. It is expensive — as much as $100 an hour — plus transportation. Find a heavy equipment operator whose shovel is equipped with a compressed-air activated chisel to break up rock in small enough pieces to be scooped out by shovel. Unlike blasting, this equipment can work very close to existing structures, and it could be what you need if rock is in the way of a coveted addition to your cottage.

It is worth a little of your time to think about rot, even if you have never found a trace. It is better to take preventive measures now than to wait and take remedial action when the cottage starts to disintegrate.

There are two kinds of rot, both caused by fungus. Wet rot and dry rot turn sturdy wood into lightweight material that crumbles in the hands. Wet rot, not surprisingly, is found in damp places, notably underneath the cottage, around posts or wood sills, possibly where a water pipe near wood has been leaking or even merely sweating, or around a dock. The wood often looks charred. Dry rot is caused by a microscopic fungus whose spores may be carried by air or on clothing. When it gains a foothold, it starts making thin white threads that thicken into sheets.

Both fungi are plants which cannot grow like decent, normal vegetation with water, sunlight and air. To germinate, they must eat wood with at least twenty percent moisture content. The wet rot fungus needs thirty percent and a continued supply of moisture. The dry rot can get its own moisture from the wood. Thus the necessary elements for control of rot are good ventilation, elimination of damp places and treatment of wood with fungicides. Take heart — beating rot is actually easier in a cottage than in a modern air-tight city house.

The most effective preventive measures are taken during construction, or even before it. If you are building on rock, take the extra time to strip away all soil and vegetation. Don't leave anything that will absorb moisture. Before you put sill lumber on a concrete foundation, lay a permanent barrier of 6 mm plastic. If you are insulating the rest of the building, install your vapor barrier very carefully on the room sides of your walls.

Even if your cottage is long since built, perhaps you can still clean up underneath it. Try to avoid storing anything under the cottage. Wood and other absorbent materials are conducive to rot but even metal or concrete may reduce the air circulation. If your cottage is on footings rather than on piers, ensure that there are adequate openings in it for cross ventilation (at least the equivalent of two or three blocks on each side for the small or average cottage). Close off the openings for winter to keep out both snow and animals.

A good test is to go outside right after a heavy rain to see the run-off from your roof. If it is going underneath the cottage, it will be necessary to do some drainage work with pick and shovel to divert it. If you are getting splash on lower wood, consider eavestroughs, which will carry the water harmlessly away and reduce the splash on horizontal pieces like window sills.

If, after all these precautions, you spot areas that still seem damp, coat the wood generously with a preservative basd on pentachlorophenol or zinc napthenate. If you are building, use pressure-treated lumber in those damp places near or below ground level.

If you find any rot, you must cut it out to about 2 feet beyond the infestation and replace the wood, for it could be the mother lode of future trouble. Then lavishly coat all nearby wood with preservative. Be especially careful if you are handling these fungicides in a confined space, for their fumes are toxic. Do not work alone. Do not stay in the confined space more than a few minutes at a time. Use fans to disperse the fumes, especially if there is a risk of them seeping into the interior of the cottage.

Don't be discouraged by the specter of rot. It is neither a common nor an insuperable problem.

ROWBOATS

The rowboat is the great workhorse of cottage water life. It is the safest and most stable of all water craft, capable of carrying large loads of people and things, and decently quiet. It is a friend to fishers and an ideal craft for a family with young children.

For these purposes, rowboats can be defined as all small craft or punts equipped with oars, though they may also have small motors or even sails. They are usually made of wood, aluminum, or plastic. Wood generally has the advantage of lower price, especially if the boat is constructed of high quality plywood with marine varnish finish rather than of individually crafted boards. It takes more maintenance than the other varieties of rowboat, but it is often more easily repaired. The aluminum and plastic boats are lighter to carry and propel over the water, and — barring misadventures — easy to look after. Aluminum boats, though, tend to be noisy and cold.

Like canoes, rowboats come in an infinite number of shapes and sizes. A flat bottom and shallow keel are qualities that provide stability and safety. Of course, a rowboat pointed at the stern as well as at the bow is easier to row, but this type is now relatively rare because so many people wish to be able to attach motors. You may as well have that capacity even if you do not intend to add engine power. Often the boat will be propelled by a single rower, but you may find great advantages in two sets of oars. Not only is the extra power handy if the whole family is along, but children will learn to row well more quickly if guided by an adult on the second set. Besides, many a cottager's idea of heaven is to have two of the youngsters rowing nobly while the Head of the Family sits serenely in the stern manipulating the rudder. The minimum length to accommodate two sets of oars is about 14 feet. If your prospective purchase has brackets for only one set of oars, sit in the second bench to find out if there is room to put in the added pair.

Rarely will a rowboat come equipped with rudder, but this is a highly desirable extra feature that you can craft yourself. A good marine supply shop will sell all the fittings — a pair of pins with brackets which screw onto the rudder, a pair of eyes in which to insert them, and a small flexible plastic stop to prevent the rudder from floating up. These modest steel and plastic trifles may cost up to $30, but it is then easy to construct a simple rudder with a horizontal board at right angles near the top, and a rope to guide it. If the boat is aluminum or fiberglass, you can still use a wooden rudder if you attach the two eyes through the aluminum stern into blocks of wood.

The best form of maintenance for the metal or plastic boat is to avoid bashing it. It is usually relatively easy to bring the boat well onshore when it is not in use. The wooden boat is better left in the water for the summer, so that the wood will not dry excessively, but do not leave it where it may be damaged in a wind. The best technique is to attach it to a buoy just offshore. (See **Buoys**.) As often as once a year, the wooden boat may need sanding and refinishing with top quality marine varnish. Unless the old varnish is in bad shape, you do not have to sand to clear wood until, over the years, you find the boat has accumulated an excessive build-up of varnish.

Oars come in different lengths, varying at least a foot from shortest to longest. The length depends on the width of your boat and on the people most often using it. The longer oars will give greater pulling power, but children may find them awkward. When buying the oarlocks, you have a choice of the older type, which requires drilling through the oar, or a more expensive type, which clamps on with bolts. The latter type enables you to adjust the oars for comfort, and use them elsewhere.

S

SAFETY

Although the recurring safety warnings in these pages may seem to imply the opposite, the cottage is generally considered a very healthy place. An awareness of the risks (many of which also exist in the city) will ensure your intact and happy return to the cottage next year. The major subjects of **Fire Precautions** and **Boating Safety** are discussed separately; here we review other challenges, some of which have been mentioned elsewhere in passing.

Mechanical Equipment

When the sedentary worker is let loose on mechanical equipment, normal prudence may suffer in the excitement. One of those most frightening statistics published each spring is the number of human toes which will be severed by whirling grasscutters left on the lawns of North America in the coming summer. Please do not contribute to the list. Never allow anyone who is not wearing proper shoes to cut grass with a power mower on your property. Steel-toed boots are rather much to ask, though you can buy steel-toed running shoes. At least ban bare feet and open-toed sandals — they are invitations to trouble. If you have procrastinated too long about cutting the grass, and the exhaust chute clogs with a thick green mass, the operator should stop the machine completely before cleaning it out. If stopping for every clog is too time-consuming, carry in one hand a stout stick with which to tap the chute from a safe distance. It is still worthwhile to stop the machine occasionally, and thoroughly clean the underside, but at least it will not be necessary on each row.

Trimmers, which work with a rapidly revolving nylon cord, can whip out stones and leave you limping. When using these machines, always wear proper shoes, socks and long trousers.

When using power-operated clippers, wear either a pair of heavy gloves, or at least a glove on the hand which is not operating the trigger. You can easily forget the clippers' power as you lift a tuft of growth for trimming, and find you have cut more than you intended.

The chain saw is the most lethal instrument on your property. (See **Chain Saws**.) It is a good idea to take two minutes each spring to re-read the safety precautions. Encourage the family to check up on you if you attempt to venture out without proper safety equipment, or when your impatience exceeds your caution. Most mishaps occur toward the end of the day, when fatigue has set in. Don't push yourself too hard. If you lend your saw, be certain that the operator is both experienced and prudent.

The first rule with power carpentry tools is to see that they are kept in top condition. On saws particularly, the guard must work faultlessly, and never be held back with elastic or tape. If you have a table or radial arm saw, never turn on the power without the guard in place — on the former especially, it is an all-too-common practice. When you are feeding small pieces of wood, always use a push-piece to keep your hands far from the blade. On a portable or table saw, sharp blades are less likely to jam and kick. With a belt sander, ensure that the motor has come to a complete stop before putting it down, or it may take off across your bench and wreak havoc. Always wear eye protectors when working with these tools, and for prolonged use, use ear protectors as well.

When using insecticide or fungicide in a pressure sprayer, be careful of the fumes. Not all mixtures are hazardous, but we have yet to encounter one that is positively healthy to breathe. Pump up the pressure before it visibly dwindles so that the mixture shoots far away from you, and stand upwind of your target. Never use these pumps indoors.

Electrical Equipment

Take no chances when working with electrical equipment. Always use the ground plug on any piece of equipment that is provided with one. If you ever feel a trace of shock when handling equipment, or simply when plugging in a light, find the cause and fix it, even if you have to buy a ground tester or call in an electrician. See that all outdoor and bathroom outlets are on ground-fault interrupters. Never take apart electrical equipment, or touch a screwdriver to it, until the power plug is detached.

If an electrical storm or high wind is impending, unplug the audio-visual equipment, computer, intercom and other electronic gadgets. Old-fashioned electric motors (on pumps, for example) also can be damaged in a storm. Even a brief power failure may lead to a surge that could make scrambled eggs of the innards of your electronic equipment. Better still, protect electronic equipment with surge protectors, for in the country the risk of power surges is higher than in the city, and they can happen when you least expect them.

Miscellaneous Hazards

When climbing, you should always have a back-up system which consists of a person or a rope holding the ladder. (See **Ladders**.) Attach an anchored rope to yourself whenever you clean the chimney or work on the roof. Never work on the roof when it is wet, for all rubber soles are slippery when damp. Even climbing a tree can be dangerous — hitch a rope around the branches as you climb in case a dead branch breaks.

Finally, check your liability insurance. You can be sued by workers or even visitors to your property. The nicest people can suddenly grow horns when they sniff money from a legal action. You must beware not just of the risk of a law suit to compensate Aunt Martha for her broken leg which may inhibit her career as a stripper, but the pain and mental torment discovered by her 23 relatives when they contemplate her suffering.

Other Equipment

If you remember nothing else from this book, please memorize the phrase "Always cut towards your buddy." This admittedly anti-social advice can save you untold lacerations, whether you are chiselling wood or carving the roast.

Though it is generally safer to use tools that are sharp, they are a hazard. Even a casual touch of certain pieces of equipment (for example, a pruning saw left on the ground), can be bloody and painful. To be truly safe, wear gloves for all outside operations with saws, axes, crowbars and so on. Please use steel-toed boots when using the axe, whether to fell trees or to split firewood.

Remember the lethal possibilities when you put a wire or chain under tension, whether with a come-along dolly or with a vehicle. For example, you may attach a line to a tree before felling it so that it does not strike power lines or a building. If that line snaps when it is put under heavy tension, it can whip with enough force to sever human limbs. Stand well beyond its range when tightening the line, or protect yourself by staying behind trees or in the vehicle.

Sitting at an office desk is more likely to cause back problems than life at the cottage, provided you do nothing foolish in the country. Practice lifting a heavy object sensibly, by grasping it with knees bent and using the leg muscles instead of the back muscles to straighten up. Watch yourself when prying rocks to ensure that you are erect and not twisted when you apply full pressure.

SAILING

Sailing, like fishing, excites an almost religious zeal in its participants, but the source of the enormous satisfaction is a little easier for the outsider to understand.

Sailing is renowned for its own occult vocabulary, and even if you never own a yacht — or a dinghy — you would be well advised to acquire some knowledge of its language. Otherwise the enthusiastic invitations to come aboard are liable to diminish. Both to feel the full pleasure of sailing (and to keep your host in a good mood), you should also know the basics of what is happening.

The thrill of sailing lies in the use of your own ingenuity, wedded to the technology that others have prepared for you, to harness the wind. You can do it with a raft and a groundsheet attached to a pole in the middle of it. Well, partly — you could go downwind, but it would be a hard paddle back. You can rig a sail on a canoe or rowboat, and learn to make slow progress upwind as well as down. In fact, there is much to be said for encouraging young people to go through these stages to gain an understanding of the elements of sailing, before you present them with a more costly boat. If you want to learn the basics yourself, you might be well advised to practice with a small dinghy for a season, before advancing to the level of your ambitions. Then you can further your education by a combination of service in an experienced friend's sailboat and your own experimentation.

The Language

If you ever expect to set foot in a sailboat, you probably will want to know at least these few terms.

boom	the horizontal pole at the bottom of the mast at right angles to it.
bow, stern	please! not front and back
centerboard	a movable fin with the same purpose as the keel
forward, aft	up there in the bow; back towards the stern
gaff	the pole (rare in pleasure boats) at the top of the mast
halyards	lines to raise and lower the sails
hull	body of the boat
jib	small triangular sail forward of the mainmast
keel	fixed flat strip along the length of the hull to lessen side drifting
leeboards	a pair of fins on either side of a sailing canoe for the same purpose as the centerboard
lines	ropes
mainsail	the main sail
mast	the big pole holding the main sail; if there is more than one, it is the *mainmast*; the shorter one towards the stern is the *mizzenmast*; the *foremast* is towards the bow
port, starboard	not left and right, as you stand in the stern and face the bow
rudder	vertical metal or wood piece at the stern for steering
running rigging	all the lines used to adjust the sails and booms
sheets	lines used to adjust *(trim)* the sails
shrouds	lines from sides of boat to mast

spars	all the poles supporting the sails
spinnaker	balloon-shaped sail, often made of colored nylon, used when sailing downwind
stays	lines from bow to mast
tiller	lever attached to the rudder

The sailboats themselves are classified according to size and rigging into *catboats, sloops, yawls, ketches* and *schooners*. The most common types seen in cottage country are the catboat, with a single mast far forward in the bow and only one sail, and the sloop, with one mast nearer the middle and a jib as well as mainsail. There are hundreds of classes of catboats and sloops. All the boats in each class are built alike, for example, the *Snipe* (the most popular sailboat in the world), the *Penguin*, the *Lightning*, and the *Star*. Thus, people can race each other with only the human factor separating them.

The boat's direction is controlled by the rudder, aided by the centerboard, which keeps it from skidding. A deep keel would serve the same purpose, but it would prevent you ever bringing your boat into the shallow waters by your dock; hence the centerboard, which can be raised and lowered. Sails are designed like airplane wings with a curved edge; on a sail, the *leeward* side (away from the wind, as opposed to the *windward* side) is like the top of the plane's wing. The wind blowing across it creates a pull towards the bow, while the wind is also blowing like crazy against the windward side of the sail. That spells happiness. With these two forces, you can go 45 degrees on each side of the wind direction, but you obviously cannot sail straight into the wind. You can do one of three things.

You can sail towards the wind (*tack to windward*) up to that critical 45-degree angle. If you gradually turn too far into the wind, the sail flaps (*luffs*), the boat stops and it is really rather embarrassing if anyone is watching. The skill comes in feeling unexpected little changes in the wind, taking full advantage of them, and not being caught at the wrong angle. Sailing across the wind (*reaching*) gives the greatest speeds and the exciting sensation of almost lifting out of the water. Sailing with the wind (*running*) is considered pretty tame. The sail is let out at right angles to catch all the wind, (with the jib *swung out* on the opposite side, or a spinnaker ballooning out, if you have either).

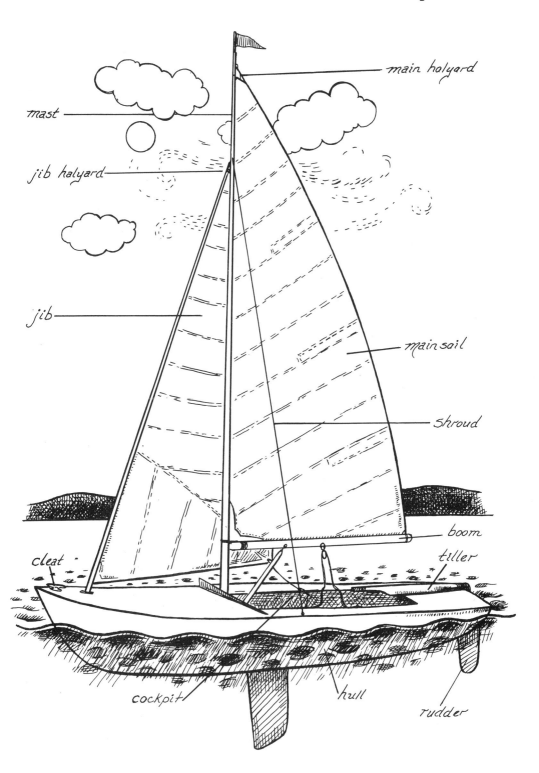

main halyard

mast

jib halyard

jib

main sail

shroud

boom

cleat

tiller

cockpit

hull

rudder

The art of sailing lies in steering the boat in relation to the wind and *trimming* the sails to take every advantage of it, tightening to get the full available force, slacking off to keep the boat from blowing over, and adjusting the placing of weight (mostly people) to preserve the ideal angle for the wind. If you are neatly tacking to windward, you cannot go on forever or you will hit the far side of the lake. Eventually you have to turn the bow smartly so that the wind crosses it; this is known as *coming about*, the commonest and simplest of sailing maneuvres, when the boom and sail shift quickly to the other side of the boat. If you try the same thing with the stern to the wind, it is called *jibing* and is certainly not recommended until you are a very good sailor. If you don't capsize, the boom, swinging at the speed of light, can knock you out.

Of course, harnessing the forces of the wind is not without its hazards. Sailors should always wear life jackets. Capsizing is an eventuality which even the novice sailor should be prepared to take with aplomb. The novice must keep alert to avoid the swinging wood and taut ropes. Good sailors can be very bad tempered if their underlings do not move with frantic alacrity when the need is evident (to the master) or when sharply bidden.

When you are sailing alone, falling out of your craft is undesirable, for it is discouraging to watch from the middle of the lake as your boat recedes over the horizon. Your first instinct should be to keep an iron grip on the mainsheet, which will not only help you to climb aboard again, but will spoil the even course of your empty boat. Possibly the worst thing you can possibly do when alone is temporarily lash down the mainsheet and even fix the tiller in place while you reach for a beer. If you fall overboard, the boat is likely to sail better and faster and farther than ever before, searching for a new owner when your estate is settled.

SAUNAS

Do you really want to build a sauna? Since the July temperature in the great outdoors may seem to provide a sauna free-of-charge, sauna owners tend to use them little in the summer months. But if your cottage stay stretches to autumn or, even better, through the winter, the sauna can add a new dimension to cottage life.

Let's look at the purpose of having a sauna before thinking about building one. The object of the exercise is to sit with maximum exposure to maximum dry heat for the maximum time, then to plunge into maximum cold. A cold shower or frigid lake will do, but the very best plunge is into soft snow. The effect of total well-being among those who survive is too extraordinary to be described in words.

Some people favor a humid sauna, which is achieved by spraying water on the hot rocks, although there are those who deplore this variation as an imitation of a Turkish steam bath. Even Finns, to whom we must defer in all things related to the sauna, use some water — they call the process *loyly*. The main reason for keeping everything quite dry is that the body can tolerate higher temperatures in low humidity, and so the purists claim that any water reduces the total heat potential. Owners of saunas may tend to sympathize with the purists, for the introduction of water raises the possibility of more maintenance problems, including rot, rust, smell and higher wear on heater parts subject to violent temperature changes.

It is well to decide which regime you prefer before starting construction. If you expect to use water, you will have to take more precautions against rot. Bear in mind that you cannot use any kind of chemical fungicide on any wood near the sauna because of the risk from fumes in the confined space. There is no choice in the lining of the room: it must be cedar. If there is going to be much water around, you should consider using cedar also in the framing of walls, ceiling and floor. Otherwise, construction-grade spruce is satisfactory.

The biggest factor to consider in designing the room is heat conservation. It is not just a matter of wasting electricity. You want a room which heats up reasonably quickly, which does not lose heat excessively when the door is opened, and which quickly regains its proper temperature again after the door is closed, so that the patrons do not sit around shivering. That means framing thick enough for R-28 fiberglass insulation. We favor it over rigid foam, which is flammable and which, under high heat, may start to melt and lose its value. You will be glad if you overbuild for super-insulation, and install a heater a size larger than the unit rated for the room's cubic capacity.

The practical place to put a sauna is usually in, or attached to, the cottage, rather than in a separate building. This will ease the problems of heat conservation, paticularly in cool weather, because the door will open into a normal room temperature rather than to the chilling outdoors. It should be close to the shower and preferably have a nearby outside door through which you really can run to the lake or snowdrift. If you expect your saunas to be social occasions, you may want to install more than one shower. Even among the friendliest of folks, only so many can effectively use one shower simultaneously.

As to size, you wish to aim for the smallest possible space to accommodate its probable clientele. We leave you to add such input as how many friends you really have or how close they are in the figurative and literal sense. The sauna is not a place for distance or privacy. If you make it larger than necessary, it will not heat as efficiently, and you may have more frustration achieving the right temperature. In a room 10 feet × 4 feet × 6 feet 6 inches high, we have seen as many as 15 comfortable patrons.

The construction of the heavily insulated walls, floor and ceiling is conventional. The walls and ceiling must be lined with cedar V-joint or tongue and groove, with the nails properly concealed in the tongues or, when necessary, well countersunk. The floor, being cooler, can be made of plywood covered with indoor/outdoor carpeting, but of course cedar, without grooves, would be better.

We assume you will use an electric heater, which is far more efficient, simpler to operate, safer and smaller than a wood-, charcoal- or coal-burning stove. The rated heater for 300 cubic feet is 5,000 watts and 240 volts; therefore, you might buy a 6,000 watt unit (designed for 400 cubic feet). Place it beside the door, surrounded by stout railings of cedar to avoid *any* possibility of bodily contact with it.

The need for two benches, one lower than the other, is evident because some people will want to start low and cool. The benches don't have to be facing one another, or in steps as in a commercial establishment. One can be three feet directly above the other, with the lower one slightly wider to serve as a step when climbing higher. Use 2 × 3 cedar for the benches, with spacings of at least 1½ inches to allow the heat to circulate. Unless the customers are all likely to be agile, make a simple ladder. Be especially careful about the solidity of your construction, because if anything came loose from excess weight or sudden movement, someone could lose balance and strike the heater.

The door requires special ingenuity in design to be as well insulated as the walls and to fit snugly with an air trap. For safety, as well as space, it must open outwards. The handles must be of wood, and no metal fittings should show on the hot side. On the inside it can have a simple wooden latch pivoting on a screw, strong enough to let the users close the door tightly, but flimsy enough that someone on the outside could yank it open in case of suspected emergency. Similarly, on the outside there should be no padlock and no latch strong enough to withstand a firm push, in case the door is inadvertently latched while the sauna is in use.

If the sauna is annexed to the cottage, we suggest installing a fan which, after sauna use, will use the hot air to heat the building. When the sauna is not being used, the door should be left ajar for ventilation.

Your sauna is working well if, whatever the outside temperature, it will reach 190°F within 30 minutes, and regain that temperature within five minutes of the patrons entering. For success, you need not only good construction, but discipline. All the users must be ready to leap in when the door is opened, and the designated last person must be ready to slam it shut. Those showing signs of chickening out early should be encouraged to sit on the floor to await the hardier users rather than to wander in and out. If you are considering drinking beer in the sauna, as has been known to happen, provide yourself with styrofoam insulated containers to hold the bottles. Don't use beer tins: the ads tell you they chill more quickly, but they forget to mention how quickly they warm up.

Come to think of it, a sauna *is* a good idea to stretch the season of cottage enjoyment.

SECURITY

As any security expert will explain, the needs of every property are different. Nevertheless, we can generalize about most cottages.

Let's start with the assumption that it is impossible to make the average cottage completely secure against robbery and vandalism. Trying too hard to do so, with steel window bars and enormous locks, may be counter-productive if it suggests that your cottage is a place worth robbing. On the other hand, it is not a good idea to leave the place completely open. A reasonable compromise is to acquire a system which scares off young offenders — cottage country's main problem — without attracting the particular attention of professional thieves.

Bear in mind, too, that the purpose of a security system is not only to protect your property during your absence. Break-ins can occur during the summer, usually when the burglar wrongly concludes that the place is vacant. A security system can deal with these people. When someone is staying alone at the cottage, the existence of a security system can be a real comfort.

There are three common kinds of security system, and many variants. Point protection, designed to protect one object — such as a safe — is unlikely to be used in a cottage. A perimeter system generally is placed on all doors and windows, the opening of which breaks a circuit and triggers an alarm. This is tedious to install, but is the cheapest form of protection, and does not sound false alarms caused by wind, the dog, cat, or itinerant squirrels. The simplest system for cottages is usually area protection, which emits ultrasound or microwaves whose interruption by a moving object triggers the alarm. Infrared, by a somewhat different approach, does the same job.

With good advice from a reliable dealer, installation can be a project for the do-it-yourselfer. If you decide on area protection, the heart of the system will likely be an ultrasound device that looks like a small radio, or an infrared unit, which is even smaller. Either is placed in the main room inconspicuously on a shelf or mounted on a wall, facing the likeliest point of entry and path of an unwanted entrant. It may be run on 12 volts or 120; in either case it is plugged into the normal electric circuit, the latter having a small transformer as an add-on or within the unit itself. If you want the system to work when your power is turned off for the winter or otherwise interrupted, you can have a 12-volt battery backup. If you want that back-up, be sure to ask if a used 12-volt car battery will work, or if you must buy a dry cell battery, which costs perhaps three times as much.

You must also have a siren, preferably placed (above the ceiling, facing out a roof ventilator, for example) so that it emits a colossal noise to be heard inside and out. The final essential element is a switch.

With this basic system, you can turn on the security by a not-too-obvious switch, have a time lapse (often about 30 seconds) to let you go out the door or into a room beyond its reach before it goes off. When someone uninvited moves across the range of the little box, the siren will sound and then shut off automatically after a fixed time (usually about four minutes). Conversely, when you come in, you have about 30 seconds to reach for the switch to avoid announcing your arrival to people across the lake.

One limitation of this system is that false alarms can occur, usually caused by animals that wander into or around the cottage at night. Nothing can be done about that except to try to exclude them from its path. You may be able to point the box in such a way that animals can walk sedately across the floor without fear of having the daylights frightened out of them and you. If you are away, the sound of the alarm may echo up and down the countryside without being heard by any human being. It is still likely to frighten away most evil thinkers, for they do not know whether your system is also connected by phone line to a security office or the local constabulary (which, for a price, you can usually arrange).

You should test the system periodically, but be sure that all neighbors within range know in advance, or they will never take a real alarm seriously. If you can persuade your neighbors to install similar systems, your area may acquire a reputation as a good place for thieves to avoid. If you do have such a cooperative effort, set a weekly or monthly time for all tests, to avoid unnecessary sound pollution or disturbed citizenry.

Even if you do install such a security system, do not put all your reliance in it. If you are going out for an evening or a day or two, set lights with timers, as you do in the city, to create an illusion of occupancy. If you have a postbox or newspaper box, ask someone to empty it daily so that your absence will not be advertised. Don't leave unnecessarily informative notes on the door. ("Sheila — Gone till Thursday. Key under the mat.")

Our final advice needs only the effort of making simple but eloquent signs which strike at an almost universal weakness in human kind. Around your property post notices: "Beware poisonous snakes."

SEPTIC SYSTEMS

Don't turn the page just because a septic system may still be, so to speak, far down the road for you. If you do not have one, there is probably a good chance that you or your heirs may eventually decide to take the plunge. A little advance planning may save trouble when you do.

Most municipalities accept "non-conforming" facilities, that is, an outhouse or other below-standard system if it is already in place, but (except in remote regions) they will not let you install anything that is below urban standards. It is common to require you to have one acre of land, so that there is enough space for a septic disposal field, but in some places half an acre is the accepted minimum. Since the principle of the system is to let fairly clear liquid drain out into the soil, the nature of your ground cover is critical. Sand will give you the least trouble, and if you have heavy clay or rocks, you will probably be told to import enough fill for the whole installation — an expensive operation. With an authorized septic system you can, with a little more care, handle anything your city sewage lines will take — except the effluent from a kitchen sink garburetor.

When you decide on a septic disposal system, most of your questions will be answered for you by municipal requirements. In some jurisdictions, you are required to begin by employing a consulting engineer to prepare a plan, which must be submitted for approval before a building permit is issued. Elsewhere, a contractor can do the design and acquire the permit.

Since a septic system requires considerable expenditures — upwards of $2,500 — you may wonder whether you can do it yourself. Theoretically, yes, but it is a major undertaking. Depending on the terrain, it requires extensive excavation, carefully layered fill, the installation of a very awkward tank (probably placed with heavy equipment), the laying of drainage pipes with extreme care, covering the pipes and shaping the surface. In the unlikely event you want to do it all yourself, consult the local authority that normally inspects work-in-progress at least three times. Unless they are sympathetic to your desire for self-reliance, you may encounter extreme difficulties. If you are thinking seriously about doing the job yourself, familiarize yourself with all of the requirements from your local authority, and borrow a library book on how to lay it all out.

Should you decide that your main role is to hold the chequebook, you will still have some planning to do. You can somewhat reduce the cost by site preparation before you call in a contractor to give estimates. You can remove all the trees, including roots, on the site of the drainage field, and cut down trees within 10 feet of its outer edges. You may know a local back hoe operator who will excavate more cheaply than the main installer. Then, if at all possible, you should get more than one estimate for installation; and do not ask at the height of the construction season. If you find that your local inspections are very careful, you do not have to worry so much about the quality of the installer's work, but you may be concerned with the timing. Try to arrange for guarantees, and ensure that the phased payments the contractor is likely to demand still leave a strong incentive to finish the job promptly. Also be very clear about the work stops, so that you do not have an installer stop at the tank and the plumber stop at the house, with a yawning gap between.

If the contractor is doing the whole job, be precise about what to do with the trees and rocks that are removed. If you want trees taken off the site, or cut for firewood with branches disposed of, you will have to explain it to the contractor, or you will be left with an ugly pile of wood and a new disposal problem. If there is much rock and gravel to excavate, decide with the contractor where it will go. Specify exactly what kind of surface will be left: does the contract call for a finishing coat of topsoil? If so, what will be its depth and quality? The inspector will be concerned that the final surface is shaped to drain properly, but is unlikely to care whether grass can ever grow on it.

When you begin your planning, one of your first decisions should be the site of the installation. The tank itself must be a minimum of 50 feet from your water supply, but it can be as close as 3 feet from the cottage. No part of the disposal field can be closer than 100 feet to the lake or well. The size of the field varies with your establishment, but for an average cottage (say, 3 bedrooms) you may be thinking of something like 40 feet by 13 feet. Not only must the site be free of trees for all eternity, but no roadway must pass over it, no car park on it, no building sit on it, and no main pathway run over it. You can, of course, encourage grass or flowers to flourish on it if good topsoil has been provided.

The tank may be steel or concrete, but the latter is more common and lasts longer. When choosing a site for it, remember that it will have to be emptied every three or four years. Therefore, you should not only know where its top is, but be certain that it is reasonably accessible. It should not be more than 50 feet from the nearest access for the pump truck.

Once the system is in, there is likely to be little trouble or expense to maintain it. Be careful about what is put into it. Warn your guests not to use the toilet for garbage disposal, and particularly not for tobacco. You will stretch the time between emptyings if you provide the washroom with a separate enclosed container for used paper, which is then burned or buried rather than flushed into the tank. If you get any whiff of suspicion that the decomposition is not working as it should, buy from your hardware store or plumber some pills which nourish the little microbes and put them in a good mood; then drop one down the toilet once a month even when the smell has gone.

An ordinary septic tank should have its sludge emptied every two years, before it starts to muck up your drainage field, but at the cottage with only seasonal use, every three or four years should be often enough. But don't forget it. Eventually — between 15 and 25 years — you will probably have to dig up the lawn and clean or replace all the perforated pipes. Be prepared for a mess. People don't usually undertake this task until there are clear signs that the liquid is ceasing to drain from the tank, and your cottage drains no longer work. Please accept this warm expression of our sincere sympathy.

SIGNS

The number and quality of signs needed to identify your cottage depend very much on your circumstances. If you have a long lane in from the main road, punctuating the uncertain distance with signs is a comfort which strangers will appreciate. You must also operate under the eternal law of cottage directions: if there is any conceivable possibility of visitors taking a wrong turn, they will.

On even a modest site, signs may be a thoughtful gesture for strangers. You might never think of labelling your tool shed until you glimpse a guest making a furtive and desperate dash towards it instead of to the privy. We can't even advise you on the protocol in such a situation.

The quality of signs depends on your own standards. Among the best are letters incised into a cedar or pine board, with the letters painted in black, and the board coated with a marine varnish or Varathane-type finish. If you have a router, a kit for signs and patience, it is not hard to do. After a couple of years the wood itself may have darkened so much that the letters no longer stand out — in five minutes you can machine-sand the face back to raw wood and refinish the sign.

Plastic letters have made do-it-yourself signs much simpler. They should be from $2^{1}/_{2}$ to 3 inches high to mount on a board no smaller than a nominal 1×4. The common type of letter, which has adhesive on the back, will drop off unless the wood has a very smooth finish. You can buy pieces of thick plastic to substitute for wood, or paint a board with undercoat and two coats of good quality enamel — with light sanding between coats.

A variant on that system is computerized lettering. The right shop will set up all your letters in just about any size, and space them so that you need only stick down the strip. This technique may be worth the trouble and higher cost if you are using more than one word on a sign, if you want really prominent notices, or if you want to combine letters with other symbols like arrows. They are guaranteed to last five years in all weather.

And, of course, you can go to a sign painter. Maybe, though, you have a natural facility. Most people make signs before they can talk.

SNOW

Though one of the main objects of cottaging is to push snow farther down into the recesses of your mind, it is well to think of it for just a few minutes before the summer ends.

Your main concern may be whether any precautions are needed if next winter breaks all records for snowfall. You would naturally prefer that your roof not collapse, but a heavy snowload can also bow down your roof without causing any visible disaster. This can be more of a problem in the country because cottages are often more lightly built than city houses, and have no heat in winter to melt off some of the snow on the roof. (Conversely, the absence of interior heat frees you of the city curse of ice build-up above the eaves.)

One solution is to hire a really reliable local person to shovel your roof when necessary. The need will depend not only on the

total depth of snow, but also on the weather. High winds during or just after a heavy snowfall may remove much of the mass from the roof without the touch of human hands. A thick layer of snow may do no harm until a very rainy thaw greatly increases the weight on your roof. Your local person should understand these things and use good judgement about when to act.

The second solution is winter roof-strengthening so that you can weather any snowfall without concern. This will require either your natural engineering ingenuity or some good advice. You want to be protected against two major risks. The roof itself could give way under an exceptional load of snow, or the roof could remain intact but drop either a little bit or entirely, and push out the side walls as it does so. Neither is to be desired.

To build a defense against the second, you need tie rods to hold the parallel walls of the cottage together — or at least to hold in the walls at the base of the main slope. You may already have that tie rod without knowing it, if you have interior partitions which are well secured to the other walls and make a continuous link from side to side. If you clearly have not, one approach is to install a tie rod. If your cottage is, for example, 20 feet across from outer wall to outer wall, find an iron works to make you up two steel rods, each about $3/4$-inch in diameter and 10 feet 3 inches long, threaded about 8 inches on each end. You also need a turnbuckle, which will tighten the rods together, two bolts for the outer ends and a plate of $1/4$-inch steel about 4×6 inches drilled with a $7/8$-inch hole in the center to serve as a large washer under each bolt. You then bore a $3/4$-inch hole though the upper plate of your outer wall, slide the two rods out through each, secure the plate and bolt, and join the two rods with the turnbuckle in the center. Tighten it while applying a plumb bob or spirit level on the outer wall to make sure it is true. If you had a cottage about 20 by 30 feet with no interior supports, you might install two of these. According to your taste, you can put in the rods for winter or leave them permanently in place. If you do the latter, you can use metal strapping to attach I-beam curtain rod and have matchstick curtains as temporary partitions. Or you can hang plants and lights on them.

The other approach to strengthen your roof — combined with tie rods or instead of them — is to erect a temporary pillar of double 2 × 4s stretching tightly from a 2 × 6 on the floor up to the ridge board. That board on the floor must stretch across your floor joists, which are either 16 or 24 inches apart, and rest on three of them: it must therefore be at least 36 or 54 inches long. If you have a ceiling below your roof, permanently install a double 2 × 4 from the ridge board to the ceiling, and subtly mark the ceiling to indicate where it is. Then in autumn you need only a shorter pillar which reaches from the floor to the mark on the ceiling. For the hypothetical cottage noted above, two such pillars would be a good idea. If you have partitions and a ceiling below the roof, chances are that the partitions reach only to the ceiling and do nothing to buttress the roof. If, however, some thoughtful building designer has run those partitions right up to the roof for whatever reason, you need not worry about pillars at all.

Snow can play other tricks. It can drift down your chimney, leaving dampness and a mess. The solution is simple — make a cap for the chimney. (See **Fireplaces**.)

Remember, too, that snow may drift in places usually safe from rain, and then it can turn to pools of stagnant water in spring, or perhaps rot-inducing damp earth, which you might discover under the cottage itself. Decide whether it is worthwhile to block the open space under the cottage with scrap building materials. Consider also places protected only by screen rather than by windows, such as your veranda, outhouse or tool shed.

If you have found it desirable to defend special trees with wire or roofing against porcupines or even hungry rabbits, remember the snow. The protection must be well above the highest level the snow is ever likely to reach when drifitng — that will usually mean eye level.

SNOWMOBILES

Snowmobiles are very useful when used to go from Point A to inaccessible Point B when no other transportation is practical, but they do cause certain problems in cottage country.

For those who have escaped to savor the tranquility of still country days, snowmobiles are one of the worst noise polluters ever invented. They can also damage vegetation that is hidden by snow.

There are few really effective defences against snowmobiles, but for whatever satisfaction it may give, you could post around your property "No Snowmobiles" signs. They may deter the conscientious drivers from flattening your gardens.

STORMS

When cottages in this vast land are spread from mountain top to ocean shore, with no small number in forested plains, local experience with storms is certainly the best guide. Cottagers may feel more apprehensive about the elements than city dwellers because cottage buildings are usually more fragile, more open to the elements, and farther from help and advice.

The two most worrying phenomena are electric storms (see **Lightning**) and wind. Especially if you have heard a Weather Watch or Weather Warning on the radio, there are some precautions which are likely to reduce damage or injury.

- Disconnect electrical devices such as audio-visual equipment, computers and motors which could be damaged by a power surge on your lines. (If any of these are on a reliable surge protector, disconnection is unnecessary.) If you can do without any electricity for a while, it is easier to open the main switch on your service panel.
- Close and securely lock all windows and firmly close doors. Close the chimney flue. This is not only to prevent breakage if a high wind slams them open and closed, but to avoid having your possessions blown about. The theory is that in a really fierce wind, the cottage with all windows and doors open is more likely to be blown off its foundations and perhaps deposited on a neighbor's lawn.
- Collapse all garden furniture and umbrellas. If you have time, put them inside or under the cottage; otherwise pile them with rocks on top.

- If the boat is on the shore, see that it is pulled well up where it cannot strike rocks if it is blown about or hit by unusually high waves. Also ensure that it is securely tied. A rowboat or canoe tethered to a buoy may be safer if it is partially submerged.
- If you are warned of a really bad storm or hurricane, move the car to an open space where it is less likely to be hit by flying branches or trees. Close its windows.
- Just in case the storm develops to hurricane proportions, choose the safest retreat for your family. Usually this would be in the cottage itself, but not when the storm seems to be reaching headline-making proportions. The best place (next to a cave, which you probably do not have) is a hollow in the ground, in the lee of a huge rock, or tight against the base of a cliff with some sheltering logs protecting you. Do not seek shelter at the base of a high tree that may be vulnerable to lightning. All this advice is subject to your judgement of where you are least likely to be blown away or to be hit by objects flying at high speeds. If, as the storm develops, you decide you should move to a different shelter, go together and stick together, taking your mobile pets with you. (They are even more frightened than you are.)
- With these chores done and time remaining, attend to other objects, such as garbage, hammock, toys, loose lumber, and flags, which may suffer from a gale.
- If you are very worried about the storm, you could also phone a friend living at some distance to report the impending severe weather, and to ask him or her to phone you back in an hour. If the phone line is down, he or she could report it to the telephone company.
- Is there any lonely neighbor who badly needs your physical and psychological help?
- When all is safely over, send a reassuring message to Mother.

T

T_{OOLS}

The number of tools you have at the cottage depend on your interests and priorities. Your tools may range from a collection that any skilled tradesperson would envy, to just a pair of bifocals with which to look up the telephone number of the nearest helper.

The following list is for those cottagers who have ambition to do routine maintenance and some minor building (shelves in the tool room, a door for the outhouse), but are not yet equipped. Each category is in descending order of average priority. Whether or not it turns out to be your priority depends on you and your cottage. Prices are very approximate indeed. Most common tools are occasionally on sale for much lower cost than listed. You can also hint at Christmas.

Carpentry

- Claw Hammer: preferably metal or fiberglass handle and of at least medium price range. Wood handles are cheaper, but they break and may become loose. Cheap metal hammers can be a curse, especially for pulling out nails. The cost is about $12 to $15.
- Screwdrivers: indulge yourself in a good set that includes at least two slot, two Robertson and two Phillips blades. Such a set is better than a 6-in-1 screwdriver. The blades in poor screwdrivers are easily messed up when you use them as stone chisels or lift the cottage with them; good ones are often guaranteed for life against all hazards except being dropped in the lake. They cost about $15 to $20.

221

- Tapeline: It should be at least 16 feet, of medium quality. On cheap ones, the spring goes and the tip breaks off when you walk on it. Don't buy the top of the line model, for you will weep when you lose it or your mate drives over it. Cost: about $12.
- Wrench: a medium-size vise-grip type is a must. (When you want more tools, consider also a smaller one and the types made for special purposes such as undoing pipes, straightening light metal, and so on.) They cost about $14.
- Utility Knife: with spare blades, about $5.
- Hand Saw: impatient people may opt for a power saw, but a beginner probably should first master the hand saw. Choose a 24- or 26-inch crosscut. It should cost about $16 to $20.
- Framing Square, 24 × 16 inches: this is a wondrous tool in the hands of an expert, but the amateur needs it for checking right angles on the simplest task. Aluminum squares do not rust, but they cost more than twice as much as plain steel or enamelled. For the cheaper ones, you will spend about $8.
- Spirit Level, 24 inches: for everything from hanging pictures to building extensions. It will cost about $15.
- Chisels: quality varies enormously. If funds are limited, we suggest a set of three lower-priced ones ($1/2$-inch, $3/4$-inch and 1-inch) instead of top-of-the-line. Expect to pay about $15.
- Plane: your first use may be to make doors, windows and drawers fit in humid weather, but it will be essential in more ambitious carpentry. A plane of about $9^3/4$-inches is handy. The cost: about $30.
- Wrecking Bar, preferably 36 inches: invaluable for leverage of rocks and buildings, as well as for erasing your mistakes. It will cost about $12.

These are the basic tools without which we would hesitate to stay a day at the cottage. When you find yourself using them effectively, indulge in hammock hours while you check the catalogues for your next acquisitions. Mark clearly each item you crave, and leave the catalogue casually but prominently where the family is bound to see it.

When it comes to power tools, the drill is usually first, even if you have never bought a hand drill or brace and bit. We are strong believers in pre-drilling wood for large nails to avoid splitting the wood, and the possession of a drill will encourage the

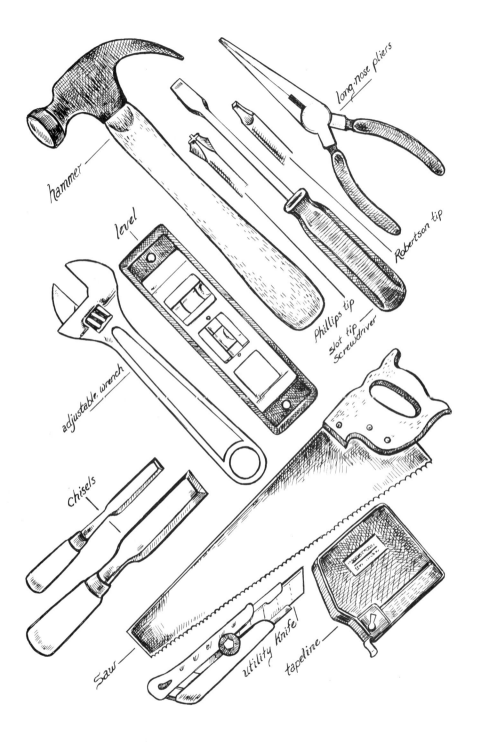

long-nose pliers

hammer

level

Robertson tip

adjustable wrench

Phillips tip

Slot tip
Screwdriver

chisels

Saw

utility knife

tapeline

laudable use of more screws instead of nails. The cheapest 1/4-inch utility drill, for light service, can be had for under $30. Variable speed drills, a great convenience if you use screws much, range from $40 to $150. Cordless drills are favored by those who may be working beyond the range of cottage electricity, but if you have only one drill, make it a 120-volt conventional type.

Power handsaws range from $50 to over $200. Before buying the least expensive model, consider safety, for you are now entering the risk zone. Has it a really reliable blade guard? A heavy saw is less likely to jump and injure than a flimsy one. Try to avoid buying the cheapest.

A sander may be the next power tool on your list. Except for a few special jobs such as vehicle repair, the fast circular sander has fallen out of favor in place of the relatively cheap ($30 to $150) orbital/straight sander, which is now the workhorse of the do-it-yourselfer. For serious carpentry, cabinet-making and furniture-crafting, the belt sander ($75 to $250) does a much faster and better job. It is advisable to buy belts of at least 3-inch width or preferably 4, rather than the smaller ones.

Sabre saws ($30 to $200) are useful not only for artistic curves, but are practical for making holes for such things as electric outlets when panelling. If you are only an occasional user, a machine for $50 will serve you well, but if you are embarking on major construction, you will appreciate the heavy type which cuts through 2 × 4s handily. Don't forget to equip yourself with a supply of various blades for different types of work; for smaller sabre saws, the best buy is a large packaged assortment.

Power planes ($85 to $150) are the luxury items of woodworking. They don't do anything beyond the capacity of a hand plane, but they do it very fast with little muscle.

There is also non-portable equipment, including table saws, radial arm saws, drill presses, planer-jointers, lathes and band saws. We make a distinction between the first two saws and the rest, for if you are into major construction, the saw is an asset bordering on necessity. Table saws are handier than radial arms for cutting large sheets of plywood, and will meet most general carpentry needs, but it is commonly believed that the radial arm saw is better for more exacting work with dadoes and routing. We are not enthusiastic about the very expensive computerized saws ($800 and up), but we would not touch the cheapest models either ($250), because they will not last with heavy work, are less accurate and probably more dangerous.

Plumbing

- Hacksaw: with lots of spare blades, of average quality, it will cost about $10.
- Pipe Wrenches: buy two, one of which is an 18-inch, one smaller. You need two to undo corroded joints. They are priced from $15 to $40.
- Adjustable Wrench: you will want a good quality adjustable wrench, of at least 10 inches. From $15 to $20.
- Propane Torch: even if you never intend to solder a metal pipe, this has a hundred uses, including the softening of heavy plastic pipe to make it slide on reluctant fittings. Don't forget a spare cylinder. Cost: about $15.
- Plastic Funnel: for pump priming, costs about $1.
- Rubber Plunger: to clear drains, costs about $6.

Don't forget screwdrivers, and the vice-grip wrench listed above.

Electrical

- Wire Stripper (and cutter): of medium quality, it will cost about $15
- Cable Ripper: about $5.
- Long Nose Pliers: about $10.
- Multi-tester: this may seem like a luxury for the beginner, but you will find many uses for it around the house in checking main electric current, batteries, continuity breaks in appliances and so on. It costs about $35.

You will also need screwdrivers, and the pliers listed above.

General Maintenance

- Oil Can: plastic or metal, with a good pumping action, costs about $5.
- Bench Vise: for repairs of everything unimaginable. Fit it to your budget, from about $30 to $75.
- Hex Key Wrench Set: you are less likely to lose the kind mounted together like a pocket knife, but loose ones work just as well. Useful for all sorts of unpredictable repairs and adjustments, it costs from $4 to $15.

- Metal Snips: at least 10-inch of medium quality. They will cost between $10 and $15.
- Wet/Dry Shop Vacuum: this can serve also as a household vacuum, and you get more power and versatility for your money with a shop vacuum. It can be especially useful as a pump to remove small pools of stagnant water from under the cottage, or for cleaning up plumbing disasters. It can also be adapted for rug shampooing. They are priced at $75 and up.
- Come-along Dolly: otherwise known as a hoist. With it you can pull your car out of the ditch by hand, straighten the cottage wall, move a massive rock, pull out tree roots, guide an awkward tree being felled. It is hard to see how a cottage can be without one. Two-ton capacity is best, and costs from $25 to $40.
- Welded Steel Chain or Steel Cable: buy 50 feet, with hooks. If this sounds too expensive (around $100), equip yourself with heavy propylene rope for diverse emergencies and projects. Have at least 100 feet of lighter rope.
- Finally, invest in some catalogues showing tools and supplies for carpentry, plumbing, electrical work and maintenance. They help you plan and dream.

TREES

In your general landscaping plan, you may want to isolate your property from your neighbors and from cars (especially with headlights) along the road. At the same time, you want to mask the less attractive facilities such as the outhouse, the garbage pit or storage area, and the carpark. One solution may be small trees transplanted from the nearby woods — cheap and indigenous.

There are drawbacks. Deciduous trees such as maples must be moved when they are more or less dormant, in very early spring, or after the leaves fall. Willows, which can be started by putting a branch in water or muck until it roots, are spectacular and fast, but don't put them anywhere near drains, which they will grow into and mess up with a passion. Hardwoods are splendid if you have long-term vision, but they are relatively slow to amount to anything. Coniferous trees, including cedar, pine, hemlock, and spruce are handsome in all seasons, and they can be transplanted in late August or early September.

There is nothing to the moving process. Just dig up the largest practical clump with minimum disturbance of the roots. If it is too heavy to lift, shift it into an old car or truck tire and drag it with a chain or rope. Dig an adequate hole. Roughly fit the clump into it and adjust the hole accordingly, so the tree remains the same depth as before with the roots spread out. When it is properly placed, put one large handful of bone meal at the bottom of the hole (more, if the tree is bigger than an inch in diameter). Now, while you can still see the roots, drive in a wooden stake without breaking them, and tie the tree to it, but not so tightly that it will bite into the young wood. (The purpose of the stake is not to keep the tree upright, but to minimize swaying, which will draw the hair roots away from the nutritious soil they need.) Fill in the hole with a mixture of decent soil well mixed with peat moss (about a quarter by volume). Soak thoroughly and press in the earth. If the trees are coniferous, water is extremely important. It is not enough to throw in a bucket. The best aproach is to leave a hose to barely dribble for days, and water constantly in the first year — right up to the first frost. Very early next spring you might throw a handful of garden fertilizer around each new and old tree in your vision. With this kind of care, you can almost double the normal rate of early growth.

The disadvantage of this kind of planting is that the trees may take some years to give the foliage you want. For attractive screening at low cost, cedars are especially good. If you are in a position to give constant watering when they are young, there is much more latitude about the time of planting, but they should not be moved in hot, dry weather. You may be able to find them locally. If so, try to get cedars that have been growing in your kind of soil. Don't take them from an oozy swamp if they are to be moved to a hot, barren knoll.

The transplanting procedure for cedars is as already described, with emphasis on the water and even more peat moss to hold moisture. (They dry out even through the winter, and therefore need a good reservoir.) And don't forget the bonemeal on anything you plant. After you transplant, you must prune them to bring foliage back into balance with the roots, some of which have inevitably been disturbed or damaged. Transplanting is a deep psychological shock which may slow down the tree's normal active life (we're not kidding). The amount of pruning — on any part of the tree — depends partly on the state of the roots. When they thrive, you should prune annually, usually by nipping the tops, so that they do not become thin and leggy, thus defeating your purpose. If you want a cedar hedge — rough or shaped — never let the trees grow higher than you can conveniently reach with a pruning hook. They should also be fed annually with fertilizer sold for the purpose.

Another part of your tree landscaping is re-directing what you already have. We hope you will be reluctant to cut down healthy trees, but sometimes there comes a moment when it is sensible. You may have poured out your life savings for that view of the lake; it doesn't seem very logical to obscure the view from the place where you most often sit. A few trees, such as cedar or hemlock, can be drastically pruned and shaped with success. You can cut off a few limbs, if artistically selected, from deciduous trees, but to really open up the view, some may have to be cut down.

Perhaps you should also consider curbing natural growth to reduce the excessive shade. Not only may you want to sit in the sun on the deck or make the interior less gloomy, but too much shade may contribute to the dampness of the building, with all sorts of bad consequences.

Whether or not you have to remove trees around the cottage, ensure that everything in sight is well managed for healthy growth. To promote models of arborial health and happiness, remove the unsightly suckers and the trees that are choking one another out.

W

WATER

It is when you go to the cottage that you may begin to realize how many services you take for granted in the city — including drinking water. Here in the country you are on your own with no medical officers, lab technicians or engineers to make your decisions for you.

Taste and appearance are not necessarily a guide to potability, though obviously you will not want to drink water which is badly discolored and has funny things floating in it. Water that smells like rotten eggs can be perfectly all right to drink. The crystal waters of that azure lake, however, may be dangerous to your family's comfort and health. Whatever the appearance of your water source, therefore, it is important to have it tested regularly. This is normally done by a provincial laboratory. You can find out how to take a sample and where to send it by inquiring at a provincial or municipal office, or by asking a plumber who installs water systems.

If you have doubts and are thirsty, there are some temporary measures you can take. The most obvious is to boil water for drinking. This means really boiling it — 3 minutes is the minimum. It is not enough, for example, to use dubious water to make coffee on the assumption the percolation will banish the germs. When you boil it, and then put it in the refrigerator, it will still taste like boiled water when you drink it. If you are on this regime for long, check that your family is not unconsciously depriving itself. You may want to disguise the water with flavoring for the young people, as adequate intake is important to health, especially in dehydrating summer weather.

You can add chemicals to purify water. The same chloride of lime familiar to outhouse customers can be used, but you must know how to mix it. Easier for small quantities are water purification pills, used by travellers to foreign lands, which you can buy at a drug store.

You can drink rainwater, but how do you collect it? Water that you catch from roof run-off into a rain barrel picks up heaven-knows-what along the way, and if it stands long it will become brackish and unpalatable at best. If you insist on rainwater you will have to put out thoroughly clean vessels, preferably moving their meagre contents to the refrigerator when the sun comes out.

Your safest bet for drinking water is a deep well, but even it should be tested. After it proves satisfactory, don't be upset if it sometimes develops a taste from minerals dissolved in it; that taste may even come and go. If it is both bad and persistent, ask a water purification firm for advice. They will probably test it for minerals without charge, but the remedial measures are likely to be expensive.

The condition of your drinking water can change in a season. Obviously, lake water, which now rarely tests out for drinking in inhabited areas, is vulnerable to run-off, which gathers up animal waste even when there are no problems of man-made sanitation systems. Run-off can also be an enemy of wells. Even a very deep well can be contaminated if the well-head is not properly sealed and graded against ground water. If sand is allowed to wash down, it could also damage your submersible pump. Check it out occasionally.

You may encounter the long-term cottager or native who has been drinking lake water for years and has never had a problem. That may be so, but the likely explanation is a well-developed tolerance for the pollution that will give newcomers bad days — and nights. In foreign lands, it is the tourists who get dysentery. You may manage to drink the water with little upset, but be cautious about exposing the young members of your family to your experimentation.

Of course, water is important for more than drinking. Lake water that is not certified for drinking may be fine for swimming. You should find out just what it is like, at various times in a season. You and your neighbors can take turns at this chore. If it is not fit for drinking, warn your family not to ingest it while swimming. If doubts have been cast even on its swimmability, seek more information from the testing authorities before you, so to speak, throw in the towel. They may be giving you important advice, or perhaps they are being over-cautious. If you have been swimming, has your family noted any problems, especially around the eyes? Are there some days when unaccustomed winds blow in obvious pollution that seems to disperse quickly when the winds change? You may want to discuss the situation with your family doctor before reaching a decision on the use of the lake. If the situation is discouraging enough to send you in search of a swimming pool, consult the municipality or provincial environmental authorities to see if they are aware of the problem and have any plans to solve it for the long-term future. It could be as simple as one broken sewer line which no one knew about until you raised the issue.

WEATHER

There are many sources of information to help you to forecast the weather including the direction of the wind, grandmother's arthritis, the almanac, and listening to the government meteor-ological service. Who can say which is the most reliable? You can enjoy cottage life more if you become your own forecaster by choosing your signs.

If you want to baffle your family with science, you can equip yourself with a thermometer, a barometer and a rain gauge. You probably have the first, but if not, read on. The second, by recording high and low air pressure, gives a pretty good indication of what is likely for the morrow. The rain gauge doesn't help with the forecasting, but it is enormously useful in learning whether those showers you dimly heard last night amounted to anything, or whether you should get out the hose. A rain gauge is a transparent glass or plastic tube (about 18 inches long and 3/4 inches in diameter) mounted on a board marked with a scale in inches or millimetres, and a funnel at the top. You can make your own by buying a tube at the hardware store, and figuring out the scale by experimentation.

If you think back to your high school physics, you may remember about high pressure areas in which the wind whirls around clockwise from the center, and low pressure areas in which it goes counterclockwise towards the center. It is the lows which bring the rain and snow because the whirling air finally shoots up the center, and the moisture in it cools and condenses. If you can spot the low pressure area, you are well on your way to forecasting.

There are lots of ways to forecast for which you will not need any equipment at all. Your hair may feel limp because humidity is rising. Some aches and pains may emerge. The far shore of the lake looks closer. There is little morning dew. Birds tend to run home and stay there. Even the family pets may know about storms before you do, and inexplicably retreat under the table. (See **Lightning**.) You may detect subtle differences in sounds: a change in bird calls, voices seeming to carry farther, a changed tone to the breeze in the pines as the winds strike them from a different direction, and other telltale signs, unique to your property, which you discover without immediately knowing their rational explanation.

Then there are the clouds. What can be more agreeable than studying them from the hammock, and then rushing in to pronounce your predictions to an awestruck family? If the clouds are very low, chances are that you have a low pressure area on your hands. If the cumulus clouds — those fluffy ones illustrated in toilet paper advertisements — stretch upwards, probably they are being pushed up by a moist updraft of low pressure. That improves the odds for rain. If they become darker and lower than other cumulus clouds, it is time to roll up the car windows. If those wispy cirrus clouds with tails change to a mackerel sky, expect the onset of rain or snow.

Here is some secret information on which to build your reputation as a seer. To estimate the temperature in Fahrenheit, count the chirps of a cricket in one minute, divide by 4 and add 27. You can then convert to Celsius or let the cricket do it for you: count the chirps for 7 seconds and add 5. (Well, crickets never were very good at mathematics.) Or listen to a Katydid. If it says "Katy did it", the temperature is about 79 degrees Fahrenheit; if "Katy did", 72 degrees; if "Kaytee", 64 degrees; if only "Kay", 57 degrees. To learn how many miles away a thunderstorm is, count the seconds between the lightning and the beginning of the thunder, and divide by 5.

Then you can put your finger up to the wind. If it gets wet, it's raining. Go inside.

That's all you really need for short-term weather forecasting. It costs less than the way the government does it.

 WEEDS

A weed is nothing more than a plant growing where it is not wanted. In your garden you want plants to show a little order and respect, and so you remove unintended intruders. They spoil the color scheme, attract snide comments from the neighbors and, worse, compete with your favored plants for nourishment and light.

Unfortunately, removing the weeds is as tiresome as painting the Forth Bridge, which has to be redone at one end by the time the other end is finished. There is an alternative: a wonderful invention called "the vernacular garden", in which plant life grows as it will. To say that you really like to see nature growing in all its profusion can be freely translated as "I hate weeding". There is a lot to be said for the vernacular garden. It can be an attractive splash of ever-changing color and texture — from a reasonable distance. It liberates the garden slave. But there are also limitations. It can propagate thoroughly unwanted plants which may spread where you do not want them, or which cause annoying or painful reactions to humans, or which encourage damaging insects. Some weeding is desirable, if only to remove anti-social weeds and a portion of the unattractive grasses which dominate less aggressive plant life. When weeds are thoroughly mixed in such a garden, mechanical removal with hand implements is the only effective solution. A hoe when the soil is fairly dry is fastest, but a small hand fork after a rain is the most thorough approach.

In a well disciplined lawn, the healthy grass should virtually smother incipient weeds, leaving only a few to be removed by hand implements. But it takes time for a lawn to be so healthy and disciplined — sometimes a century or so. Meanwhile, though some of our neighbors say "tut tut", we go for chemical "weed and feed". Its application requires extreme care if you are not to burn your lawn grossly. Do not use it in the year the lawn is seeded. Follow directions on the bag scrupulously. Never use it until after the lawn has been cut three times that season. Take the fertilizer spreader off the lawn to fill it, and be very wary of spillage. If you fertilize and water the lawn well, that one application in the second season should never have to be repeated.

This small counsel is familiar to the city gardener. The new dimension for the cottager is found in the so-called weeds which grow in profusion beyond the tended plots. Like the flowers in the garden, there are annuals, biennials and perennials, and it is helpful gradually to learn which is which. If an unwanted species is annual, and therefore dependent for survival on re-seeding, you can control it by cutting it down before it bears seed. Unwanted perennials must be terminated with extreme prejudice. This is not always easy with growth such as brambles or sumac, which have root networks of enormous tenacity and extent. Of course, the path of least resistance is to leave things as they are, but there are other alternatives:

1. Remove all nasty weeds within the largest practical distance. This operation includes plants like poison ivy, poison oak, or nettles, which are dangerous to people who come into contact with them. They must be removed from areas frequented by humans; if you merely mark such weeds with warning signs, they will continue to spread. It would include also weeds which are painful to victims of allergies, such as ragweed and — depending on your family and friends — goldenrod and sumac. It could include weeds which are unfriendly to other plant growth.Bindweed, wild pea, virginia creeper and bittersweet all have their own charms, but they can smother other plants and even kill trees if left. Wild gooseberry is the carrier of white pine blister rust; if it is not eradicated, it can destroy all the white pines on your property.

2. Improve on nature. In nature's race, the survivor is not necessarily what is best for the human environment. Fragile plants of delicate beauty may be trampled or smothered by aggressive contemporaries. You can add to the attraction of country lanes and meadows by removing or just cutting down the grosser species to give the little plants a better chance. It may not be a matter only of saving uncommon examples of precious types, but allowing ordinarily hidden blossoms to flourish in incomparable carpets of color.

3. Flatten nature. A meadow of wildflowers/weeds is one of the uplifting pleasures of cottage life, but all too often meadows turn into visually impenetrable bush which gradually destroys most of the flowers you treasured as well as the view of far horizons. If you catch the weed-trees in time, you can control them with pruning shears or a saw, but when that job becomes too much, you may want to hire someone with a tractor to cut or even plough the whole area. Next season the wildflowers/weeds will be flourishing again.
4. Tame nature. You can make an attractive garden just by transplanting a few indigenous weeds/wildflowers. (See **Gardening**.)

In the development of a policy towards weeds, you face interesting dilemmas and tough judgement calls. Do you really have to declare war on goldenrod, one of the most beautiful and dramatic flowers of the field? That tree, completely enveloped in virginia creeper, is such a dramatic flaming symbol at the height of autumn coloring, that you may wonder whether to save the tree or the vine. (With patience, the moral compromise is to save the living tree, and to transplant virginia creeper — not difficult — to the base of a dead tree. Surely no one would want to eradicate the relatively uncommon bitter-sweet, but detaching it from the trees is an exercise in patience.

A public debate rages on the subject of chemicals for the control of weeds and nourishment of growth. Obviously, care must be exercised in the use of chemicals and respect must be accorded to the most recent stage of knowledge reached by science and technology, fallible though it may be. To use chemicals indiscriminately is negligent and often illegal. If you decide to use them to control growth on your property, it is best to treat them with respect. Judiciously used, chemical treatments are a very effective method of taming unwanted plant life. Those who oppose the use of chemicals to control noxious weeds in public places — on the grounds that chemicals *might* be conducive to cancer or halitosis — may forget the agony which is *certainly* caused by some noxious weeds. They may have never seen a child in state of shock because of extreme sensitivity to poison ivy, or a young member of the family trying desperately to breathe on the panicky drive to the hospital because of an allergy-induced asthma attack.

We therefore urge that, in the elimination of noxious weeds, you use the best available weapons and scientific advice.

If your cottage property is adjacent to agricultural land, bear in mind your social responsibility. It may be that local farmers are engaged in a costly battle to eliminate certain weeds that you are unconsciously propagating en masse. Before warfare breaks out, quietly ask a few questions to learn if there are any such difficulties and how you might become part of the solution instead of adding to the problem. You could talk to neighboring farmers or seek out the local agricultural representative of the government.

#

If you decide to dig a well instead of relying on lake water or drilling a well (see **Water**) the first question is where to put it. It must be far (100 feet or more) from any present or future septic disposal system or outhouse, and not too far from the cottage, but that usually leaves a lot of latitude.

Ground formation is the main clue. You are hoping to reach the water table or tap into an underground spring. The water table, which rises and falls with the season, rain and use, may be very near the surface, or hundreds of feet down. Because of the changes in the level of the water table, the best time to make a well is usually in the dry later part of the summer; a glorious well in May could be a dry hole in August. While a spring may be running close to the top of a hill, the odds are against it. On the other hand, you do not want a low marsh where you are likely to get the brackish seepage. Vegetation which indicates deepish soil in a cleft between rocky slopes may be promising. If your land is flat and homogeneous, you may as well put on a blindfold and choose a spot.

Or you could call in a water diviner, or dowser. The art of finding underground water with a cleft stick in the hands of the right person is ancient. Nowadays the tendency to deny the existence of what we cannot explain makes many people cynical about water diviners. You may wish to try it, if you don't think that the experience of 20 centuries can be written off just because we don't yet understand it.

The diviner may not be easy to find, because many people who "possess the power" are sensitive to ridicule by strangers, especially city people. A Protestant Church minister advertised his services in our local paper (he was known as the water divine), but you are unlikely to be so lucky. If tactful inquiry brings someone to your doorstep, he or she is likely either to use a forked stick from a willow or hazel, or bring a metal rod. Holding the forks in two hands, the diviner walks slowly in parallel lines until the end of the device twists or shakes suddenly. Then the walker goes at right angles, and if the same reaction is repeated, the intersection of the two lines is the place to try.

You can then hire a back hoe or small shovel to dig a well as deep as the equipment will reach, or you can dig one yourself by hand. This is hard work, and sometimes risky. You must make a hole more than 3 feet in diameter to give space for a person to work. While you are digging, the hole must be protected from cave-in with a temporary structure extending from the surface to where the ground becomes stable. The best solution is a 4-foot length of 42-inch-in-diameter old steel culvert which you might be lucky enough to borrow from a Highways Department shop. With something like that in place, you go on digging, passing the soil up by a bucket on the end of a rope to a lucky buddy who waits at the surface. You continue until you strike water, but even then you do not stop. The water should be coming in faster than you can bail it out by hand. If that does not happen after 15 or 20 feet, you should try a new hole.

When the happy moment of flowing water arrives, you line the well with stones until you near the top. For at least 3 feet from the surface, you should then line it with brick or stone set solidly in mortar, or acquire concrete culverts with water-impervious mortar between them. They save a lot of work and later main-tenance, but they are very heavy and expensive. The High-ways Department may be able to guide you on buying imperfect "seconds" which will serve your purpose at much less cost. This solid wall, whatever it is made of, must extend far enough above ground to prevent surface run-off. The whole must be capped. Though a concrete cover is ideal, a very sturdily built plywood cover, well treated with wood preservative, is far cheaper and easier to handle.

If your well is less than 20 feet deep, you can get your water by an electric shallow well pump in the cottage, by an old-fashioned hand pump on the well cover, or by some mechanical invention of your own devising to let you bring up a pail by pulley, winch or lever.

Don't forget to test the well water before drinking it. (See **Water.**) The well should be cleaned occasionally. If it is less than 10 feet deep, you should do so annually, for it is a simple operation when you acquire a shovel made for the purpose. The roundish metal part is set almost at right angles to a long handle so that, from the top, you can scoop up sand and gravel without spilling. If the well is deeper, you go down it on a ladder when the water is at its lowest, and scoop up all the loose sand or gravel which may have accumulated. The punishing part of this task is having the cold water splash down on you as your buddy lifts the pail by rope over your head. You can postpone that operation to two- or three-year intervals if you are not getting much loose stuff. While you are down there, check that the mortar in the upper part is in good repair. You may also wish to brush down the sides. When the operation is over, run off a great deal of the drinking water you have been sitting in — otherwise the family might object.

WINTER

Before the summer wanes, consider the possibility of winter visits. If you have in mind overnight stays, it is a good idea to start early on the fight against the cold, even though your cottage may not be insulated for year-round use. It is wisest to assume that the temperature will be well below freezing and that you will want the interior to be an oasis of comfort.

Of course, much depends on the size and condition of your cottage. Most often it may be wise to concentrate on heating central space, leaving the bedrooms and bathroom in their icy fastness. Not only have you a good chance of making the living room comfortable, but to do so will take much less of your time and effort than heating the whole place. If that is your approach, next winter you will be glad if you left electric blankets or sleeping bags ready for your visit.

The major job may be to close off the area to be heated. If your bedrooms lead directly from it, all you need do is close their doors. If there is a corridor, decide whether you now would like to install a permanent door to block it, or make a temporary winter barrier with light plywood or heavy blanket. Then equip yourself with a roll of plastic sheeting to reduce the heat loss and drafts through the living room windows. You may as well go for the heavy 6 mm grade which looks better because it will have fewer wrinkles and which can, with care, be salvaged for re-use; of course, watching the infinite peace of the snowy lake through any plastic will make you think that a visit to the optician is overdue. You can staple the plastic to the inside of the windows. You can tape it, which damages the woodwork less and may make it a tighter fit. Or you can make thin, reuseable batten strips to hold it down with light nails or number 4 screws; if this is your solution, mark the strips with their proper location for future use. Keep an old blanket to hang over the front door, which may have drafts you never suspected in summer.

The next important step is to gather enough firewood for all your projected visits, and stack it indoors handy to the stove or fireplace. Not only is this more convenient than digging through deep snow to find it and then cleaning snow from it, but the wood will be guaranteed dry and will gradually heat up to room temperature, making for easier burning.

Then consider the sanitary arrangements in the absence of running water. We will not inquire closely into your decision, but here are some possibilities. Get an old toilet seat from a garage sale (don't pay more than $2 for it), and make a simple mount for it over a 5-gallon metal pail equipped with a heavy plastic bag. If you have no such pail, ask your friendly hardware merchant if he will save you one. At the end of the visit, remove and tie the plastic bag. Since you are not likely to want to include it as cabin baggage on the way back to the city, store it far from the lake for disposal in spring.

A simpler alternative is a portable toilet such as recreational vehicles use, which may cost around $100. One advantage of that investment is that it will always be there for standby use if, perish the thought, your water system ever goes temporarily out of order in summer.

Finally, there is the old-fashioned chamber pot, which has stood the test of the centuries. Just be careful of which area of your grounds you favor with its contents, for with spring comes the moment of truth. You will find its contents easier to dispose of if you persuade its users to deposit their paper in a paper bag you thoughtfully place beside it and burn towards the end of your visit.

In winter you will want to reduce to a minimum the supplies you must bring in by sled or backpack. Consider, therefore, what you can safely leave in autumn. This excludes all liquids, with the exception of overproof rum. If you can sacrifice something on gastronomic quality, you have many groceries from which to choose. After all, in the Arctic, explorers regularly left tins of foodstuffs in caches, sometimes for many years. If there is no visible evidence of damage to tins or contents, you are not taking a big chance. Don't forget lots of matches. Just be sure that matches and food not in tins (such as macaroni) are left in a place safe from mice — in the oven, for example. Why not leave a supply of disposable dishes and cups, because the midwinter shortage of water is not conducive to dishwashing?

Equip yourself with at least one snowshovel and leave it in an accessible place outside; you will not be occupying your time cleaning walks, but you may have to shovel out the front door. Or you may want to take some exercise by reducing the snowload on the roof. Also, have available either an ice chopper or an old axe, in case nature has perversely frozen in your entrance.

To be really well organized, you could cache sleds near where you are likely to park in winter so that you do not have to clutter the car with them when you come up. Ideal sleds for the purpose are made of plastic with rim all round and no frills; they cost only about $8 each. They accommodate cardboard boxes the size of a 24-bottle beer carton. If you have rough and steep terrain to cross, you can easily rope in your cargo, using the plastic handles or holes that you drill yourself in the rims. Toboggans are more inclined to spill.

You can make your own decision about bringing in water. If you do, use a collapsible plastic container which is light, unbreakable and spillproof. Alternatively, you can rely on melting snow. The risk of pollution may not be high enough to worry about, but it is a slow process and melting snow will not help your efforts to warm the interior fast.

On the happy assumption that you have electricity in winter, you can use it to help thaw the cottage quickly, even if you do not have electric heating. Turn on the electric stove to full heat with the oven door open, and use one of those summer fans to spread the heat while you tackle the woodstove or fireplace. That electricity will also make possible the glorious use of electric blankets. In your anxiety to produce warmth quickly, be careful about the risks of chimney fires. (See **Fire Precautions**).

The cottage in winter is a wondrous new experience in a wholly different world. You may well have chosen to spend the daylight hours skiing, but do not overlook the lesser-known joys of snowshoeing. Don't worry if you have never done it before; you can learn enough to thoroughly enjoy yourself quite quickly. You will be surprised at the speed with which you skim through the woods, going places you would not choose for skiing, and on routes too difficult for leisurely hiking in summer. The chances of accident are also relatively slim.

But don't forget the precautions. The sense of freedom may lead young people especially to take off imprudently fast and far where they may soon be lost in an unfamiliar landscape. Solitary forays and travel when dusk is approaching are to be discouraged. Each person or party should have a compass and be impressed with the importance of memorizing the route in the course of travel. A piercing whistle is another wise precaution.

Travel on frozen waterways requires large amounts of good sense. The biggest risks on a lake are at the beginning and end of the season. In the height of winter, the chances of immersion are relatively low for those on skis or snowshoes, both of which spread the human weight more widely than boots do. But no one should ever venture onto the ice alone. Rivers require far more respect, because the flowing water below the ice may have done mischievous things with the apparently safe crust of ice above. If a river is dammed even miles downstream, the water level may have been suddenly changed by human intervention, creating dangerously thin areas and crevasses. The best rule is to spend the shortest possible time on a river, but if you must travel on it, do so in groups with a 50-foot length of reliable light rope in the pack of one member of the party.

Great though these outdoor winter adventures are, you are likely to enjoy equally the long evening when the room is lit only by the flickering flames of the fire and lights so dim that you can watch with awe the pristine world outside the window. For you, this will no longer be just a summer cottage.

WOOD CUTTING

If you are new to sawing and expect to be doing much of it, there are a few techniques worth picking up fast, whether you are using a bow saw or chain saw.

First there is the felling of that big tree. By all means, follow the cutting technique summarized below, but if you are not experienced enough to have confidence about where the tree will fall, take a little time for extra preparations. If the tree is anywhere near a power line or building, these precautions are a must for the amateur. Even in the depth of the woods, where seemingly no harm can come, they may be worth the trouble to avoid having the tree drop into the lake or snag on a neighboring tree.

Either find a professional baseball pitcher who can throw a string and weight neatly around the trunk very high up, or ascend an extension ladder to do it yourself. Then secure to the tree a chain or rope of appropriate strength. If it is a massive tree threatening the cottage or a power line and tending to lean where you do not want it, only a welded steel chain will make you feel really secure. Bring out your come-along dolly (see **Tools**) and connect it to the chain, anchor it, and put moderate tension on it. If your buddy is handling the rope or chain, the time to leave the scene for safety is before you start sawing.

Your first cut is at a convenient height and on the side towards which you wish it to fall. Cut straight in about a third of the way through the trunk and stop. You now want to make a notch with an angle of 45 degrees at its point, inside the tree. At the appropriate height to meet the bottom of the first cut, make a second cut at the 45-degree angle. Saw until the wedge is loose and can be lifted out. Make your third cut on the far side of the tree an inch or two above the first cut. As soon as you see the tree start to fall — in whatever direction — shout some dramatic word like "Timber". If it is creaking slowly towards its doom, switch off the chain saw, put it down and move smartly away. If the tree is going suddenly, make your leap away your first priority, in case the tree hits something that causes the severed trunk to pivot upwards to where you were standing.

With luck that will do it, but some things have been known to go wrong. The tree could have such a perverse lean on it that it starts to fall on the side where you are making your final cut. That is when you wish that you had inserted wood or plastic wedges in the cut behind your saw blade, for otherwise the saw will now be firmly stuck. This is where the ropes or chains come in. With the dolly, human power or even an accessible car, pull on the tree while someone stands by ready to remove the saw as it loosens. But don't use a car unless you have also rigged a pulley to let the vehicle do its work from a safe direction where the tree cannot possibly fall. When the tree reaches dead center, be ready to retreat.

In the unlikely event that you cannot budge the tree, or the rope breaks, you have three choices. Let it fall where it wants to — provided nothing precious is in the way. Or go and borrow more chain and keep on pulling. Or get a professional.

Once the tree is down, cut off all the branches which are standing free of the ground or other trees, and remove them from the site. Examine carefully any branch which may be under tension to avoid a sudden whipback or unexpected rolling of the trunk when you cut. Be sure also that you cut from the side which will not cause your saw to jam. When only the trunk is left, cut about half way through it at 16-inch intervals. Then employ a peavey (you brought one, didn't you?) to lever the trunk half a turn around, and cut the rest of the way. With your scientific eye, note the pressure on the trunk where you are going to cut. If the saw is in danger of jamming, use those wedges behind it.

Just one other point. If you are not felling a century-old elm but smaller trees whose roots you may later wish to remove by come-along dolly and axe or by bulldozer, make your original cuts as comfortably high as you can reach: perhaps 4 or 5 feet from the ground. This will give you much greater leverage for stump removal.

Well, that is the toughest sawing job of the year. Now you have to cut the branches into stove lengths. Two devices that you can make yourself will stand you in good stead. One is the traditional sawhorse, or sawbuck. Take 4 pieces of 2 × 4 about 3 feet long, and nail them together in pairs in the form of two separate Xs; the crossing should not be in the middle but about two-thirds of the way up, and the angle at the top of the X should be about 70 degrees. Strengthen each X with a piece of scrap 1-inch lumber nailed across the bottom. Have your buddy hold the two Xs upright, flat sides facing each other and about 28 inches apart. Nail a scrap board joining one to the other just below the cross on both sides. Then on each side nail another board diagonally from the end of the first board to the bottom of the cross: or fill in each lower side with scrap plywood of at least 1/2-inch thickness. You can make it much more beautiful and sturdy if you like, but avoid letting it be overly elaborate or too heavy for comfortable lifting. Chances are pretty good that, if you are using a chain saw, it will slip down and chew away your transverse supports. Don't make it a big project, but assume it will often need easy repair.

You probably have never seen the second device, but it deserves to be used constantly. It consists of two pieces of 5/8- or 3/4-inch scrap plywood. The first is about 15 inches square. In the top of it you cut away a triangle from the edges to a center point about 6 inches down. In the bottom you cut a slot 4 inches long and as wide as the thickness of the plywood. The second piece of plywood is 15 × 8. Midway along one long side you cut exactly the same slot as in the first piece. Have you guessed what it is? If you now fit the two slots together, you will have a neat little cradle to slip under a heavy log before cutting it. Placed judiciously, it will prevent the log from binding the saw. It also gives space for an undercut without dulling the saw chain by getting it in the dirt. Just carry those two little pieces with you into the woods, assemble them in an instant, and impress all the passing birds.

There is another old invention which is helpful when you have a lot of logs to cut. You may have been doing a lot of felling, leaving the straighter and larger pieces in four- or eight-foot lengths. You can make a real production line by driving four posts in the ground, with three or four feet showing, to make a square about two feet each way. Join the two north posts, so to speak, with a wire or rope at the top, and do the same with the two south posts to prevent them from spreading. Now you can slide all those logs under the ropes to lie north-south, and slice through the whole pile with one cut. The width of your pile depends on the length of the blade on your chain saw; the maximum width is just less than double the length of the free part of your blade, since you can cut from both sides.

For safety's sake, don't overuse the chain saw. To trim the small twigs off branches, pruning shears or a hatchet are less likely to cause accidents.

Now you have all that wood, what do you do with it? Please see **Wood Storage**.

WOOD STORAGE

When laying master plans for wood storage, your first decision should be location. However strictly rationed the space inside your cottage may be, you will be glad if you can spare some of it for firewood, including both kindling and logs. It will not only save inconvenience on that rainy or snowy night when you don't want to go outside but it will contribute to a supply of super-dry materials for easy starting.

If space inside is at a premium, one option may be a wood cupboard on the outside with a door opening beside your fireplace or near your stove. That has the added advantage of allowing you to replenish the supply from outdoors without dragging wood over the oriental rugs. Particular housekeepers may also note that it distances the bugs that may lurk in firewood. We doubt, however, that this is major consideration to most cottagers, who generally offer their hospitality to a wide spectrum of the small animal world.

Outside storage should be near the cottage, for obvious reasons. If unusual circumstances, like a tornado or the clearing of a site for new construction, leads to the sudden acquisition of a wood supply that will last for years into the future, you may want to put the reserve supply farther away. It still deserves some simple sheltering storage structure to forestall rot and decay before you get around to using it.

The purpose of a storage shed is not only to keep the wood dry, but to dry it in the first place, on the assumption that some of it is green when cut. Stacking it against the cottage, therefore, is not always a good idea. It will not help the cottage siding, and the air will not circulate as effectively as it would around a free-standing woodpile. If you have a foundation of cement blocks, you might erect a small shelter against it, to keep wood that is already reasonably dry; since firewood is more aesthetic in most eyes than cement foundations, you will add to the appearance of your estate and have a supply that is handy. All you need build is a roof made from sheets of 1/2-inch sheathing-grade plywood cut in half lengthwise and supported by 2 × 3 spruce posts at 4-foot intervals. Also running 2 × 3s under the roof from each post to the cottage wall will stop sagging. Well, most sagging. If you want a woodshed that will qualify for a mortgage, you will design somewhat more elaborate bracing. You can cover the plywood with roll roofing, with shingles, or just with wood preservative.

Whether for this simple lean-to or for a shed, you will need something on which to pile the wood away from the ground. Poles made from trees about 4 inches in diameter are simplest. You will save some time in later years if you choose dry ones, strip off the bark and apply wood preservative generously (see **Paints and Preservatives**) before laying them with their centers about 12 inches apart.

The dimensions of a free-standing shed depend on the available space and the expected wood supply. It should be placed where the sun and wind can get at it. The length is easy — 8-foot units to conform to available lumber lengths — and as long as you need. If you have lots of space, use a full sheet of plywood for each unit, making the width almost 4 feet — it will be not quite that because of the slope. If you don't want such an obtrusive structure, you can get away with a 3-foot width, which will still accommodate two rows of firewood back to back, each in 16-inch stovelengths. In this version, there will be hardly any space between the rows and the meagre roof overhang will not keep rain from wetting the ends, but that is not critical.

If you have soil not too hard to dig, you can support the structure with fence posts, ideally sunk below the frost line (at least 3 feet in most places). Less sturdy, but far less work and usually satisfactory, is a frame which sits on flat stones, cement blocks or logs. The 2 × 3 uprights can be 6 feet high at the front and 5-feet 6-inches at the back. They are set at 4-foot intervals; 2 × 3 horizontals on edge run along the top of the front and the back. Join each pair of opposite posts at the bottom with 2 × 3s. Put 2 × 3s across under the roof at either 2- or 4-foot intervals, depending on your standards. Most important is the bracing, which can be made of a 1 × 3 spruce. It will go diagonally in an X from the top to the bottom of the front and back at the two ends. If your shed is longer than 8 feet, put the bracing every 8 feet. That will prevent your shed from falling over backwards or forwards, but you don't want it to fall like a line of dominos either. The longitudinal bracing goes in the middle, so that it will not be in your way when piling wood. Run the same kind of light strapping from the middle of the 2 × 3 under your roof at the end of the shed, to the middle of the 2 × 3 with which you thoughtfully joined the posts just above the ground at the 4-foot interval. Then, put the next strap up from there to the roof at the far end. Do this in each 8-foot section.

The structure is now so impressively solid that you can throw on the roof plywood and even climb on top to nail it without much danger of collapse. If the shed has more than one unit, cover the plywood with roll roofing, or you will get rot where the plywood sheets join.

This structure is relatively light: will it all blow away? Not likely, especially when it is full. Even if it is not anchored to the ground, those pieces joining the pairs of posts will be held down by the weight of the firewood. Also, if your wood is piled well, it should be an immovable object before the gale.

Piling well is a small art in itself. The main hazard is probably not wind, but animals that like to play wild games. If you have the usual variety of firewood, from heavy logs to light kindling, keep the heavy stuff towards the bottom; then each 4-foot section will have a good variety. It is better to use the wood by sections in that way, so that you do not always take from the top along its whole length and end up with bottom layers that are not touched for years. You can also keep track of your consumption. With two rows back to back and piled 4 feet high, each 4-foot section holds one stove cord. If the pile goes right up to 6 feet, you have 1¹/₂ cords.

There may be a contradiction between piling loosely (to get the drying air) and piling tightly (to make the pile more secure). Having suffered a few collapsed wood piles, we prefer the latter. If you have really rambunctious beasts who consider the woodshed as their own, you can usually forestall spills by tying a rope along each front a bit higher than mid-way up, but good piling is usually enough to curb them.

WOODSTOVES

Why woodstoves? Because they are economical to run if you have your own wood or access to a cheap supply. Because they can heat a space quickly and are far more efficient than a fireplace. (The fireplace sucks in so much cold air through every crevice in the cottage and shoots so much carefully heated air up the chimney, that its only passing marks are in the charm division.) Because they seem right for the cottage.

The woodstove's disadvantages are that it requires more work than electricity or liquid fuel and it can present a fire hazard to the careless operator. If it also needs more skill than the turning of a thermostat, it is skill that is easily acquired and proudly displayed. The work is in obtaining the fuel, tending the stove, and cleaning it and the chimney. If you are really keen, you can buy a wood cookstove that heats the room, makes hot water and lets you prepare the meals. Beware that solution for summer use, though. On many days you would not want your whole cottage heated by a cookstove.

In recent years, the variety and quality of woodstoves has increased enormously. An antique stove may be great to look at, but the fact is that modern designers have beaten the pioneers at their own game — today's stoves are both beautiful and efficient. Up to a point, you can be guided by price. The better airtight stoves use only the air they need for efficient combustion. They may have baffles and chambers to burn gases and capture heat that went up the chimney in the olden days. The engineering designs and even the construction materials vary widely. If you seek efficiency, ignore the Franklin Fireplace and realize that a stove with doors which open in the front will be really efficient only when the doors are tightly closed. On the other hand, such a stove may suit you well — it will look charming when you are sitting in front of it, and burn long and efficiently at other times.

Steel is commoner than cast iron, partly because so many companies seeking to meet the explosive demand in the 1970s could tool up far more cheaply with steel. Cast iron has some drawbacks, such as its susceptibility to damage from a heavy blow or sudden temperature change (from throwing cold water on it, for example), but it retains heat far longer and radiates it gently.

In the selection of a stove, resist accepting the word of one salesperson. The first step is to borrow a book from the library. While you are there, you could check out any *Consumer Reports*. Then find, by advice from friends or diligent search, a retailer who is a true stove specialist and knows the subject thoroughly. You are entitled to much free advice before you buy. Beware specials of foreign origin in a department store. After you buy the stove, you may still want expert advice for fine-tuning in the cause of maximum efficiency. You are the only one who can decide properly on the size of your investment, the importance of sophisticated extras for heat control, the trade-offs between burning efficiency and price, the importance of appearance and the value of seeing an open fire.

If efficiency is your main concern, remember that you cannot let even the best stove purr along forever like a small electric heater. It will burn low overnight without nocturnal feedings, and will then coat your pipes and chimney thickly with creosote. You must periodically have hot fires burn some of it off, or you will be spending your days cleaning flues. Also, do not be talked into a size larger than specified for the cubic contents of your room. That is a good idea for electric heating, but not for airtight woodstoves: you would usually be running it below capacity and thereby encouraging the build-up of creosote.

The selection of the stove is not the last of your difficult decisions. Will you use a conventional stovepipe or a far more expensive insulated type? The great advantage of the latter is, of course, safety and a sense of security. Even a chimney fire is not likely to be catastrophic if you have insulated pipes. On the other hand, if their cost seems high, careful installation and continuous prudent operation of conventional stovepipes should save you from disaster. As with so many other appliances around your cottage, one factor in your decision is whether you are likely always to be there to operate it yourself. If tenants, friends or teenagers may sometimes be in charge, the argument for more money for less trouble and higher safety becomes stronger.

It is possible that you will be planning a stove and fireplace at the same time. Building a good, tile-lined single chimney with more than one flue is an economical way to proceed if the placing of the chimney lends itself to stovepipes. You may not want stovepipes trailing across your room, though it was a common practice in Victorian homes as an effective heat-recovery system. Whatever you do, never try to connect both a fireplace and a stove into a single flue. It will be the wrong size for one of them, it will cause trouble, and it may be illegal.

If the stove has its own exit to the heavens, consider carefully the placing of the stove before you make that irreversible hole in the roof. Although you will lose more heat by putting the pipe straight up from the stove, you may get a somewhat better draft, you will have less cleaning to do, and have less chance of creosote build-up and chimney fire. But you must know precisely where the stove will sit.

It should sit on non-combustible material. This could be a slab of concrete alone or covered with tile; it could be a sandbox with sides of about $3^1/_2$ inches; or it could be a sheet of steel and asbestos that you can buy from the stove store. The last is by far the simplest, though it is expensive. Your stove probably has legs at least 4 inches long. If it does not (like a cookstove), you have to place it on two layers of hollow-core masonry blocks about which the retailer will advise you. Your protective material on which an ordinary stove sits must extend 18 inches in front of the fire door, so that hot ashes will not drop on the planks, and 6 inches on each of the other sides. The back and sides of the stove must be a minimum of 12 inches from the wall; that distance can be reduced by as much as half if the wall is protected by a layer of asbestos and steel or equivalent. Don't reduce the clearance from stove to wall unnecessarily. The front must be 48 inches from anything combustible. If your pipe does not go straight up through the ceiling, but does a right angle out a wall, that joint must be at least 18 inches below the ceiling. The top surface of the stove itself must be at least 36 inches below the ceiling, which is rarely a problem. The reason for all these clearances, is to reduce the risk from any nearby combustible material: don't spoil everything by placing the stove beautifully and then allowing kindling to be stacked dangerously close.

When you are installing the pipe, remember that you will be taking it down each year to clean, and design it accordingly. It is handy to have at some place along an ordinary pipe a collar which slips over two adjacent ends and tightens with (what else?) stove bolts. This collar easily slips off and makes the dismantling of the rest very simple. Not many places will sell you the cheapest lightweight stovepipe these days: if they offer it, decline in favor of the heavy black or galvanized.

Each year when you clean, look for signs of rust, for which unoccupied cottages are famous. It is likely to show up first in right angles. Take no chances, but replace the piece immediately. If much of your pipe has angles, keep a spare.

How do you keep the stove and pipes looking presentable? If you have bought the heavyweight black pipes, you need do nothing with them. If you have galvanized pipes, you can paint them with high-heat black paint, but you may have trouble getting the paint to adhere well. First, thoroughly rub the pipe with fine steel wool dipped in Varsol, and wipe it off with paper towels. The traditional treatment is then to rub the galvanized surface with vinegar, let it stand a few minutes to etch into the surface, and wipe it off. Doubt has been cast on the effectiveness of this operation, but at least it will do no harm. For the stove itself, use stove polish, remembering to give it a thorough coat before winter starts. Almost any treatment you give pipes and stove will cause some odor the first time you light a hot fire — you may want to start up the stove on some mild day when the windows can be comfortably opened.

We have talked about the stove and what burns in it. (See **Firewood**.) There remains only the problem of the ashes. Unless the stove has been out of use for days, always insist that ashes be shovelled into a metal container which is doused with water, or left on an incombustible surface for a day. If you want to take the time, you can screen those ashes through a scrap of wire lath or similar coarse screening (window screen is too fine). Then you can use the ashes on lawn or garden without a visually unpleasant residue of charred remains and nails, or you can save it to throw on icy walks or to put in the car trunk for winter use.

WOODWORKING PROJECTS

This section is for cottagers whose energies and creative instincts sometimes lead them in search of improvements to the family's Quality of Life. Usually, dreams of projects far outnumber their fulfillment, and that is what cottage relaxation is all about. But there are times when some people feel like adding to the Gross National Product by the work of their hands. What follows are general directions from some simple cottage projects, for space does not permit the inclusion of detailed plans. Anyway, the truly creative woodworker may not need plans. Some of these projects can be made with the wood from the forest or the supplies of lumber you probably have on hand; others require more planning and special ordering.

Benches and seats

For semi-permanent benches near the barbecue or in front of your favorite view of the lake, one step beyond sitting on a log is to take two sections of that tree trunk you had been hoping to split, and put a 2 × 10 or 2 × 12 plank on top. If you are handy with the chain saw, an alternative top is a slab cut lengthwise down the felled tree. Put the curved (bark) side down, and slip 4 wooden wedges underneath to keep it from rolling.

If that is too simple for your creative juices, take that same type of slab (ensuring it is at least a couple of inches thick) and drill four 1-inch holes $1^{1}/_{2}$ inches deep for the legs, angling them out about 15 degrees. Make legs out of poles about $2^{1}/_{2}$ inches in diameter and 18 feet long. Taper one end of each down to 1 inch to fit the holes, and glue them in.

For a coffee table which will be the envy of all who pass by, you need only a 3-inch slab cut from an enormous tree — and endless spare time. Choose hardwood (with no trace of rot) that is at least 2 feet in diameter. Make a precise chalk mark around the trunk and use a sharp chain or sawblade to make a very careful cut from one side to the other. (Don't cut in from both sides to join at the middle.) While you are at it, you may as well make 3 or 4 such slabs to have spares, or to sell and make your fortune. The next step is not absolutely necessary, but it may reduce the risk of unwanted splitting: with a turnbuckle and heavy wire, encircle the slab as tightly as you possibly can. Leave the slab to dry until next summer in a place where it will receive drying winds without direct sunlight. Remove the wire. Now smooth the surface. This step is where the patience comes in. You will probably find it easiest to use a belt sander, but it will have to be finished by fine hand-sanding. When all traces of sawcut and sanding lines are erased, use a finish such as 3 or 4 coats of matte Varathane, sanding lightly between each. Then add many coats of wax. The 3 or 4 legs are made as for the bench noted above. What a creation for indoors or out!

A very simple country bench has at each end a vertical 1-inch board, 16 inches long and the same width as the top, instead of a pair of legs. A V-notch is cut about 4 inches deep in the bottom of each vertical to leave 2 outer points about 2 inches across for more stable use on uneven ground. Nail through the top into the unnotched ends of the vertical boards. Cut 2 triangles of 1-inch wood with sides each about 10 inches. They are braces for the 2 end pieces, placed between the bench top and the middle of the vertical, just above the notch. They are simply nailed through the top and through the vertical. To make the whole thing stable, attach a side piece of 1 × 6 along each side of the top, and nail it also to the vertical boards. That is crude but effective, and the pioneers made thousands of them — fast. If you have high standards, you can improve on the design by dadoing and glueing all the pieces together, but for the outdoors, early carpenters rarely did.

If you are in the mood for a little more challenging carpentry, you could turn out a "tench" — a combination coffee table and bench strong enough for a heavy adult to jump on. It is best made of ³/₄-inch plywood, which can be painted, with floor tiles, ceramic tiles or plastic on top. As with the old-fashioned bench, use solid ends instead of legs. Make a frame with a cross piece 2 feet shorter than the length of the table top, and about 8 inches in width, dadoed and glued into the middle of the two ends, with a few screws to gild the lily; the top of the cross piece is flush with the tops of the ends. Center the frame on the bottom of your table top and mark it for dadoing. Glue it together. Make a trim for the edges of the plywood top.

The same construction can make an almost indestructible stool. Apart from being shorter than the tench, the only difference is that your final trim around the top can stick up a couple of inches to hold a cushion in place.

For the truly immovable seat, take advantage of a felled tree. Instead of laving an ugly stump, cut the tree off 3 or 4 feet from the ground. At about 18 inches from the ground, make a horizontal cut $2/3$ of the way through the stump, at a slight downward angle. Then slice down from the top to meet the bottom of that cut, remove the block, and you have a high-backed throne.

Carport/Boat shelter

This is hardly the item to build on a Sunday afternoon, but it can be simpler than you might think if you want to build lightly and are prepared to accept the nuisance of support wires. The boat shelter is similar to the carport, but scaled down appropriately for your craft.

We are suggesting a carport whose flat roof is 14×24 feet. If a medium car is parked with reasonable care, its doors will open on both sides, even if they land beside a post. If this cramps you, make it 2 feet wider.

Probably the toughest step of all is to make a perfect rectangle on the ground. Be sure that it is perfect, checking and rechecking to ensure the 2 diagonals are equal, adjusting and rechecking. Ensure that the centers for 4 posts on each side are precisely marked. The centers of the two lines of posts should be exactly 12 feet apart. From the front post to the back post should be 22 feet. They are spaced equally along each wall.

If you have soil to dig in the posts, the extra work will be compensated in ease of construction. If not, don't be discouraged. For permanence, it is worth making concrete piers by digging until you hit rock and placing 8-inch cardboard tubes (available from the builders' supply) in the holes and about 6 inches above the surface. At exactly the same height on each, measured very carefully with levels, push a nail through the side of the cardboard. Fill each tube up to the nail with concrete — dry mix if you want to save trouble and don't mind the few extra dollars. Before the concrete sets, place a 5-inch common nail (or larger) point up, with half of it showing, in each pier along the exact line of each side While waiting for the cement to cure for a couple of days, assemble all your other supplies and start cutting lumber. You will need two beams 24 feet long and 4¹/₂ inches wide. You make them by nailing together 2 × 8s in such a way that no 2 end joints come opposite one another: for example, one line could be made of boards 8 feet wide and 16 inches long, the next 12 feet and 12 inches and the third 16 inches and 8 inches. For a 12-foot wide carport, the rafters can be made of 2 × 10 spruce 14 feet long with 16-inch centers. Cut for 4 × 4-inch cedar posts 6-feet 6-inches long, and four posts 7-feet 6-inches long. Drill a ¹/₄-inch diameter hole 2 inches deep in one end of each.

When the concrete is cured, place the posts on the protruding pins and temporarily secure the posts securely upright by scraps of lumber or with the 2 × 10s you will be using for rafters. Now you and your buddies will lift the beam and secure it to the perfectly upright and perfectly equidistant posts by 4-inch spiral nails. If nothing has fallen over yet, put the two end rafters in place and toenail them to the beam. Then temporarily put two more rafters just over the two inner posts to be sure that you are keeping those two beams perfectly straight. Now, mark the places for all the rest of the rafters at 16-inch centers, and toenail them in.

Before you go any further, you should put cross bracing between each rafter to spread the roof load. You can use scrap 1 × 3 from the top of one rafter to the bottom of the next, adjacent to one going the other way. On a 12-foot width, one set down the middle of the whole length will serve you. Be sure to do this before installing the ⁵/₈-inch tongue and groove plywood roof. You can cover the whole thing with roll roofing.

Whatever you do, don't remove those temporary supports on the posts yet. The whole structure could quite easily collapse, especially when you work on the roof. How, then, do you make this light structure safe?

If you want cupboards in the sides or end of the carport, construct them with generous use of plywood sheets and they will give you most of the stability you need. If you want to keep all sides open, use heavy galvanized wire with eyebolts, thimbles and turnbuckles. You will have to make an X along each wall and across the end, thereby producing an interesting hazard for pedestrians. The eyebolts will go right through the posts near the bottom or the top, and the wire will be tightened with heavy turnbuckles as you check with spirit levels and plumb bobs.

An alternative to be used in whole or in part is to attach guy wires to objects such as large trees or rocks near the structure. Be sure to put the wires well above head level on trees. Four wires should suffice, provided they are angled out from each post and are reasonably symmetrical.

Fences

By far the easiest fence to build is made with fenceposts and fence wire. If you lean to something more visually pleasing, there is an infinite variety of challenges. Here are a couple for people who have lots of trees to use.

Lowest on the difficulty scale is the so-called sawbuck fence. Two logs are crossed as in the sides of a sawbuck or sawhorse (See **Wood Cutting**), except that where the two pieces cross, one should make a half-lap joint by cutting through each log half-way. These X-brackets are dug a little way into the ground at about 11-foot intervals to accommodate the horizontal poles that are 12 feet long. The poles rest in the crotch, overlapping each other and nailed together. This type of fence will satisfy only your senses of property and aesthetics, for it will exclude no man or beast. It can be made into more of a barrier by adding horizontal poles, nailed to the sawbucks below the crotch. An advantage of this design is that it can be used where digging is impossible.

The most basic type of log fence uses standard, dug-in fenceposts with 2 or 3 horizontal rails nailed to them. Or you can put your fenceposts in pairs less than a foot apart, joined with short horizontal pieces on which the rails can rest, with or without nailing. A third version, which uses more rails for a more secure barrier, is to take those twin posts without their joining rails, and pile rails on top of one another from just above the ground to the top. Since the rails overlap at the twin posts, the space between each will be the width of one rail. If you decide on this technique, use two $3/4$-inch threaded steel rods to bolt together each pair of posts. The lower one will go through one post, through the lowest rail and through the other post, and the upper will do the same with the top rail.

For more class and less wood, you can notch the fenceposts to let the two or three horizontal rails (however many you decide) slide into the notches. You can make the notch long enough so that 2 meeting rails, one on top of the other, can fit in. Or you can make a smaller notch and taper the ends of the horizontal rails so that they fit in side-by-side. To make the notches, you can make holes with a brace and bit or drill, and chisel out the wood. It is much quicker to notch with the chain saw, but you must be extraordinarily alert to the danger of the blade kicking back. It is easy for those who have acquired skills with the chain saw, but even they must be careful and wear safety equipment, including hard hat.

Garbage shed

It is not as striking as a sculpture for the front lawn, but a garbage shed will exclude unwanted marauders, which are messy beyond belief, eliminate the eyesore of cans and boxes, and reduce clean-up.

The box is framed with 2 × 3-inch spruce, with hinged $1/2$-inch plywood top. The sides are covered either with plywood or, more attractively, with board and batten. In addition to the hinged top, there are 2 wide front doors so that light refuse in bags can be lowered from the top and heavier items can be pushed in through the doors. The outside dimensions are roughly 7-feet-6-inches × 2-feet-6-inches × 3 feet high. This permits a hinged top of 8 × 3-foot plywood to overhang the 4 sides. Put a vertical center post in the front so that you can secure the 2 doors to it with handmade wooden turn-buttons; if you do not, the raccoons can open it. The doors can be about 3 feet wide to give easy access.

On a flattened site, make a foundation of 4 cement blocks, stones or thick logs. Make the floor frame, preferably covered with used 2-inch planks with a space of about a $1/2$-inch between each; plywood will also do, but it gives less ventilation for drying. Make the walls as in conventional house framing, with the front 6 inches higher than the back (or the reverse). When the wall frames are nailed together, you can add two 2 × 3s from front to back to discourage the roof from sagging —

in the middle, and out both ways 16 inches from it. Install the
8 × 3 plywood with 6-inch strap hinges secured with bolts
through the plywood and either heavy screws or lagbolts into
the back. For the doors use 4-inch strap hinges with the same
technique — extremely well-secured hinges are important.

This shed will be proof against the entry of all animals except
a rare and determined bear, which could push the whole thing
over. If you are unlucky enough ever to have to face that
problem, you could vary the design by using 4 corner posts
embedded at least 3 feet into the ground.

Flower boxes

Flower boxes below your windows are attractive from inside
and out. Boxes lining your deck have the added purpose of
preventing people from falling off. In either case, the plants
are handier to weed and tend than those in the garden. Flower
boxes can be made easily and quickly by any cottager.

If you have access to a supply of rough, unplaned pine
boards about 10 feet wide, that is the most attractive material,
and it is cheaper and stronger than planed 1-inch pine, cedar or
spruce. You have a choice of vertical sides, or one or both sides
splayed out at an angle of about 10 degrees. The latter look
better, but they are more awkward when meeting at a corner.

No matter what the length of a deck, don't make any box
more than 6 feet long; filled with earth, it will be very heavy
to shift. The ends will be the width of the bottom board, less
twice the width of the side ones, for the side boards will go
on top of the bottom. Attach the sides and bottoms to the ends
with 2-inch number 10 flat-head Robertson screws. For added
strength, add a vertical of 2 × 2-inch spruce at each corner
and across the centre about $2/3$ of the way up from the bottom.
To raise the box from the floor, make plinths out of three 2 × 4s
on edge; cut each end at an angle of 30 degrees for aesthetics,
so that the top edge is the width of the bottom of the box and
the bottom stretches out an extra couple of inches. Nail the
3 plinths to the bottom at equal distances. When you have
drilled about eight $3/4$-inch drainage holes, you are finished.

Before adding earth, do two things. Apply preservative very
generously, especially to the inside; in fact, do it twice. (See
Paints and Preservatives.) Now, fill the bottom quarter of the
box with loose scraps of rigid foam insulation at least $1^1/2$ inches

thick. This will contribute to drainage, lessen the quantity of earth you need, and make the boxes a little lighter. If you have none, ask the lumberyard for broken pieces. If this is too much trouble, you can line the bottom with stones, but they will eventually become solidly embedded with earth and not really effective. Before putting in the earth, mix it thoroughly with $1/3$ peat moss.

Window boxes are made the same way, but are much smaller and have no plinths. Eight inches deep and 6 inches wide is generally large enough. The easiest way to attach a window box to a wooden wall is first to cut a horizontal piece of 2×2-inch spruce the length of the box. Screw it into the wall with 3-inch number 10 Robertson screws where you will hit studs, for this is the piece that will fit under the bottom and take all the weight. Lift the box onto it, and attach the box to the wall by $2^{1}/_{2}$-inch screws near the top — at least 3, no matter how short the box. You need not screw the bottom into the 2×2-inch support. If you want to be able to lift off the box more easily for maintenance, an alternative to those last screws is a pair of stout gate hooks, which will hold it in place.

Garden shed/Tool shed/Beach shed

Roughly the same design and size is suitable for sheds to accommodate garden tools, fertilizers and supplies; general maintenance tools when you do not contemplate a walk-in workshop; or beach supplies, oars, paddles, towels and out-door games.

Adjust the size to your needs. It is tempting to make the roof 8 feet long to use the length of a sheet of $1/2$-inch sheathing grade plywood; you can also use the full 4-foot width and provide for an overhang of 3 or 4 inches on each side. The roof will slope backwards, with the front wall about 6 inches higher than the back. A minimum height for the front wall is 6 feet, so that you can extract long-handled tools over stuff stored on the floor.

The approach for the foundations and framing is the same as for the garbage shed, but the center post in the front is unnecessary and a nuisance to the maneuvering of big articles like a lawnmower. The two doors reach from just below the roof frame to the floor, and the full width of the frame less 6 inches on each side. They are big enough to need 8-inch